The All Colour Book of
VEGETABLE GARDENING

H·G·Witham Fogg

Sundial

Contents

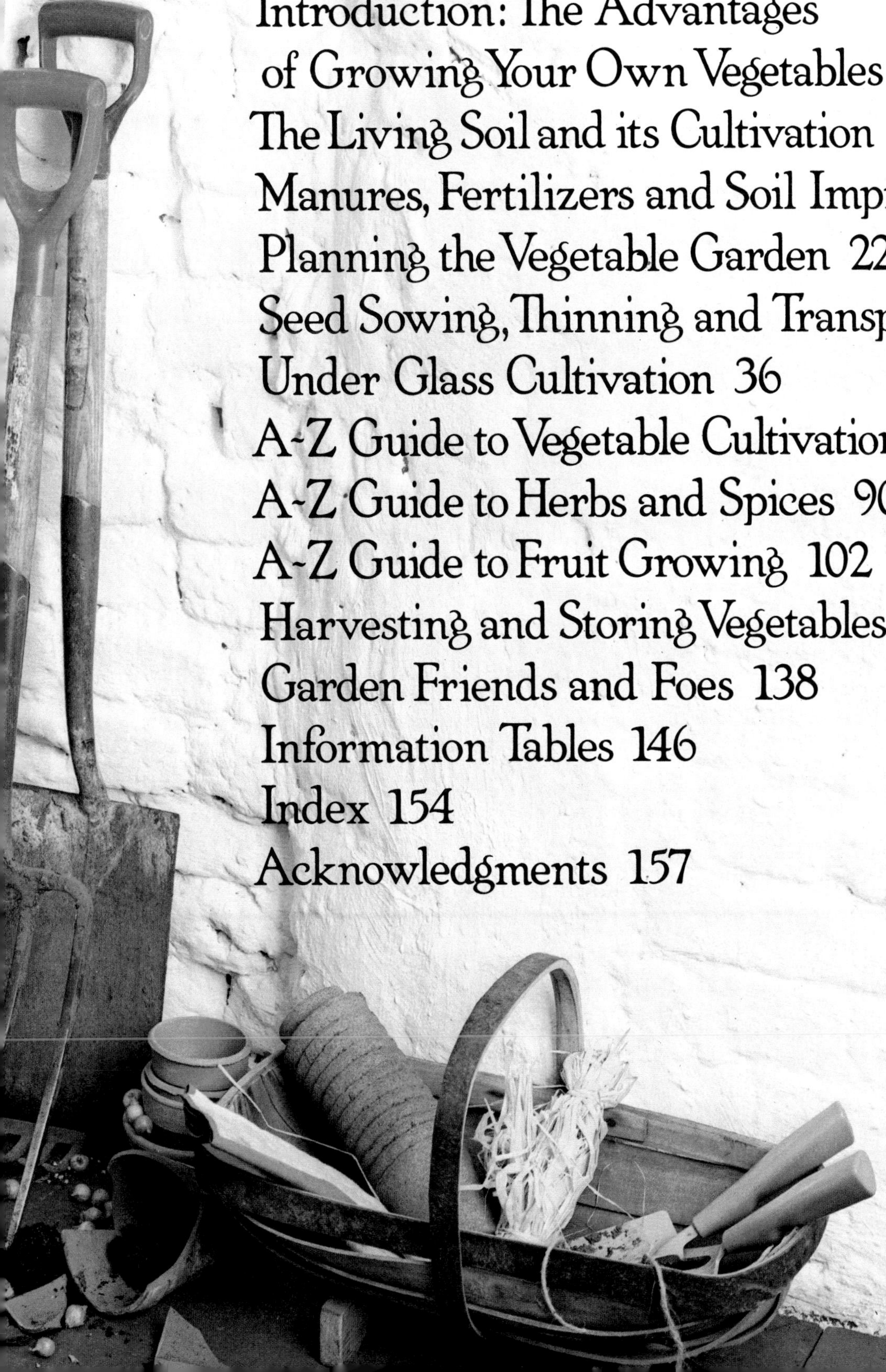

First published 1977 by
Sundial Books Limited
59 Grosvenor Street
London W1

Second impression, 1978

© 1977 Hennerwood
Publications Limited

ISBN 0 904230 32 5

Printed in Great Britain
by Jarrold & Sons Limited

At the time of printing,
names of varieties
given in the text
were widely available

Introduction: The Advantages of Growing Your Own Vegetables

As the population continues to rise in almost every part of the world, the necessity for increased food production becomes obvious. The price of vegetables in shops and markets is a further great incentive to gardeners to grow edible crops instead of cultivating almost exclusively ornamental subjects. Beyond these motives there is the question of freshness and flavour, experienced at their best with produce newly harvested from your own garden.

In addition, the vegetable grower can select his own varieties, choosing those subjects which he and his family like and those having nutritional and vitamin values. It is no more difficult to grow the best varieties than those of poor quality. By careful planning it is possible to obtain a continuous supply of vegetables throughout most of the

Decorative food plants like runner beans look perfectly at home in the flower garden

year, particularly if care is taken to store the right crops for use in mid-winter. There is also a great deal of satisfaction to be gained from eating fresh food which you have grown yourself.

There can be very few people who do not eat some vegetables, for apart from those that are eaten raw, there are others that can be canned, frozen, boiled, stewed or fried. We use various parts of vegetable plants including roots or bulbs, stems, leaves, seeds such as garden peas and broad beans from the pod, and fruits, notable examples of the latter being cucumbers, sweet corn and tomatoes.

A number of vegetables are natives of widely separated parts of the world. Potatoes, sweet corn and tomatoes come from South America, onions originated in Egypt, radishes and soya beans were known in China centuries ago; carrots are said to have come from Greece while the lettuce was known to the ancient Romans.

With such examples of the background of some of our popular vegetables it is hardly surprising that many stories and superstitions have arisen, some of which make interesting reading even if these days they sound a little far fetched. We can mention only a few beliefs once held by many people.

Onions were said to be a cure for all sorts of physical disorders. A bulb cut in half and rubbed on the forehead was claimed to cure head-aches, while if the heart was taken out of a roasted onion and put into the ear, as hot as could be borne, it relieved earache. More likely it was the warmth which did the trick. According to an Oxfordshire remedy to cure advancing baldness, it was said that the juice of a raw onion should be rubbed into the skin or baring patch until the skin was red and felt hot. Onions were also hung in doorways to scare off witches. The onion, due to its aroma, could hardly be thought likely to arouse thoughts of love, but according to one old country belief, girls searching for a husband had to eat plenty of raw onions. There is every reason to believe that 'onions are good for you' and this includes garlic which, in small quantities, gives a subtle flavouring to many dishes.

Rhubarb, generally thought of as a fruit, was used medicinally as long ago as 2700 BC by the Chinese, but although often mentioned in old herbals it was not grown in kitchen gardens for culinary purposes until the early nineteenth century. Many old gardening books refer to rhubarb being grown for ornamental purposes, the tall spike of whitish-yellow flowers being the attractive feature, with the large leaves and rosy-red or green stalks.

On their introduction into Europe potatoes were not used in the human diet but fed to livestock. Even then, some people were prejudiced against eating animals which had fed on potatoes, saying that the vegetable caused leprosy and fevers, and that human beings could so catch them from the livestock. One of the first to popularize the potato was King Louis XVI of France. He not only ate them with his meals but had large parts of his garden planted with them for the flowers which he was so attracted to that he wore a spray every day while they were in bloom. During the reign of Napoleon Bonaparte the potato was widely used in France to make a love potion. Josephine is said to have drunk it and so did many single ladies at Court seeking a husband.

Brought to England as early as 1596 from South America, it was not until the eighteenth century that the tomato began to be commonly eaten. Because it is in the deadly nightshade family, many members of which are poisonous, the tomato was also thought dangerous. So it was grown as an ornamental plant, for its flowers, scent, and brightly attractive coloured fruits. Who first tasted them in England is unknown, but afterwards a belief arose that eating tomatoes made a person temporarily passionate and so the fruit was given the name 'love-apple'.

Some of our everyday vegetables were once associated with romance. Nine peas in a pod was considered a very lucky signal. If an unmarried girl found one, she nailed it over the door of her house. The first man who came through the doorway after that, excluding her male relatives, would become her husband.

In medieval times lettuce juice was used in love potions and charms. Girls who wanted a husband also ate large quantities of raw lettuce supposedly to increase their powers of attraction.

The Romans thought so highly of the cabbage that it was included in their mythology, and at their orgies large bowls of raw wet cabbage leaves were placed on the tables to eat between the rounds of drinking. The Romans believed that the cabbage leaves absorbed the fumes given off by the wine and so they could return home without any trace of alcohol on their breath.

To come back to more practical things we find in vegetables something more than luxuries — we find food of the highest order, from which may be derived strength and good health. Today more than ever before, there is an appreciation of naturally grown fresh food coupled with an urge for self-sufficiency and a 'back-to-the-land' approach. This in part, is a reaction against processed and frozen convenience foods. In addition, the cost of buying vegetables rises continuously and we are now in a 'belt tightening' era. One does not need to be a financier to notice the difference in cost or a gourmet to appreciate the difference in taste between freshly harvested crops and those that are wizened through having been gathered days previously.

Most vegetables lose at least some of their vitamins as soon as they are gathered, so the sooner they are eaten the more beneficial they will be for health and a well-balanced diet.

When growing for the table, large size is not the criterion as it may be on the show bench. Giant Brussels sprouts, huge beetroot, carrots and leeks are less likely to be as tasty as smaller specimens gathered and eaten when young. Very often vegetables are cooked far too long and may become tasteless and lose their vitamin value, especially cabbages which are a natural provider of vitamin C.

Fortunately there are now very many varieties of cabbages and it is possible to have a supply throughout the year by selecting the right variety and sowing at different periods.

It is pleasing to realize that while everyone cannot travel to far distant places, we can grow vegetables originating from all parts of the world. While they may have been raised in greatly differing conditions from those in this country, a number of them are out-

Even a small garden can produce a variety of vegetables

standing in growth and flavour. As we shall see in detail later, east meets west in the garden, through Japanese cucumbers, onions, winter radishes and melons. From China come mung beans, Chinese mustard, Chinese cabbages such as 'Pe tsai' which are first class as a salad crop or can be cooked like ordinary cabbage but with much less of an unpleasant 'cabbagey' smell. The range of vegetables from the United States increases annually. Green celery, lettuce 'Salad Bowl', tomato 'Big Boy', various large pumpkins and squashes are all proving to be worth growing.

Whether you grow the very new subjects from far distant places or rely on well-tried favourites, it is advisable to plan the garden so that gluts and shortages are avoided. This means not only sowing little and often to spread out supplies, but making sure to grow certain items which will keep or store well. Whether or not vegetables are being stored for winter and spring use, the way the crop is harvested is of importance both for the actual plant, as well as the portion being taken off the plant.

As the result of official trials by experts from many countries, it has been decided that identical varieties of vegetables, known and grown under more than one name, must now be known by their original name. This means that some names we know so well are now not offered in seedsmen's catalogues. This does not indicate that these favourite varieties have been discarded or are unsatisfactory but simply that they are now offered under the name originally given to them.

For instance beetroot 'Showbench' should now be catalogued as 'New Globe', lettuce 'Sugar Cos' as 'Little Gem' and Brussels sprouts 'Continuity' as 'Early Half Tall'.

Although the loss of some favourite names will be regretted, it will avoid the possibility of growing two or more varieties of the same vegetable under different names, only to discover this when the crop matures.

The Living Soil & its Cultivation

The majority of garden owners have to continue coping with the particular soil they inherit. In the case of a newly built house there may be special problems caused by the relics of building works that have churned up the site and left immovable rocks behind. Thorough cleaning of the site is essential; if really serious damage has been done it may be necessary to pave over the area. Nevertheless, there are many ways in which a poor patch of ground can be improved and made more healthy to give heavier crops. First we should realize that the soil does not consist of inert dead matter but myriads of living organisms, which must be present if crops are to flourish.

The various types of soil are usually based on clay, sand, loam, chalk or peat.

Clay soils become sticky and glue-like when wet. On drying, they harden into lumps, making it difficult for roots to penetrate.

Sandy soils are porous and easy to work but they drain rapidly and are liable to dry out badly in summer. Chalky or limy soils are usually shallow, lacking in humus and need feeding heavily. In dry seasons, particularly, the leaves of crops turn yellow, growth is stunted and yields are poor. Such soils can be made productive by adding plentiful supplies of organic matter each year.

Peaty soils are usually very sour. They contain plenty of organic matter, and because they often remain wet, they need to be drained. This is especially so in the case of the black heavy boggy peats.

The air spaces in the soil are also most important; air is essential for plants' roots have to breathe to live and grow. If the soil becomes too wet air is driven out and roots stop growing.

The so-called loamy soils are the best for they contain an ideal blend of clay and sand. The sand keeps the soil warm allowing moisture to seep through, while the clay prevents quick drying out as well as helping to retain plant food. Whatever the type of soil being cultivated, get to know its organic content so that the right feeding programme to sustain plant life can be worked out. Loams differ in

their composition, and regular applications of humus in the form of old manure or garden compost as well as an occasional liming, will normally ensure that good crops are produced.

It is not easy to state exactly what humus really is, but it has been described as a complex residue of partly oxidized animal and vegetable matter, together with substances synthesized by fungi and bacteria used to break down these wastes. It is hardly surprising that it is of complex character, since it is formed by the work of worms, animals, insects and many kinds of bacteria with numerous live and dead organisms combined with the residues of plants and animals. These produce the marvel we know as humus and upon which the organic gardener relies. It is not dead, in the way we usually understand that word but is part of an organic cycle in which constant changes and processes are going on.

The scarcity of farmyard manure should not cause us to give up our quest for bulk manures for there are substitutes which make it possible to build up good, fertile, 'easy-to-work' soil. These include composted vegetable refuse – including kitchen waste and leaves, which should not be burned – seaweed, sewage sludge, shoddy, spent hops and poultry manure. To these may be added organic fertilizers such as bone meal, hoof and horn and soot.

Very often manure is dug in too deeply, for many of our most useful plants and trees have a rooting system fairly near the surface. This is why mulching is so valuable and why it is so needful for the top 45 cm (18 ins) of soil to contain a high percentage of the organic materials that provide the humus material essential for proper development.

The beneficial soil organisms are the vital link in the chain of fertility, for it is through their functions in the decomposition of organic matter in the soil that a circulation of the necessary elements for plant life is possible. Most of the many soil organisms are to be found near the surface and in the area close to plant roots. Their

To manufacture the carbohydrates necessary for healthy growth by the process known as photosynthesis plants must have fresh air, adequate light from the sun, and water. Fine root hairs (shown many times magnified) absorb mineral salts in solution from the earth.

number falls off rapidly in soil deficient in organic matter. We can only refer to a few of the living agents in the soil, not only for space reasons, but because little is known of some of the others.

There are the mycorrhiza, a name covering various fungi which among other activities excrete substances which appear to stimulate growth. Quite a number of plants grow much better when these fungi are present. There is reason to believe that they thrive on decaying vegetable matter and do not live on the actual soil.

The soil bacteria vary considerably in size and function, while algae are soil plants without roots or distinctive form. They are in various ways connected with the protozoa some of which are not at all helpful to plant life. Another group of soil inhabitants is known as the actinomyces which appear to be related to both bacteria and fungi. Other lesser known organisms act in a different way in that instead of breaking down material, they build it up making it useful to plant life. Since we do have so many microbes working for us in the soil it is to our advantage to see that we provide the organic matter essential for this work to be carried on.

If there are multitudes of soil inhabitants we cannot see with the naked eye, there are other beneficial living agents working for us and whose appearance we know well. The most important of these are the earthworms. While they may not be wanted in the lawn because of the casts they throw up, elsewhere they should be made welcome and encouraged. The tunnels that they make as they burrow through the soil increase aeration and assist drainage, creating an environment in which beneficial bacteria can thrive, and worm-casts have a useful manurial effect.

The earthworm greatly helps to renew and maintain the film of top soil. While it is difficult to fully understand how the earthworm can make the soil more fertile, as a result of experiments in the USA and in Britain, worm casts have been found to contain more nitrogen, phosphates and potash than is present in the top 12–15 cm (5–6 ins) of normal garden soil.

Worm burrows may penetrate up to 1.20–1.50 m (4–5 ft) into the ground. The size and appearance of worms seen when moving the ground will give a good guide as to the fertility of the soil. Fat, red rather tacky glistening worms indicate a good soil, where these creatures can work and breed freely. Greyish-red slow moving perhaps curling specimens suggest that the ground is in great need of humus matter.

A useful function of their work which can often be seen happening is the pulling down of decaying leaves and other organic matter into the soil. Old pieces of grass or weeds as well as other pieces of vegetable matter such as loose skins off shallots or onion sets are also pulled into the ground where they are broken down and dampened by the excretions of worms and become useful to the plant as well as improving the physical condition of the soil.

Various chemical fertilizers may retard the increase of the worm population which is why they need using with care and should never be applied heavily.

It is possible to have soils analysed to obtain an accurate idea of their constituents. The horticultural departments of most county colleges will perform this service for a small fee. Alternatively small soil testing outfits are readily available and for a small plot these are usually quite satisfactory. Another way of determining the type of soil is to observe which type of weeds are growing.

The very common chickweed which can be seen thriving in fertile soil indicates that there is plenty of nitrogen available. Nettles flourish in ground containing plenty of humus and do not grow nearly so well where the soil is sandy, stony or very chalky. There is

Fat Hen, or White Goosefoot, was once eaten as a spinach substitute

Sheep's Sorrel will not grow on chalky soils

therefore much truth in the saying that where nettles thrive the ground is good and crops are likely to flourish – after the nettles have been removed!

Fat hen is another extremely common annual weed which can be found growing freely in light loamy soil and indicates the ground contains plenty of plant foods. The presence of horsetail on the other hand, tells us that the soil is wet and badly drained. Sorrel and dock plants have deep roots which like dampness at the roots and grow strongly in deep clay.

The presence of self-sown clover in a lawn shows that the soil is alkaline. In this case apply a dressing of sulphate of ammonia which will destroy the large leaves of clover, make the soil more acid and strengthen the grass. Care is needed not to apply too much of this fertilizer since only a little (25 g (1 oz) per sq yd is usually adequate) may be needed to correct the imbalance between acidity and alkalinity.

Not all soil organisms are beneficial to plant growth: some compete for soil, space and nutrients in the battle for existence. Certain soil fungi are responsible for diseases such as damping off, mildews, root and stem rots. Nematodes or eelworms will attack roots and the upper parts of plants, while certain bacteria may cause galls and leaf spot diseases.

Everything that is done to keep the soil in good condition by feeding and by the improvement of the chemical and physical properties favours the well-being of beneficial soil organisms, so helping to maintain their dominance in the soil population.

Experience shows that the presence of organic matter leads to an increase in desirable soil fungi which play their part in pest control and in increasing soil fertility for the higher plants.

A now well-recognized method of helping to keep the soil in good condition, preventing the surface from drying out and encouraging the increase of the beneficial living soil inhabitants, is the practice of mulching.

The word 'mulch' simply means a layer of material placed over the soil, usually to cover the root area of the plants. Mulching serves several purposes including the conservation of moisture and preventing the drying out of the surface soil especially where there may be only a few young fibrous roots, while some mulches are applied as a means of feeding plants. Moisture from rain or watering

cans infiltrates more readily through mulches without the repeated stirring necessary to keep the surface soil broken and receptive to water.

Mulches have other functions in that they help to keep down weeds and according to what is used, feeding matter is eventually washed down to a good depth. Earthworms flourish in the humus formed by organic mulching materials, further improving the soil.

Crops which are gross feeders will derive most benefit from a surface covering of material which supplies plant food as well as preventing loss of moisture from the surface. Well-grown runner beans, late peas, cauliflowers, marrows and cucumbers and tomatoes under glass are specially responsive to mulching.

Do not apply mulches too early but wait until the soil begins to

Horsetail will take over damp areas if not checked by hoeing

13

Applying a springtime mulch to a plum tree

Heavy harvests will be the reward from well-nourished soils

warm. The middle of May is usually early enough for cauliflowers, mid-July for runner beans and for peas from June until late July, according to variety. Outdoors, tomatoes on light soil should be mulched by late June. Cucumbers under glass will benefit from several applications since this will prevent the roots from surfacing.

Make sure the soil is moist before applying any surface covering. Apart from materials which provide feeding matter and soil improvers, such as compost, leaf mould, peat moss and hop manure, there are many others which can be used. These include black plastic sheeting, which hinders weed growth, and sawdust which, when fresh, leaches nitrogen from the soil which needs to be replaced. It may also attract woodlice and ants. Grass clippings are also useful but they sometimes become messy and harbour flies. Small stones too, can be used. Anyone who has moved stones in the driest of weather will have been surprised at the amount of moisture in the soil beneath them.

Frequent hoeing often produces a dust which acts as a mulch to the soil beneath, a practice once greatly relied upon. While material with feeding value is much more beneficial, we should not too lightly disregard successful methods relied on for many years.

For some years experiments have been made in growing vegetables and other crops by the no-digging method. This is not because certain gardeners are lazy and do not like the idea of the work involved in turning over the soil, but because they are keen to get the best results. Gardeners who have seriously tried 'no digging', are unlikely to go back to moving the soil.

Instead of using a spade, fork or hoe in the autumn, the non-

digger places a layer of compost all over the vacant ground in his garden. Advocates of this system, which in certain cases has much good to be said for it, argue that in nature, plant wastes are not buried but become incorporated with the soil by the effects of the weather and the functions of worms and other soil inhabitants. Bulky material is reduced by natural decomposition without the help of man. In addition, surface applications of compost provide the right conditions for the fungi which are present in fertile soil. Many weed seeds brought to the surface by ordinary digging could lie buried in unturned soil for many years.

There is reason to believe that surface mulching gives greater freedom from pests and diseases, while regular dressings of composted material placed on the surface result in better flavoured vegetables even though the size of the crop may sometimes be smaller. It is worthwhile trying a no-digging experiment on a small plot to compare results with conventional methods of cultivating the soil.

The success of the organic surface cultivation really depends on the amount of compost available. Mulching places the raw materials where nature allows the natural workers to process it. If it is buried very deeply organic material cannot be properly processed: it must be near the surface. Among other advantages of organic surface cultivation are that weeds are gradually eliminated and are not dug up again as they would be if the soil were turned over. Worms are not disturbed and therefore go on with their valuable work of aerating the soil, while soil bacteria are kept sufficiently near to the surface to function properly.

Plants grown by this method of cultivation show a vigour that is never seen where the gardener depends on continued supplies of artificial fertilizers, which not only cause the soil to become thin and lifeless but never encourage the production of a bunch of fibrous roots which plants need if they are to produce good crops.

How to Build a Compost Heap

One of the best substitutes for organic manures may be the plant food organic waste provided by a compost heap. This is made by composting all garden and kitchen waste so that it is acted upon by soil bacteria and fungi and so converted into humus.

Before considering the material to use on the heap, some thought should be given to selecting a site, for the more favourable the position the easier and quicker will be the process of decomposition. The heap should not be fully exposed to the sun, wind or rain, while a very low lying position, or one where there is dripping from overhanging trees should be avoided. Where low ground is the only position available, it is not necessary or even wise to dig a hole; in fact, if this is done, water will collect and hinder the process of decomposition.

On level ground, a shallow excavation may be made for the base of the heap and in very dry areas where rainfall is always low, pits of 45–75 cm (18–30 ins) may be taken out. Fork over the foundation of the heap and if brushwood, cabbage stalks, coarse hedge trimmings or bricks are first laid in position, they will provide valuable aeration and drainage. Over this base, place a layer of peat and well-rotted manure or even ripe compost from the previous rotting down. Once this has been done, the various materials are placed upon the base and mixed so that decay is quick and even. Therefore coarse and fine, wet and dry, fresh and old material should be used together, and will lead to proper breaking down.

The shape and size of the heap affects the rate of decomposition and the ultimate quality of the compost. For preference make the heap in the shape of a pyramid or a rectangle avoiding a flat shapeless mass, as is so often seen. For the average garden a heap 1 m (3 ft) long, ½ m (1½ ft) wide and 1 m (3 ft) high is the easiest size to manage. Wooden compost boxes may be employed to keep the material in place. Alternatively, use proprietory compost bins which retain heat, yet ensure adequate aeration of the decomposing waste.

To build up the heap spread a layer of manure or soil, or sprinkle dried blood or fish material, or some other organic manure on each layer of waste matter, then add a good sprinkling of soil and ground chalk. Sandwich the layers until the heap is complete. Then leave it for three weeks before turning it, placing the outside to the middle. Then cover the heap entirely with a layer of soil, which will increase fermentation, or in the case of bins, plastic or even wood may be placed on the top to keep the heat in.

Depending on the materials used, a compost heap takes anything from three to 12 months to become ready for use. It is therefore a good plan to make a new heap every autumn, so the material is ripe for use by adding to the soil when winter digging. Two heaps are needed, one being built up as the other becomes ready to use.

Anything organic that rots down easily can be put on the heap, including plant remains, leaves, grass mowings, kitchen peelings, and tea leaves. Woody, bulky material such as cabbage plants can also be added to the heap but before doing so, it is wise to crush these with a hammer so that they rot down more easily. Although the heat from a well-made compost heap is sufficient to destroy many weed seeds, generally speaking perennial weeds such as couch grass, docks and bindweed are best burned.

Twigs laid beneath the first layer of compost ensure aeration. A sturdy framework keeps the heap neat and maintains its temperature

Build up material for compost in layers 15 cm (6 in) deep, watering each one and adding 15 g (½ oz) sulphate of ammonia to alternate layers

After 3 weeks turn the heap over, outside to centre, before covering with soil and leaving it to rot down completely

Manures, Fertilizers & Soil Improvers

As we have seen, the soil teems with life, but it is doubtful if any of us appreciate its true worth. It is the gardener's stock in hand, and as Sir Albert Howard, a pioneer conservationist, some years ago once wrote, 'a fertile soil means healthy crops, healthy livestock, healthy human beings and a healthy nation'.

It is therefore imperative that we keep the soil in a really good healthy condition, building it up and replacing those nutrients removed by growing plants. The aim should be to keep the soil well-nourished and not simply to feed the plants.

Quick acting fertilizers will certainly speed growth but they will do little to benefit the ground or replace feeding matter which plants have used. The law of return should be followed, for it is nature's way. It implies growth and decay – the passing back into the soil what has been taken out. That is, using organic matter from vegetable, animal and human waste. This is why a compost heap should be regarded as essential. Where space is very limited a bin can be used and properly made, the compost will be sweet and odourless. Actively decaying humus-forming, organic matter works wonders for all soils. As food for the various forms of soil life it is digested and broken down.

In the garden we can open up and feed the soil with compost and manure. Farm and poultry manure although not always easy to obtain are often offered in processed form and sold in bags at garden centres and stores.

It is not advisable to dig in fresh strawy manure because it usually has a de-nitrifying effect on the soil — wait until the straw is broken down. It should be kept in heaps until the straw has shortened and breaks easily by which time there will be no 'smell'. Place the heap in a sheltered position and cover it to stop rain leaching out plant foods.

Mixed farmyard manure can be used for all purposes but horse or stable manure is considered to be of higher quality although its nutrient value depends on how the animals were fed. Cow and pig manures are heavier and therefore particularly useful on light sandy soils. Sheep and goat manures are reckoned to be richer in nitrogen.

When so few of us can keep animals it is fortunate that there are quite a lot of good substitutes available. Seaweed has long been known to benefit the soil rendering the poorest soils fertile. It can be dug into the ground up until three months of sowing or planting and also added to the compost heap. Dried and powdered forms are now offered under proprietary names. These can be forked into the surface during autumn and winter.

Sewage sludge improves the physical condition of the soil rather than supplying a great deal of feeding matter. It is valuable for adding to the compost heap.

Spent hops are useful for digging in. They help to retain soil moisture as well as supplying nitrogen. The bag analysis will show whether potash or phosphates have been added.

Poultry manure has its uses. It can be worked into the compost heap or dug in, in the usual way. It is now possible to obtain dried poultry manure for working into the top 5 cm (2 ins) of soil in the spring. Pigeon manure from lofts can be used in the same way as poultry manure, but it should not be added to seed compost. Bark fibre is an excellent soil improver. Somewhat similar to leaf mould in appearance, it is an attractive light brown colour and a useful alternative to peat. Easy and clean to handle, it is cheaper than leaf mould, lasts longer in the soil and its 'aroma' tends to keep away soil pests. As it does not pack down or form lumps, it allows roots the air and moisture they need for free development. Bark fibre

1. Bone meal 2. Moss peat 3. Dried blood 4. General purpose fertilizer 5. Hoof and horn meal 6. Sawdust 7. Peat 8. Superphosphate 9. Proprietary humus-type enricher 10. Nitrate of soda 11. Sulphate of iron 12. Seaweed-based fertilizer 13. Sulphate of potash

lightens heavy soils and gives more bulk to light ground, enabling it to hold moisture. Used as a mulch, it prevents the surface soil from crusting in dry weather and suppresses weed growth, while it can be added to potting composts with advantage.

Green manuring is a method of increasing soil fertility in the garden, usually resulting in heavier crops of good flavoured vegetables. Green manure plants are among the best natural soil conditioners. They improve the soil's texture and make it easier for nutrients to be absorbed by the plants. Green manure can be said to grow humus, which prevents plant foods from being washed out, and in the case of legumes they increase soil nitrogen without causing soft leafy growth.

If the green manure crop is well worked in, in naturally clay soil, it will break down quite fast and render the soil easier to work. It also tends to increase a plant's resistance to pests and diseases.

While it is possible to use certain annual weeds, such as groundsel, as a green manure crop, and many of them are really fast growing plants, some are liable to seed when quite small and a continual crop of self-sown weeds is a nuisance.

Whenever a piece of ground can be allowed to lie fallow for a period of six weeks or more, the site can be dug or hoed deeply and sown with quick growing seeds of plants that make ample foliage. These include peas, beans, lupins and tares, all of which add nitrogen to the soil. In addition, flower and vegetable seeds, surplus to your needs, also make first class green manure if the plants are dug in at the peak of their leafy growth.

Mustard is one of the best plants to build up fertility in land that has been stripped of its top soil by building operations. One should avoid using mustard where club root has crippled a recently harvested crop, since it belongs to the order *Cruciferae*, and is liable to be attacked by this disorder.

Sunflowers are highly recommended if the land is not being used for several months in early summer. This crop must be dug in before the stems become too tough, otherwise they will take a long time to decay.

Lining a trench with manure in single digging (digging to one depth of a spade)

The blue field lupin, *Lupinus angustifolius*, and the white flowering form, have often been used as green manure crops. They are quick growing and ideal for sowing from late April to July. Dig them in as soon as their flower spikes can be seen and while the stems are still fairly soft. It is helpful first to knock down the growths before chopping them up and putting them in the trench as digging proceeds. Any plants not dug in can go on to the compost heap.

Winter tares are often sown in late summer, but they are equally suitable for sowing in April or early May. They can then be dug in during August and September. Buckwheat, *Fagopyrum esculentum*, is another useful green manure crop. The large seeds are best sown in rows 30 cm (1 ft) apart. One ounce of seed sows approximately 30 m (100 ft) row. Sown from April onwards growth becomes very leafy, so much so that all except the coarser, more persistent weeds, such as ground elder, are smothered.

Crimson clover, *Trifolium incarnatum*, is best grown as an annual and, if left, it will grow 50—60 cm (20—24 ins) high. As a bonus it will be of use to bees which never fail to find and regularly attend plants in flower. Sow the seed in April making sure the site is not lacking in lime. Growth is usually quick and once the flowers begin to fade, break down the stems and dig in the plants. Another way of using crimson clover is to sow it in August or early September after a crop such as potatoes have been lifted.

Whatever green manure crop you decide upon, every endeavour should be made to take out deep-rooted persistent weeds such as couch grass, ground elder, convolvulus, thistles and docks before turning in the sown crop.

Apart from the bulky and green manures there are quite a number of organic fertilizers which can be used with perfect safety and which will build up strong healthy growth. Among these are the following which can be used on all soils.

Bone meal slowly provides phosphates and is used for a very wide range of plants. It is best applied in autumn or winter. Bone flour is quicker acting but its value is more quickly exhausted. Dried blood is rich in nitrogen but expensive. Hoof and horn meal, also expensive, provides nitrogen fairly slowly and is used in potting mixtures. Hop manure provides bulk and is useful for working into the ground in the early spring. Leaf mould, or leaf soil has little feeding value, but is a useful source of humus. It lightens heavy soil and helps to retain moisture in light ground. Oak or beech leaf mould are the best. Fish meal is useful for supplying nitrogen, phosphates and trace elements. Liquid manure has many bases, varying from the liquid left after soaking a bag of manure in water to a variety of named proprietary brands.

Peat has little feeding value but provides bulk, darkening and warming the soil. It can be used with success when making up seed beds and for mulching and digging in, while it is an important ingredient in seed sowing and other composts. Soot provides nitrogen, and soot water can be applied with advantage to many plants. Wood ashes contain potash which varies according to the quality of the wood. The ash must be kept under cover for if left exposed to the elements, its value is less.

Sawdust is a cheap, useful source of humus but rots very slowly. It is best spread 15—20 cm (6—8 ins) on spare ground and mixed with a sprinkling of sulphate of ammonia to quicken decomposition. Leave it for four or five months before digging it in.

All fertilizers depend on the amount of nitrogen, potassium or phosphate they contain to do their work. Farmyard manure has equal, though tiny, quantities of all three, its chief value being its bulk. Organic fertilizers release their nutrients rather slowly.

Inorganic Fertilizers

The point often stressed about inorganic or artificial fertilizers is that they are quick acting. Most of them are easy to handle and completely free from the pests that some animal manures contain. But they are not long lasting, and they do little or nothing to improve the soil structure or supply 'bulk'. Most need handling carefully to make sure that not too much is applied, while in some cases they cause discoloration of the foliage if they touch it. Their chief value is in supplementing food already in the soil or where quick results are required.

A number of inorganic fertilizers are readily available. Nitrate of soda and nitrate of chalk both supply nitrogen fairly quickly. Superphosphate supplies phosphorus and is fast acting. Kainit is a good means of providing potash although sulphate of potash is better, and benefits growth longer. Muriate of potash is sometimes used but is not so pure and could have harmful effects if used too freely. Nitrate of potash and potash nitrate supply both nitrogen and potash, and do this quite rapidly.

Sulphate of ammonia is one of the cheaper forms of nitrogenous fertilizers. It is not readily washed away in the soil and can be mixed with superphosphates and sulphate of potash: as a spring dressing it releases nitrogen steadily. It is best kept off the foliage.

Whichever of these fertilizers is used, be careful to apply it at the rate indicated on the container, for too much may do much harm. Many compound fertilizers are available under proprietary names and usually the manufacturers provide a full analysis of the constituents.

Trace Elements

Besides nitrogen, phosphorus and potash the other main elements required by plants are calcium, magnesium and sulphur. Magnesium is a mobile nutrient like nitrogen and phosphorus. When a deficiency occurs it appears first in the old leaves since these yield up their stock to the younger leaves. Since magnesium is an essential component of chlorophyll, a deficiency results not unnaturally, in chlorosis, or a yellowing of the leaves between deep green veins.

Calcium is necessary to bind the cells of the plant together. This may be the reason why calcium deficiency causes poor bud development and the death of the root tips, since cell division is most active in these regions. With calcium deficiency the young leaves may become distorted, the tips hooked back and the margins curled and ragged. Scorching may also occur and the root system is poorly developed and often appears gelatinous. Symptoms vary according to the level of deficiency and with the species involved.

Sulphur is necessary for the formation of proteins, vitamins and enzymes. Its absence results in reduced shoot growth. The leaves may be tinted or yellowed, the stems stiff, woody and thin.

Small quantities of other chemicals are also required and these are referred to as trace elements.

Trace elements are needed by plants, animals and man in a number of ways — quite how many, nobody knows. But there is one way in which trace elements are known to be essential, and that is in forming part of the enzymes which initiate and control many of the processes vital to the plant. One of these is the use of carbon produced by photosynthesis to help make fats and sugars. In seaweed fertilizers they are present in beneficial proportions. This is important because it can be dangerous to give an overdose of a particular trace element. Excellent commercially prepared seaweed fertilizers are available.

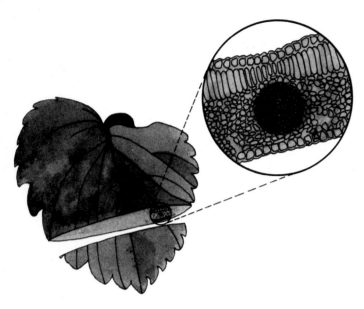

Internal structure of leaf. The stomata are the spaces between the protective cells which lie just underneath the leaf's thin waxy surface. They are the crucial connection between the air outside and the cells within the leaf. The wide central band of cells surrounding the vein contain the chlorophyll essential for photosynthesis

The following are the main trace elements which play an important role in maintaining balanced, healthy growth.

Iron plays a crucial role in chlorophyll formation. Most growers are familiar with iron deficiency and they have been helped to combat it by seaweed fertilizers complexed with iron. It appears as severe chlorosis, young growth being the worst affected. Deficiencies are common in soils of a high lime content where it is referred to as 'lime induced chlorosis'.

Boron deficiency is not common but its lack may result in several disorders involving disintegration of plant tissue. In many cases the stem and root tip dies.

The other trace elements required are manganese, copper, molybdenum and zinc.

Foliar Feeding

Although the long accepted way of feeding plants has been through their roots, foliar feeding is an alternative method by which nutrients are supplied to the plant via the leaves.

There appears to be no conclusive evidence as to the manner in which nutrients enter the leaf, although it is thought to be possible by two routes: through the imperforated cuticle or through the breaks (stomata) in the cuticle.

The upper and lower surfaces of a leaf are covered with single layers of flattened epidermal cells. The main purpose of these cells is protection. The epidermis is so thin that transpiration can take place through it, but before the leaf is very old a layer of a substance called cutin forms over the surface of the leaf and prevents further transpiration. This continuous covering of cutin, which is a resistant fatty material, renders the outer walls of the leaves more or less water- and gas-tight. Very often the cuticle is coated with wax, which increases this water and gas resistance. This wax is present to a high degree in evergreens and gives these leaves their characteristic shiny

appearance, much valued in ornamental gardens.

It is believed that plant nutrients sprayed on to the leaf might be absorbed to some extent through this protective layer – first the wax, then the cuticle, and then the epidermal cells. This could occur by diffusion if this protective layer is slightly porous. But it is more likely that nutrients are absorbed through natural breaks in the leaf. The most common of these are the stomata, which are slit-like openings between two guard cells. The guard cells enable the stomata to be opened and closed.

The purpose of the stomata is gaseous interchange; carbon dioxide finds its way into the leaf and oxygen finds its way out via the stomata. It has been suggested that the plant nutrients could find their way into the leaf through the stomata, but there is one obstacle in the path of this argument. That is, the guard cells which surround the stomata are so shaped as to make the entry of drops of water impossible unless forced in under pressure. If the plant nutrients were being absorbed by the stomata, then anything which reduced the size of the water droplets should increase the absorption of the foliar nutrients.

There are other natural openings in the leaf, for example the hydathodes which are water secreting glands and present on the edges and tips of the leaves. However, these are not present as frequently as stomata and not in sufficient quantities to be the route for the considerable absorption of foliar sprays that takes place. Absorption rates are greater for young leaves than older leaves and usually absorption is greater on the underside of the leaf than on the exposed surface.

Foliar feeds have a wide and diverse range of activities. They increase yield, improve quality, increase resistance to pests and diseases and extend the storage life of crops.

Moisture

Moisture is essential if the living soil is to function properly. Growing plants need water for it acts as a carrier of nutrients throughout their structure. Since it is lost in transpiration into the atmosphere it must be regularly replaced. If, however, too much water is present, air is expelled from the soil which becomes sour. The roots are then unable to breath and cease to function, gradually rotting away.

For proper growth, the top soil must, by cultivation, be made moisture retentive and yet allow excess water to drain away. This involves a knowledge of the type of soil we have. When the soil is gravelly or sandy, we can, by adding humus-forming organic matter, help it to hold moisture. The subsoil which receives moisture from the top soil, must itself drain efficiently, otherwise saturation and flooding may result. This could mean draining the site by underground pipes or breaking up the hard layer or 'pan' of sub-soil which prevents moisture escaping.

When it becomes necessary to water growing crops during the exceptional conditions caused by very dry weather, it is advisable to give a few really heavy soakings rather than frequent dribblings which simply bring the fibrous roots to the surface where they may be damaged by the sun's heat. Remember that plants can only use the foods in the soil if they are dissolved in water which must be applied when the soil is moist, otherwise dry concentrated fertilizers around the roots may drain them of moisture, causing a severe check or even death through dehydration.

Luxurious as it looks, a comparatively small proportion of this garden has been devoted to the vegetable patch

20

Planning the Vegetable Garden

There are many good reasons for growing vegetables. It is usually cheaper than buying them and the crop may be gathered fresh. The exercise is not only rewarding but, in these days of stress and strain, there is release of tension in working on the land and great satisfaction in watching crops develop.

Few of us are able to choose a perfect site for our garden; we have to use the ground adjoining our home. Even with an allotment, the position may not be ideal. That being so, we need to select with care the subjects most likely to succeed in the type of soil available.

A well-planned vegetable garden will yield crops throughout the year, especially if there is some form of glass protection. Insufficient or hasty soil preparation will be reflected in the quantity and quality of

the crops harvested. Another advantage of making a definite plan is that the varieties to be grown and the amount of seeds required can be fairly accurately determined in advance. This will ensure that a lot of ground is not taken up by crops that are not so popular in the kitchen, as sometimes happens.

There is much pleasure to be gained by laying out a culinary herb garden. In the past, many elaborate and perhaps not very practical designs were planned, involving a great deal of work to keep them in shape. Annual herbs such as basil, chervil, dill, coriander and summer savory look best grown in clumps. Thyme, parsley and chives are useful for edgings. Since herbs vary greatly in height and spread, the larger growing species should be placed so that they do not shade the

dwarfer subjects. It is certainly possible to make a decorative herb garden since many subjects produce colourful flowers and foliage, as well as providing a spicy and aromatic extra to many dishes.

In considering any plan for the vegetable garden, the fences and walls should be used by growing runner beans against them or disguised if necessary by Jerusalem artichokes. In certain positions, cucumbers and squashes are also valuable for clothing fences, although this often means supporting the fruits which can be weighty.

Rotational Cropping

Rotational cropping is the system whereby closely related vegetable crops are grown on different plots each year. If they are grown for several years on the same site then the essential food supplies may be exhausted, pests and diseases may build up and crop growth deteriorate.

The soil and nutritional requirements of a particular group of vegetables are likely to be different from those of another group. By grouping together plants with the same requirements and moving them to a fresh site each year we are able to carry out the appropriate soil treatments such as manuring, liming or application of fertilizers.

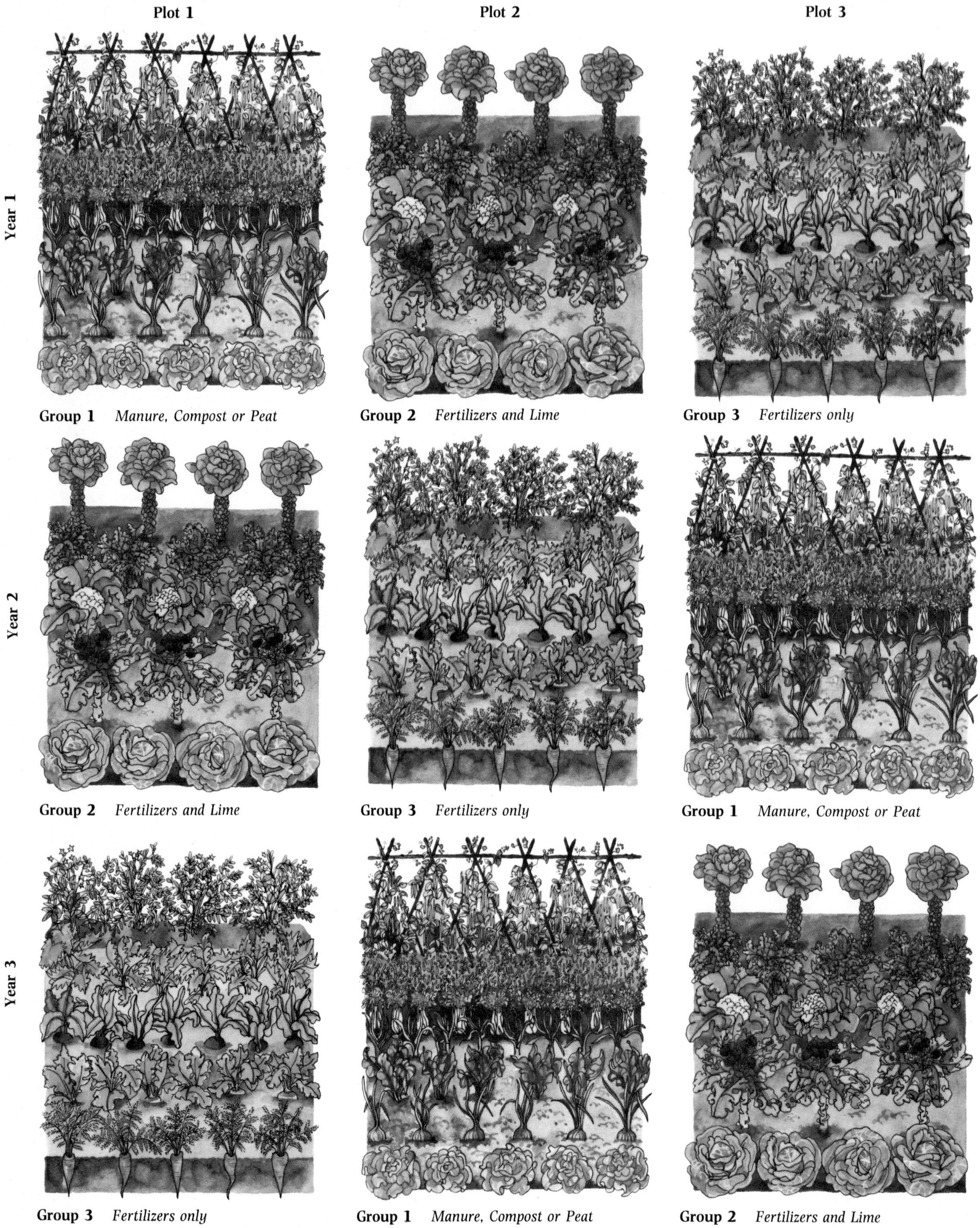

	Plot 1	**Plot 2**	**Plot 3**

Year 1

Group 1 *Manure, Compost or Peat*

Group 2 *Fertilizers and Lime*

Group 3 *Fertilizers only*

Year 2

Group 2 *Fertilizers and Lime*

Group 3 *Fertilizers only*

Group 1 *Manure, Compost or Peat*

Year 3

Group 3 *Fertilizers only*

Group 1 *Manure, Compost or Peat*

Group 2 *Fertilizers and Lime*

The whole plot can then be kept in a fertile condition without the build-up of pests and diseases. Root crops such as parsnips, carrots and beetroot need a deep soil and can be followed by the brassicas – cabbages, cauliflowers, Brussels sprouts, broccoli, kales and so on. Peas and beans form the third group and are capable of storing nitrogen in their roots. This remains in the soil when the aerial parts are removed and, as the peas and beans are gradually rotated around the vegetable plot, the overall fertility increases.

However diligent one may be at controlling pests and diseases there is always a danger that some will remain in the soil in the form of eggs, larvae or spores. If the same crops are then grown again the next year the organisms are certain to attack even more severely. This is particularly obvious with the fungus causing club root which will attack all members of the cabbage family.

It is not always easy to arrange a planned rotation since household needs vary and there may be a demand for more peas, beans and salads rather than root crops. The area of each crop within a particular rotational plot may also vary according to individual needs. There may be a temptation – encouraged by tradition – to keep crops such as onions on the same site for year after year. This is dangerous since populations of stem eelworm can build up rapidly.

In very small gardens, plants have to be grown just where space is available. This sometimes means in odd corners and even boxes and other containers. Runner beans are often grown at the end of the plot, so that it is easier to gather the crop, while the plants can act as an attractive screen.

The simplest rotation extends for three years. For this purpose the vegetable garden is divided into three plots. Although by no means perfect, it does ensure crops are moved round methodically. The example shown opposite is based on the plan suggested by the Royal Horticultural Society. The Groups are (1) Peas, Beans, Salad Crops and Onions, (2) The Cabbage Family, and (3) Potatoes and Root Vegetables.

The usual size for an allotment is 27 metres (90 feet) by 9 metres (30 feet) which is sufficient for most families. It is best to measure and peg out the three plots on both sides of the allotment so that the position of the rows can easily be determined. Attempt to make three approximately equal-sized vegetable areas and rotate the crops as indicated on the plan even if you are using part of the garden.

A four-year rotation is more complex but may be better suited for your requirements. The extra plot is just for potatoes with the other root crops remaining on their own. The four groups would then be:

Group 1.
Early, main crop and late potatoes.
Group 2.
Peas, broad beans, dwarf and runner beans, celery, leeks, onions.
Group 3.
Root crops, carrots, beetroot, parsnips, salsify. Root crops should be grown on land manured the previous season, otherwise they may become forked and mis-shapen.
Group 4.
The cabbage family: cabbages, Brussels sprouts, broccoli, kale, cauliflower, turnips and swedes. This group will benefit if the ground is limed before sowing or planting.

Crops such as lettuce, radish and spinach have not been mentioned but these can be grown as catch crops and could follow early potatoes or early peas. Herbs, including parsley, chives and sage, can be fitted in at the sides of the beds.

Lettuces are a useful subject for catch cropping

Successional Sowing and Catch cropping

There is no need to make one large annual sowing of individual vegetables such as carrots and beetroot, many of which become old and tasteless before they can be used. It is far better to make small-scale repeated sowings throughout the season (successional sowings) and to practise catch cropping by sowing vegetables that mature quickly between rows of those that occupy land for a long time. The type of soil and the location of the site will have some influence on the varieties chosen, since the same variety will mature earlier on light loamy soil than it will on heavy clay ground.

Globe beet and shorthorn carrots can be sown at intervals up until the end of July. Peas can be put in until the third week in July, using the first early dwarf varieties such as 'Kelvedon Wonder'.

If a sowing of dwarf French beans is made about mid-July the crop will mature after the last of the runner beans. Ground can be cleared after the early peas have finished in July and sowings of early maturing cabbage can be made. Alternatively, 'All the Year Round' cauliflower or savoys make good follow-on crops.

Endive and lettuce are other crops to grow after earlier subjects have been cleared. Salad onions such as 'White Lisbon' can be sown from April until late August, while maincrop onions, including 'Ailsa Craig' and 'Bedfordshire Champion', if sown in August, will mature the following summer and will store much better than when sown in spring. The new varieties of Japanese onion such as 'Express Yellow' now available in Britain, are also sown in the autumn for lifting the following July.

Radish can be sown in succession and can often be fitted in between other crops or will grow in odd corners so long as there is full light and the soil is in good condition. Winter spinach and spinach beet may also be sown in summer.

Turnips can also be used for catch cropping and will be much more appreciated from early autumn onwards, when many vegetables are becoming scarce, than in summer. Bush marrows can be sown as late as mid-July, giving a crop which is often more tasty than that from

earlier sowings, as well as extending the season.

The secret of successful catch cropping is to prepare the soil well and ensure that it is fertile. The land should not be dug or moved deeply after the first crop has been cleared, and the soil should be brought to a very fine tilth so that the drills can be drawn out easily.

Food Crops in the Small Garden

The imaginative garden on the left has been designed to make the most varied use of an average-sized plot facing south-west. Assuming that it is attached to the house of a family who will want to relax and play in their garden as well as enjoy its visual appeal, only half has been given over totally to the cultivation of fruit and vegetables.

Immediately next to the house, a tiled terrace offers a convenient site for container-grown strawberries (in a barrel) and a bay tree (left), with chives and tarragon (right). In contrast to the neatly ordered vegetable patch, the decorative area is deliberately informal: the lawn circular, the edge of the terrace uneven and broken up by ground-cover plants. The flower beds are not all they seem, giving a home to some plants that are both attractive and edible. On the left, a peach tree is trained in fan-shape against the wall. Lettuces fringe the lawn, bush marrows grow plump in the centre of the bed, while globe artichokes occupy a permanent position in the corner. The trelliswork archway (placed *off*-centre) supports scarlet runner beans; more lettuces and marrows in the right-hand bed, plus tomatoes, sunflowers (for their seeds) and in the warmest corner of the terrace, a grape vine.

The greenhouse shelters houseplants as well as some unusual sun-loving vegetables: aubergines and green peppers in pots (they could stand on the terrace on really hot days).

A crop-rotation system is being practised in the vegetable garden proper. On the left, nearest the house, are rows of cabbages and cauliflowers; beyond them, onions, celery, leeks and peas with a catch crop of lettuce between. On the right of the path, root vegetables at the far end (carrots and beetroot) share the plot with celery and a block-planting of sweet corn behind the trellis. Fruit trees are trained on both walls: apples are shown here, but pears or plums would do equally well. Two blackberry bushes are fan-trained against the far wall, with black and red currant bushes in front. This bed will be semi-permanent.

No tidy garden should lack a shed, and where better to put it than in the shade of your neighbour's great tree, where very little would grow successfully anyway. In time the ivy will trail over the shed and conceal its unlovely façade from view.

That other essential of the vegetable garden, the compost heap, is situated as far as possible from the house, but in a convenient corner for digging in the compost when it is ready.

Growing Vegetables Without A Garden

There are few situations in which it will not be possible to cultivate some vegetables, even if only salad sprouts on blotting paper or mustard and cress on a window sill. The best solution to growing in a limited space is to use growing bags, large pots, or barrels. You will have the advantage of being able to monitor very closely the condition of the growing medium. Suitable crops include tomatoes, peppers, runner beans (with support), many herbs, and strawberries.

A word of warning: soil-filled clay pots can be very heavy, so do not fill your balcony with them unless you are sure it can take the weight.

Above: Large pots and (below) growing bags save precious space. Container growing makes it easier to control pests and diseases

Successional sowing

Successional sowing or planting of vegetables on a particular piece of ground will ensure a constant supply for the kitchen.

Such successional cropping can be achieved either by sowing or planting the follow-on crops.

FIRST CROP			FOLLOW-ON CROP		
Crop	Sown/Planted	Crop harvested by	Crop	Distance between rows	Distance between plants in rows
Sprouting broccoli (purple or white)	Planted June–July from an April–May sowing	April–May following year	Dwarf French beans	45 cm (18 in)	Thinned to 15 cm (6 in)
Early carrots (for pulling when young)	March sown	End May	Dwarf French beans	45 cm (18 in)	Thinned to 15 cm (6 in)
Kohl rabi or Summer turnips	March sown	Mid-June	Main crop carrots (for pulling young)	20–30 cm (8–12 in)	Thinned for use
Early peas	February–March sown	June–July	Autumn lettuce	30 cm (12 in)	Thinned to 30 cm (12 in)
Early broad beans or Early summer cauliflower	November sown Planted March from September sowing under glass	Beginning July Beginning July	Winter turnips or Carrots or salad onions	20–30 cm (8–12 in) 20–30 cm (8–12 in)	Thinned for use
Shallots	February planted	End July	Winter turnips or Winter spinach	30–40 cm (12–16 in)	Thinned to 20–30 cm (8–12 in) Thinned to 15 cm (6 in)
Second early potatoes	Late March planted	End August	Salad onions	20–30 cm (8–12 in)	0.5–1.0 cm ($\frac{1}{4}$–$\frac{1}{2}$ in)
Maincrop potatoes	End April planted	Beginning October	Early broad beans (November sown)	45–60 cm (18–24 in)	15–20 cm (6–8 in)

Successional planting

FIRST CROP			FOLLOW-ON CROP		
Crop	Sown/planted	Crop harvested by	Crop	Distance between rows	Distance between plants in rows
Summer spinach	Late March sown	Early June	Sweet corn or Ridge cucumbers	45–60 cm (18–24 in) 90 cm (36 in)	45–60 cm (18–24 in) 90 cm (36 in)
Early peas	February–March sown	June–July	Leeks or Late savoys	40–45 cm (16–18 in) 45–60 cm (18–24 in)	20–30 cm (8–12 in) 45–60 cm (18–24 in)
Early potatoes	Mid-March planted	June–July	Autumn cauliflower or Late heading broccoli (winter cauliflower)	60 cm (24 in) 75 cm (30 in)	60 cm (24 in) 75 cm (30 in)
Second early peas	March sown	Beginning July	Leeks or Late savoys or Late heading broccoli	40–45 cm (16–18 in) 45–60 cm (18–24 in) 75 cm (30 in)	20–30 cm (8–12 in) 45–60 cm (18–24 in) 75 cm (30 in)
Autumn-sown bulb onions or Late broad beans or Shallots	August sown March sown February planted	End July	Tom Thumb savoys	30 cm (12 in)	30 cm (12 in)
Second early potatoes or Stump-rooted carrots	Late March planted March–April sown	End August End August	Tom Thumb savoys	30 cm (12 in)	30 cm (12 in)
Spring sown bulb onions	March sown	Early September	Spring cabbage	45 cm (18 in)	30 cm (12 in)

A Succession of Greens

It is not possible to obtain regular supplies of greenstuff (brassicas) from a single sowing. Different varieties mature at different times and once ready they will not remain in good condition indefinitely.

A large seed bed is not necessary and one of approximately 2 m × 1.50 m (6 ft × 4 ft) will provide sufficient room for many sowings.

Seedlings should be transplanted when they have made four or five true leaves and are about 6 ins high.

Allow 75 cm (2½ ft) between Brussels sprouts, 45–60 cm (1½–2 ft) between cauliflowers, whilst 60 cm (2 ft) can be allowed between kales; the spacing distance for cabbages varying from 30–38 cm (12–15 ins).

Right: Good planning will ensure regular supplies

Harvesting Period	Crops and Cultivars	Sown	Planted
January–March	**Late Brussels sprouts** 'Market Rearguard', 'Citadel', 'Achilles'	early April	late May
January–May	**Winter Cauliflower** 'St Buryan', 'Early White', Snow White', 'Late Enterprise'	April–May	June–July
January–February	**White Sprouting Broccoli**	mid-April	June–July
March–April	**Spring Greens** 'Flower of Spring', 'Offenham', 'Wheeler's Imperial', 'April'	late July sown in final positions and thinned to 8–12 cm (3–4 in) apart in the rows after emergence	—
March–April	**Purple Sprouting Broccoli**	mid-April	June–July
March–April	**Curly Kale (Borecole)**	April–May	July–August
April–May	**Spring Cabbage** cultivars as Spring Greens	July–August	September–October
May–June	**Rape Kale**	July (thin to 45–60 cm (18–24 in) apart in the rows after emergence)	—
May–June	**Early Summer Cabbage** 'Extra Earlhead', 'Golden Acre' 'Greyhound'	February	April
May–June	**Early Summer Cauliflower**	Late September (plants over-wintered under cold frames or cloches)	March
June–July	**Summer Cauliflower** 'All the Year Round'	January (under heat) March (outside)	March–May
July–August	**Summer Cabbage** 'Greyhound', 'Hispi'	mid-March	mid-May–mid-June
late July–September	**Green Sprouting Broccoli**	April–May	May–June
August–September	**Early Autumn Cabbage** 'Winnigstadt', 'Best of All'	April–May	June–July
August–November	**Early/mid-season Brussels Sprouts** 'Early Half Tall', 'Peer Gynt', 'King Arthur'	late March	late May
August–December	**Autumn Cauliflower** 'Kangaroo', 'All the Year Round', 'South Pacific', 'Brisbane'	March–May	May–July
October–February	**Winter Cabbage** 'Ormskirk', 'January King', 'Christmas Drumhead', 'Winter Salad'	April–May	June–July

Seed Sowing, & Thinning Transplanting

A properly prepared seed bed is essential if maximum germination and growth are to be obtained. Seeds and seedlings need four things: moisture, warmth, air and, after germination, light.

The majority of seeds are small and need a fine crumbly bed which should be prepared well in advance of sowing time. If seeds are sown in lumpy soil they may lie in a pocket of air and when the tiny roots emerge these will soon dry out.

Never make the seed bed when the soil clings heavily to your boots and tools. Particularly where the land is heavy, it should be turned over and left rough in winter. After frosts, it will break down and produce the tilth which is almost impossible to secure even by much labour. Very heavy ground can be improved by the addition of sharp sand which will provide aeration, while finely ground peat will keep heavy soil open and prevent it drying out rapidly and cracking, which sometimes occurs on heavy land, to provide a suitable medium for growth.

Although dryness will not spoil germination before the process starts, once the seed coat opens, the young growth will soon die if the soil becomes dry. There are also seed-borne diseases which hinder germination, and insect pests and other hazards. This underlines the necessity of sowing seed in really good soil, containing humus matter which encourages even germination and a plentiful root system. Discourage soil-borne diseases by practising crop rotation.

Very shallow sowing is successful only if there is sufficient surface moisture present, from frequent showers, or irrigation. Deep sowing will only give good results if the weather remains dry enough to keep the surface soil open. The rule should be therefore, to sow rather more deeply on light, easily drained ground and more shallowly on soil which is heavy and holds moisture for a long period. For most crops, one should aim at having a seed bed which is firm at the base and fairly loose at the top.

There are various ways of sowing seeds, the most usual being to draw out drills and then to sprinkle seed along them. Some gardeners mix very fine seed with sand, powdered peat or dry soil so as not to sow too thickly. Alternatively, a little lime may be added to the seed so that it will be easier to see where it falls into the drill.

There are various seed distributors on the market, some having a number of holes like a pepper pot. It is usually possible to adjust a distributor to regulate the number and size of the holes. Seed shaken from the corner of the packet rarely falls out evenly.

Drills can be scratched into the soil with the point of a draw hoe or a stick. Flat-shaped drills are usually made for peas and beans, especially if sowing double rows. Care is needed to ensure that the base of such drills is level so that the seed does not become covered with varying depths of soil.

It is certainly wasteful to sow seed too thickly and then spend time thinning out. Apart from this, the scent that carrots and onions give off when handled, attracts carrot and onion flies. There is less trouble from these pests if thinning out is avoided.

Take out straight drills with a hoe against a taut line

Sow large seeds from the packet, but use your fingers for very fine seed

Once the seed is sown a covering of fine soil should be given. Using the rake deeply may disturb the newly sown seeds. Afterwards firm the soil, which can be done with the head of the rake, to help the tiny roots to gain a hold.

A further *very* light raking of the surface soil will ensure that moisture seeps through evenly and does not settle along the drills.

Should there be a prolonged spell of dry weather during which it is essential to sow the seeds, encourage germination by watering the opened drills generously before sowing the seeds. Runner beans and peas can be soaked for a few hours before sowing but this is not always satisfactory as some seeds may rot before growth starts. Another method some gardeners adopt is to place carrot seeds between layers of damp cloth or muslin. After a few days the germination process begins and the seeds can be sown in moist soil in the usual way. This does require care since wet seeds usually cling together and are difficult to separate.

Many early sown seeds, including peas and beans, may be attacked by a soil fungus which disrupts growth. This pre-emergence damping off can be prevented by dusting the seeds with a fungicidal powder available from garden shops.

Pelleted seeds enable you to sow them individually at the required distances apart. A drawback is that since the coating disintegrates slowly in dry soil, it is essential for the soil to be moist so that the material breaks up quickly and there is no delay in germination. Some pellets are made to split into two halves, leaving the seed free. Expensive F_1 hybrid seeds may be sold in pelleted form.

It is sometimes an advantage to sow vegetable seeds in containers and there are four main types to choose from. The seed box is particularly useful where a lot of seeds are to be sown and where they are expected to germinate freely. The standard seed boxes, measuring $20 \, cm \times 36 \, cm \times 6 \, cm \, (8 \times 14\frac{1}{2} \times 2\frac{1}{2} \, ins)$ deep, are a convenient size and can be placed closely together thus economizing in space. Wooden seed boxes have a comparatively limited life while plastic trays last longer and are easier to clean and sterilize.

The square earthenware seed pan is a useful container, although seldom used today. It is convenient where large quantities of slow germinating seed is being sown. Where a seed box would be too large, the $13-15 \, cm$ ($5-6$ ins) round seed pan is a good receptacle for small quantities of seeds. The $13 \, cm$ (5 ins) pot is not quite so good as the $13 \, cm$ (5 ins) pan, since it is deeper than is necessary. Pots and pans smaller than $13 \, cm$ (5 ins) in diameter dry out rather quickly and are less suitable.

Having chosen the container, the next thing is to provide drainage material. Crocks should be placed over drainage holes to prevent them clogging with soil, and it is a good plan to place a layer of fibrous peat or leaf mould or even rough loam, over the crocks before filling in with compost. As far as the crocking is concerned, one large piece should be placed concave side down over the drainage hole, and two or three smaller crocks around it. If a deep container is used, several layers of crocks are advisable.

John Innes seed composts are very suitable for vegetable sowing although not essential, since a simple mixture of loam, a little peat or leaf mould and some sharp sand is sufficient for seeds to germinate evenly. Fill a pot or seed box by lightly pressing the soil in with the fingers, slightly over-filling the container, and then striking it off level with a straight-edged, tapping the receptacle several times before finally pressing level with a round or square presser or the base of an empty pot. This should leave the compost in the pot perfectly level and evenly firm but not compacted.

If the compost is nicely moist at sowing time, little water will be needed until germination takes place. The compost must never dry out but do not allow the surface to become caked from too frequent waterings. If it does, it may prevent the emerging seedlings from developing properly.

Thinning Seedlings

However carefully one may sow seed outdoors there is always some thinning out to be done. Do it when the seedlings are small, so there is a minimum of root disturbance to neighbouring plants. The best plants should remain in position, while weak and indifferent specimens should be removed.

Above: Sowing seeds in trays by hand. Never allow compost to dry out

Water the rows lightly some hours before thinning. Refirm the soil after thinning and if the weather is dry, water the rows. Do not do this unless really necessary or the roots will come to the surface and may be scorched by the sun.

With some crops, notably carrots and onions, thinning out is best done twice; the later thinnings being used in salads. Never delay the final thinning or the crop may be harmed by overcrowding.

Never leave unwanted seedlings lying on the ground, for disease spores may gain a hold and spread on to healthy plants. In the case of onions and carrots, flies may lay their eggs on the roots of the plants, attracted by the scent of the discarded seedlings.

1,2,3,5: Clay pots, saucers and seed tray 4,6,10: Plastic pots 7,8: Peat pots 9: Plastic seed trays 11: Strawberry pot 12: 'Jiffy' peat pots

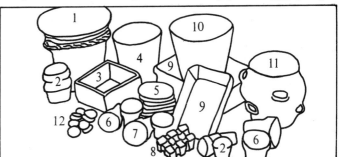

Planting leek seedlings

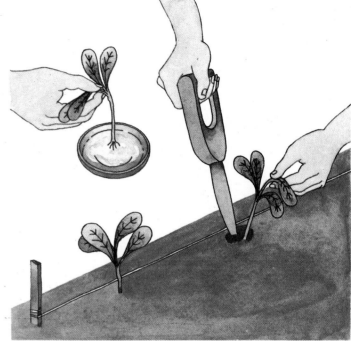

Before planting, dip cabbage seedlings in calomel paste to deter root fly

Transplanting

Some crops including cabbages, cauliflowers and Brussels sprouts, transplant very easily, as do beans, leeks, tomatoes and celery, especially during showery weather. While all seedlings must be firmly replanted, make sure not to bury them too deeply. This is particularly important with cauliflowers, which if put in too firmly, show a tendency to become blind, producing robust leaves but no curds. The crown should always be clear of the ground, allowing no soil to lodge in the centre. When planting cauliflowers and other brassicas, dust the holes with calomel, or dip the seedlings in a paste of 4% calomel

dust mixed with water and flour, to lessen the risk of club root attacks.

Shallow drills can be drawn out and the plants set in them on high ground or where strong winds are frequently experienced. Cauliflowers need extra support by earthing up firmly round the stem. The drills will give protection from ground winds, help to prevent the roots from drying out in very dry weather, and aid watering since moisture will penetrate directly to the roots. When planting out in summer, some protection from strong sunshine must be given to newly moved seedlings, otherwise the young plants may wilt and die.

The planting can be done with a trowel or dibber. The advantage of

'Station' sowing. After germination, discard weaker seedlings

Prick out into pots holding seedling by its leaves

Above: The vegetable garden can be as beautiful as it is useful

Below: Harden off seedlings before planting out

using a trowel is that holes can be made to receive roots with a ball of soil, which means less disturbance to the finer roots and in turn, a less severe check to growth. The handle of the trowel can be used to press the soil firmly around the roots. If a slight depression is left around the stem, and should watering be necessary, it will ensure that moisture reaches the roots and is not dispersed around them. Once plants are growing well, the loose soil can be worked towards them, filling in the depressions to encourage sturdy growth.

A dibber is a useful little tool but it is advisable to make sure that air pockets are not left at the bottom of the hole. If this happens, water may drain into the hole and drown the roots. After withdrawing the dibber, make another hole at an angle to the first hole, levering soil against the stem to anchor it in position, and fill in any air pockets. The second hole can be left for watering the plant. Wherever possible, members of the cabbage family should always be planted with a dibber, excepting cauliflowers which do best in trowel holes. Cucumbers, sweet corn and tomatoes also do better when planted with a trowel.

When seeds have been sown in boxes or pots of John Innes compost or a peat-based mixture, they will have to be pricked out. Lift them carefully from the box – all of them – and replant them with more space into other receptacles or into their final positions in the garden. They must be lifted carefully by using a garden label, trowel or some other pointed implement. Transplant them immediately when the soil is nicely moist.

When moving seedlings take care to hold them by the two leaves brought gently together, never by the stem.

Seedlings raised under heated frames or in greenhouses must be gradually hardened off before being moved outdoors. Particularly in the case of brassica seedlings, a watch must be kept to ensure that flea beetles do not attack the young plants. As a precaution it is a good plan to dust the seedlings with flea beetle powder. This prevents attacks which can ruin a whole batch of plants.

Under Glass Cultivation

There are many advantages to growing vegetables under glass and the use of cloches in the cultivation of vegetables and salad crops is in no way difficult.

Since cloche culture can bring forward by several weeks the date of maturity, it is a great help in successional sowing. So often the supply of salad plants falls off in the autumn and no more home grown produce is available until early spring.

It was French market gardeners who first used handlights or cloches to bring on early crops, particularly lettuces. The continuous cloches now so much in use are a great improvement, as they can be placed in continuous lines, the ends of which can be sealed with a sheet of glass or plastic, to prevent draughts. The tent type is ideal for lettuce and various catch crops, but the larger barn type makes it possible to grow taller plants successfully. Ventilation is provided by openings at the top of the cloches.

There is no difficulty in raising globe beetroot such as 'Boltardy' and 'Detroit' under tent cloches. Seed should be sown in a crumbly fertile soil, first working in a balanced fertilizer at 112 g (4 oz) per sq yd. Make the drills 10 cm (4 ins) apart and 2.5 cm (1 in) deep. Sow one row under tent cloches and three rows, 20 cm (8 ins) apart, under the low barn type. This tasty crop adds colour to any salad.

For first-class produce, fairly rich moist soil is of prime importance. Ground manured for a previous crop is suitable for all cloche and frame varieties. Rake the surface soil finely, or put down a 5 cm (2 ins) layer of compost in which to sow seed. Carrot 'Early Horn' can be grown similarly and young raw grated roots are excellent in the salad bowl.

'Golden Self Blanching' celery can be sown broadcast under barn cloches. Thin the seedlings so that they stand 20 cm (8 ins) apart, or plant at the same distance under cloches. Close planting encourages natural blanching, which can be helped by placing straw between the plants when they are growing well.

Celtuce is a two-in-one vegetable, for the leaves which have a high vitamin content, are used as lettuce, although the delicacy is in the heart of the stem, which is crisp and crunchy with a nutty celery-like flavour.

Dandelions are plants we usually regard as weeds, but the leaves are first-class used in salads. Sow under cloches in rows 25—30 cm (10—12 ins) apart. Plants must not be allowed to flower. For blanching cloches must be darkened, or inverted pots placed over the leaves, otherwise they are bitter. Roots can also be lifted in November and packed in boxes and kept in the dark for blanching like chicory.

Lettuce remains the base of most salads. Thin sowing pays as plants have room to develop; eat the early thinnings. 'Tom Thumb', excellent under cloches, and the newer 'Hilde' form compact hearts. 'Little Gem' is a superb cos variety of medium size and unbeatable for crispness and flavour. Always plant firmly but not deeply.

Salad onions are fast growers so long as the soil does not dry out. Sow in drills 20 cm (8 ins) apart and keep the cloches closed until growth is seen. 'White Lisbon' is one of the best for pulling young for salads, although the thinnings of the bulb varieties can be used.

Radishes bring colour to salads. They may be grown alone, six or seven rows to a cloche, or as an intercrop with lettuce. Here again moisture is necessary for quick, succulent growth. 'French Breakfast' is half red and half white, while 'Cherry Belle' is a fine scarlet globe variety with crisp, white flesh. Both are reliable croppers. 'China Rose' and 'Black Spanish' are autumn and winter-maturing varieties.

Garden Frames

There are four standard patterns of garden frames, determined by the size of the glass or light. The English frame is 2 m (6 ft) long by 1.20 m (4 ft) wide, usually glazed with 16 sheets of glass each measuring 45 cm (18 ins) by 30 cm (12 ins). A smaller one, often known as the Lady's Light, measures 1.20 m (4 ft) by 1 m (3 ft), and is easier to handle. The Dutch light measures 1.90 cm (59 ins) by 78 cm (31¾ ins) and is glazed with a single pane of glass, which means it is expensive to replace the glass if it is broken. The French frame is easily made and measures 1.25 m (4 ft 4 ins) by 1.26 m (4 ft 5 ins).

Sectional frames of cast aluminium or steel are on the market, while many satisfactory portable frames are available with single or span roof. These have sliding tops, easily removable for access.

The size of frame you buy or make will depend on the purpose for which it is to be used, although the aim should be to have one as large as space and pocket allow. Many frames are made with 1.20 m (4 ft) extensions, so that any length of run can be achieved.

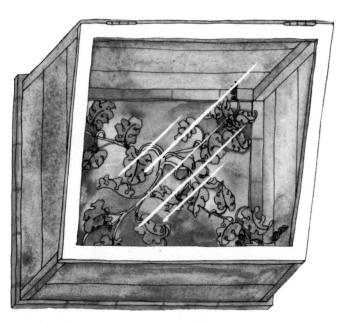

Melons need protection all their growing life. For frame cultivation prepare the planting hole towards the back of the frame by filling it with good compost and replacing the soil in a mound on top. Plant the young plant firmly on top and train it to fill all 4 corners of the frame

Where possible, place the frame due south and not under or too near trees. If backed on to the greenhouse or other building giving protection from north winds, so much the better. Avoid hollows or ground liable to become waterlogged.

The body of the frame can be of tongued and grooved timber, brick, breeze blocks or metal. Frames must be constructed on a proper draught- and damp-proof base. Provide a firm footwalk round the

structure, or it will become muddy making it difficult to attend to plants in winter or wet weather.

Keep the glass clean. Carefully seal any cracks with putty so that rain drips cannot penetrate. Make sure that it will open and shut properly without water getting between the panes or hinge joints. Give water with care to avoid excess moisture in the frame. An old-fashioned remedy for keeping out dampness is to place a lump of quicklime under each light. This takes up air moisture in winter, lasting for several weeks.

Heat escapes through the bottom of the frame into the surrounding soil. A 5–7.5 cm (2–3 ins) deep bed of cinders placed at the base of the frame area before soil is added, greatly reduces the loss.

Many small frames are available, but none less than 1.20 m (4 ft) by 1 m (3 ft) gives much scope. A lot can be done with two or three of the 2 m (6 ft) by 1.20 m (4 ft) size. These yield worthwhile quantities, instead of handfuls, of edible crops. An ideal soil depth is up to 60 cm (2 ft) at the front and 75 cm (2½ ft) or more at the back.

Provided the main electricity supply is nearby, you can heat your frame by soil cables which should be laid on 5 cm (2 ins) of sand and covered with another 5 cm (2 ins) before 60 cm (2 ft) loamy soil is put on. Make sure there is no crossing or touching by different sections of the same heating elements. Cables must be totally insulated against damp. Always buy cables specially made for greenhouse work, and carry out regular safety inspections of any electrical equipment.

Damp and draughts cannot be kept out just by keeping the top closed. Without air, mildew and rotting will occur. Ventilation is needed daily, except in very cold or frosty weather. Never let cold winds blow into a frame. For this reason the sliding light is better than the hinged type, for it can always be kept open away from the wind by using little blocks. Frost-resisting mats are valuable during severe cold, but should not be used when they are wet. It is an advantage to have duplicate mats so that the wet ones can be dried.

With heat you can force chicory, rhubarb and seakale in January,

Left to right: Glass barn cloche, rigid plastic cloche, tent cloche, polythene tunnel

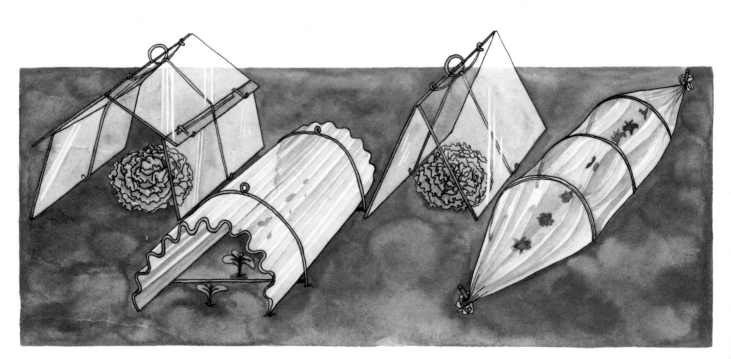

and plant early potatoes like 'Home Guard' and 'Arran Pilot'. Lettuce sown in September will heart by Christmas, while partially-grown lettuce, cauliflower and endive plants can be placed in frames to mature. Parsley transferred to frames in October will give winter pickings. Continuous supplies of mustard and cress may be harvested by sowing on canvas stretched over the soil.

Dutch Net or Cantaloupe melons can be grown in frames. For each plant, prepare a trench a foot deep and wide. Fill this with fermenting manure, topped with a mound of soil on which to plant the melon. Apply water and keep the frame closed for four or five days. Shade from hot sun and avoid excess moisture. Wait for four or five female flowers to open simultaneously, then hand pollinate them, so the fruits develop evenly. Spray the flowers with water in early mornings. Give liquid manure each week. Cut the fruit when a circular crack appears at the base of stem.

Greenhouses

What can be grown in a greenhouse depends largely on the temperature that can be maintained. Instead of having an empty greenhouse after the autumn crops are over, use it for growing tasty winter salads. The best place for these is in the border and in many cases it is possible to move the staging to make more room. Since light is important, a house with glass almost to ground level is particularly suitable. Good ventilation is essential especially during periods of mild weather.

In smaller houses with a brick or wood base, it is better to make a bed on the staging. If this is slatted, asbestos or slates can be placed on the staging before putting on the compost. Bricks or something similar will be required for the front of the staging to prevent the compost from falling off the edge. Some crops will grow well in pots or boxes of good fertile, rather porous soil.

Lettuces are always wanted. Sowings made towards the end of October will be ready for cutting from late January onwards. Sow the seed in pans or boxes and prick off as soon as the seedlings can be handled. After 2 or 3 weeks they will be ready for their final quarters. Space them 18–20 cm (7–8 ins) apart. Sometimes one can buy strong young seedlings but only do so from a reliable source. Good varieties are: 'Cheshunt Early Giant' and 'Kloek'. The Dutch variety 'Kwiek' is specially suitable for the cold greenhouse. Plant them 20 cm (8 ins) apart each way, watering with derris if aphids appear.

Dwarf French beans can be sown in pots (25 cm (10 ins) diameter being the best). These should be well crocked, and three parts filled with a good compost. Then place 5 or 6 beans 4 cm (1½ ins) deep around the edge of the pots. The soil should be just moist and no water given until the plants are growing nicely. Moisture encourages damping off. As the plants develop more compost is added until it comes to within 25 mm (1 in) of the top of the pots. When the flowers open, syringings of water twice a day should be given to encourage a good set.

Delicious young carrots can be enjoyed in winter if a short horn variety is sown. Boxes can be used but the border is best. Good, but not over rich soil is recommended. Sow in drills 13 mm (½ in) deep and 13–15 cm (6 ins) apart. Dibble in pelleted seed at 7.5 cm (3 ins) apart to avoid wasteful thinning. Keep the soil uniformly moist but not wet. Good varieties for this purpose are 'Early Gem' and 'Amsterdam Forcing'.

Turnips can be treated similarly and are best used while small. Radishes are no trouble and can be grown on the staging or in the border. Sow thinly 13 mm (½ in) deep, firming the soil after sowing.

Melons are a rewarding and delicious greenhouse crop

Keep the compost moist to encourage quick growth. 'French Breakfast' and 'Sparkler' are particularly suitable.

Mustard and cress call for a temperature of around 13°C (55°F). Boxes or pots can be used, or the staging or border where larger quantities are needed. Well firm and water the compost and when most of the moisture has drained away, sow the seed rather thinly, but do not cover it with soil. Sheets of brown paper or hessian laid over the soil help to draw up the seedlings. When they are about 4 cm (1½ ins) high, remove the covers. So that they mature together, cress should be sown four days before mustard.

Mint can be grown in pots. Once growth is seen, give mist-sprays of water to provide the right atmospheric conditions.

To obtain an early crop, cauliflower 'All the Year Round' can also be sown in the greenhouse. Alternatively, plants from earlier outdoor sowings can be brought in and potted up. If they are to mature under glass, space them 45 cm (18 ins) apart about the middle of January. Keep the temperature around 18°C (65°F) during the daytime.

Where a temperature of not less than 18°C (65°F) can be maintained, a sowing of tomatoes made during the last week in November or early December, will with proper management, produce plants from which you can start picking from late March onwards. Sow in trays or pans and prick out and pot on in the usual way.

From seed sown in late November, plants will be ready for their fruiting quarters in January. Between these months, water with care to prevent roots rotting. It will usually be convenient to plant a row of tomatoes beside the cucumber bed just before the cucumber plants are set out. But it will only be possible to obtain two or three trusses of fruit, which will not be so weighty or the quality so good, as the later crops. Their value, however, will more than make up for the reduced crop.

Chicory is another useful winter vegetable. From seed sown in May, the roots are ready for lifting from October onwards, and will produce chicons in January.

39

Greenhouses are usually categorized by the amount of heat that can be provided. The cold greenhouse is one that is never heated by anything but the sun and it is pleasant to realize that good crops can be had without any artificial heat. In extra cold weather some protection can be given by providing blinds or similar covering which can be used as necessary.

The main problem with a cold greenhouse is that the air may become damp, which is why some ventilation should be given whenever weather conditions are reasonable.

The cool greenhouse is one where a minimum night temperature of 4–7°C (40–45°F) can be maintained. This must be controlled, which means adequate ventilation. It is perhaps plants in smaller greenhouses that suffer most when air conditioning is wrong, especially if sufficient ventilators have not been provided. Fresh air is important and though when the air vents are opened this naturally lowers the temperature, it moves the stagnant, dank air, leading to the buoyant atmosphere so vital for plant health.

The intermediate or warm house provides a winter night temperature above 8–9°C (48°F). This allows for a wide range of plants to be cultivated. Such houses are usually very strongly built on firm foundations and sited where they benefit most from the sun's heat.

Here again ventilation plays an important part in keeping the plants healthy. It pays to install automatic ventilation which is governed by the weather conditions and greenhouse temperature. Automatic ventilators cost nothing to run and are easily fitted. They comprise a narrow cylinder filled with a mineral substance which expands or contracts at the smallest change in temperature to operate a ventilator push rod.

In a hot house the winter temperature never falls below 16°C (61°F). Few amateur gardeners can afford this degree of heat.

There are various methods of heating greenhouses, including the hot water system, using solid fuel, a boiler and pipes; electricity, gas or paraffin. The hot water method is satisfactory for warmth is distributed evenly without creating a dry atmosphere. It is doubtful whether a solid fuel boiler is best for the owner who is away all day, since it needs stoking at least twice a day and regular cleaning. This applies even though solid fuel boilers have been modernized and can be kept going longer without attention.

Electrical heating is time and labour-saving and requires no boiler

Extend the season for lettuce by using a frame

Get French beans off to a good start with cloche protection

or fuel storage. With thermostatic control, a pre-determined temperature can be maintained so long as the right heaters have been chosen and there are no power cuts! There are various ways of using electricity for heating:

1 By a wire grid over which air is blown by a fan.
2 By a convector heater exuding warm air. Rapid warmth is produced although distribution is not so even.
3 By radiant tubes, plates or strips.
4 By immersion heater used for hot water pipes.

Soil warmth can also be provided by electric cables. This is used to provide bottom heat for propagating seeds or growing cuttings and does not substantially increase air temperature.

Oil heaters are popular but call for special vigilance with safety measures. Use high-quality paraffin or heating oil that will not give off poisonous fumes. Always keep the burners clean so that incomplete combustion does not release harmful gases, and stand the heater itself in a place where it cannot be knocked over or where severe draughts might catch the flame. For large greenhouses, heaters with outside chimneys should be used but for small houses, several portable models are available. These need little attention other than re-filling. Choose one producing a blue flame which results from complete combustion of the oil. A yellow flame indicates the formation of carbon particles but does not necessarily indicate that harmful fumes are being emitted.

Manufacturers usually indicate how long a heater will burn with one filling. More important is how much heat is produced. Heat is lost through ventilation, but stagnant air encourages fungoid and other disorders, and particularly with paraffin heating a degree of ventilation is always needed, except during the most severe weather.

Growing Fruit Under Glass

At one time it was customary in large gardens to maintain an orchard house. This was usually a structure in which fruit trees were grown either with or without heat. The trees were planted out in borders or grown in pots, in fact they were often grown by both methods since then every part of the orchard house could be fully occupied in the production of fruit.

Vegetables Under Glass in Winter

Vegetable	When and How to Start	Where to Grow	Growing Instructions	Ready for Use
Asparagus	October–November – dig up roots after the foliage has died down	Heated greenhouse (21°C/70°F) or in a frame over a hot bed	Use 3 or 4 year old roots. Pack roots tightly together in boxes or the ground. Cover with 8–15 cm (3–6 in) of soil	Cutting begins 3–4 weeks after the start of forcing
Bean – dwarf French	January–February – sow seeds	Heated greenhouse (13°C/55°F) or warm frame	Sow 6 seeds round the edge of a 25 cm (10 in) pot	March onwards
Bean – climbing French	January–February – sow seeds	Heated greenhouse (13°C/55°F)	Sow seeds in double rows 30 cm (12 in) apart with 75 cm (30 in) between double rows. Thin plants to 20 cm (8 in) apart in the rows	March onwards
Carrot	January–February – sow seeds	Warm or cold frame	Sow short-rooted cultivars. Broadcast seed to give each plant 4 sq cm (1 sq in) of space. Rake in lightly	Early May
Cauliflower	September – sow seeds and then plant into pots/frames in March	Cold greenhouse or cold frames	Space sow seed in frame at 5 cm (2 in) square. Transplant into 25 cm (10 in) pots or into frames at 45 cm (18 in) square	May–June
Chicory	November onwards – lift roots before frosts. Store in frost-free place and force successively	Heated greenhouse (15.5°C/60°F) or warm cellar/shed	Pack roots tightly together in pots or boxes. Cover with straw or stable manure	Hearts or 'chicons' are ready 4–5 weeks after the start of forcing
Chives	January – lift plants from outside	Heated (13°C/55°F) or cold greenhouse/ frame	Pot up plants into 9 cm (3½ in) pots	As soon as new shoots are produced
Endive	July – sow seed outside and lift plants in October	Cold frame	Grow plants at 30 cm (12 in) square. Replant into frames at 30 cm (12 in) square. Blanch heads as required	1 week after start of blanching
Lettuce	September onwards – sow seeds and transplant young plants	Heated (13°C/55°F) or cold greenhouse or frame	Plant successively in heated structures throughout winter. Plant in either November or February in cold houses/frames. Set out plants at 25–30 cm (10–12 in) square	December onwards from heated houses. March–May from cold greenhouses/ frames
Mint	November – lift roots from outside after the foliage has died down	Heated greenhouse (15.5°C/60°F) or frame	Pack roots tightly together in pots or boxes. Cover with 5 cm (2 in) of soil	January onwards
Mustard and cress	September onwards – sow seeds	Heated greenhouse (15.5°C/60°F) or frame	Sow thinly in pots, boxes or on moistened tissue paper. Sow cress 3–4 days before mustard	2–3 weeks after sowing
Peas	December–January – sow seeds	Heated greenhouse (13°C/55°F) or frame	Use dwarf cultivars. Sow 6 seeds round the edge of a 25 cm (10 in) pot or sow thinly in narrow drills	April onwards
Potatoes	December – plant tubers	Slightly heated (7°C/45°F) or cold greenhouses or frames	Plant 2 or 3 'chitted' tubers in a 25 cm (10 in) pot. Alternatively plant tubers 30 cm (12 in) apart in the ground and grow as for outdoor crops	April onwards
Radish	January onwards – sow seeds	Slightly heated (7°C/45°F) or cold greenhouses or frames	Use short-topped cultivars. Broadcast seed at 8 g per m² (¼ oz per sq yd) and lightly rake in	March
Rhubarb	November onwards – lift roots from outside	Heated greenhouse (13°C/55°F) or warm cellar/shed	Pack roots loosely in boxes or on the ground. Cover with soil and maintain complete darkness during forcing	4–5 weeks after start of forcing
Seakale	November onwards – lift roots from outside	Heated greenhouses (13°C/55°F) or warm cellar/shed	As for Rhubarb	5–6 weeks after start of forcing
Tomato	December onwards – sow seeds and subsequently plant into pots or the soil	Heated (17°C/65°F) or cold greenhouse	Raise plants in 9 cm (3½ in) pots. Transplant into 25 cm (10 in) pots or glasshouse soil with plants 35–45 cm (14–18 in) apart	Picking of heated crops begins in April. Cold crops are ready from June onwards

Today things are different and apart from grape vines, it is doubtful whether any gardener would buy a greenhouse solely for the purpose of growing fruit. Not the least advantage of growing any kind of fruit in the greenhouse is that it can be brought to perfection before those growing in the open air. This is especially so if it is possible to heat the house sufficiently to exclude frost during the flowering period and for a few weeks afterwards.

Pot grown trees can be plunged outdoors after the fruit has been gathered and this helps the wood to ripen and form fruit buds for the following year.

The span roofed house with a low brick wall forming the base is best for this purpose. Ideally, it should be sheltered from the north and east and should be capable of receiving full measure of uninterrupted sunshine. Staging is not required, for the pots can stand on beds of gravel.

Grapes are grown on their own roots, being raised from 'eyes' while figs are propagated from cuttings. Other fruit trees grown in pots should be on dwarfing stocks. For apples, the East Malling stock IX is reliable and for pears, Angers Quince or Quince 'A' are suitable. Peach stocks too are favoured by some growers. Peaches themselves are best on Mussel stocks which can also be used for plums.

So long as one is prepared to wait for fruiting, well-grown one-year-old trees can be considered ideal for starting in the 45 cm (18 ins) size pots. Compost on the lines of the John Innes No 2 mixture is quite suitable. Sometimes these young trees have thickish roots and these are best trimmed back with a sharp knife sufficiently to enable the root system to be placed in the pot without cramping. It is important to retain undamaged all the fibrous roots which of course, arise from the thicker roots.

Three- to four-year-old trees, planted very early in November are most suitable. Sometimes they can be bought already in pots from the nurserymen although they cost a little extra. Alternatively, they are sold removed from the pots in which they were started, so they can be easily repotted.

With these older trees some root pruning will be necessary to enable the roots to fit easily in the pots. Although some of the longer top growths can be shortened at the time of potting, any necessary pruning should be done in February when the roots are beginning to grow again.

Plenty of crocks should be placed in the bottom of the pot in the usual way for good drainage and after putting in some of the compost the young tree is placed in the pot and the soil carefully worked among the roots. If, as the soil is added, the base of the pot is tapped sharply on the bench, it will ensure that the soil and roots are in close contact and expel any air pockets. A potting stick is very useful for firming the soil, although care must be taken not to knock off or bruise any of the fibrous roots.

With the one year or maiden trees, it is best to plunge (sink) them in a bed of weathered coal ashes or something similar, leaving them in the open air for one year to become established. After the second year the pots can be taken into the greenhouse each January, where sufficient water with overhead mist sprays should be given from January onwards to encourage early growth.

Older trees can be taken straight into the greenhouse after being potted, and if 60 cm (2 ft) is allowed between them it will permit air to circulate freely. Excepting during frosts, the ventilators should be left wide open until the end of January.

During the early part of the year the soil should be allowed to become almost dry, subsequently give it a good soaking. About the second week in February the ventilators can be kept closed at night and opened just a little on dull days.

It is important not to allow the temperature to attain more than 8°C (46°F) at night, or 12°C (54°F) by day. From this stage onwards, as the flowers begin to open, more heat will be required while regular ventilation will help to set the fruit.

The trees should be encouraged to develop properly by disbudding which takes the place of summer pruning and they are repotted every second year.

During summer frequent watering is necessary, often as much as twice daily. Some liquid feeding will be beneficial from the time the fruits begin to swell, liquid organic manure being ideal for this purpose. Routine spraying with insecticides and fungicides is carried out in the same way as for outdoor trees.

Apples, pears, plums and cherries are not forced but grown under cooler conditions. Plums perhaps, appreciate a little more warmth than the others. Apples and pears can be placed outdoors in a warm sunny spot once the fruit begins to colour and mature.

Peaches can be forced to ripen their fruits in May, and if it is possible to have some trees plunged outdoors these can be brought into the greenhouse once the earlier batch of trees has fruited. Peaches and nectarines are frequently grown as fan trained specimens placed directly into the greenhouse border.

The following varieties are reliable.
Dessert apples: 'Ellisons Orange', 'Ribston Pippin', 'Cox's Orange Pippin' and 'James Grieve'. Cooking apples: 'Annie Elizabeth', 'Newton Wonder' and 'Monarch'.
Pears: 'Doyenné du Comice', 'Louise Bonne of Jersey', 'William's Bon Chrétien'.
Plums: 'Early Transparent' Greengage, 'Victoria' and 'Czar'.

Figs grow well in pots especially 'Brown Turkey' and 'White Marseilles'. Leading shoots must be pinched back when they have made up to 30 cm (1 ft) of new growth and all side shoots stopped two leaves beyond the fruits.

Cherries need selecting with care because of pollination requirements. 'Early Rivers', 'Governor Wood', 'Frogmore Early' and 'Bigarreau Napoleon' are suitable for growing together and two or more varieties should ensure fruit.

The best varieties of grapes for indoor culture include:
'Black Hamburgh', well known for producing good crops with or without heat. It is excellent for growing in pots or very early forcing and also as a pollinator for some shy fruiting varieties. The fruits are large, round and blackish, with a sweet flavour and tender flesh.
'Buckland Sweetwater', is an early sweet variety requiring similar treatment to 'Black Hamburgh'. The large round berries have a bright green, transparent skin which often shows as amber.
'Gros Maroc' is a large thick-skinned grape of a rich reddish-purple colour darkening with age. The tender flesh is sweet and juicy and this is really a first class variety for growing in warmth.
'Madresfield Court' is an early muscat, producing medium sized, tapering bunches of dark purple firm fleshed berries which are tender, juicy and rich. A free setting variety, it likes just a little warmth. The foliage is an attractive reddish-crimson when it fades.
'Royal Muscadine', synonymous with 'Chasselas de Fontaine-bleau' is an early variety, with medium-sized bunches of small golden-yellow berries which turn a cinnamon shade when exposed to bright sunlight. It is excellent for growing in a sheltered garden or cold greenhouse.

Opposite: Amateur growers of greenhouse grapes will get best results from 'Black Hamburgh' which is easiest to pollinate

A-Z Guide to Vegetable Cultivation

The health of a nation or individual is its greatest attribute and a knowledge of food values is of primary importance. Although on reflection it may seem obvious that we ought to eat foods that make us fit and keep us well, we do often ignore this fact.

Well documented experiments tell us that a very large proportion of a healthy diet should consist of fruit and vegetables, both raw and cooked. When cooking vegetables, more of the vitamin content will be retained if the cooking time is as brief as possible. If boiling in water, use very little liquid; or better still, use a steamer. This has the added benefits of retaining food colour and texture.

To obtain the maximum value from ground used for vegetable growing, cultivate those crops most suited to the soil available. Some vegetables are easier to grow than others but there should be no problems with beans, beetroot, carrots, cabbages, lettuce or peas. It is advisable to concentrate on crops which are expensive to buy, those which mature in autumn and winter and those which are scarce in the shops when required.

Successional sowings of many crops during spring and summer ensures a long harvesting period, while intercropping and catch cropping means that the ground is always fully occupied.

Vegetable gardening may seem less glamorous than growing colourful flowers but with the rapid increase in prices many gardeners are now growing their own vegetables to save money. In so doing they are getting their vegetables fresher and provided varieties are selected carefully, they

will enjoy the best in flavour and quality. There is a great deal of pleasure and satisfaction to be gained from growing your own vegetables well and trying out unusual species along with the old favourites.

The regular eating of salads in which green stuffs predominate will provide vitamins and valuable salts which are usually lost in cooking. All too often what are served up as salads are limp lettuce leaves, hard beetroot and tough skinned pieces of tomatoes. There are literally dozens of other items which are easy to grow and which enliven any salad with colour and taste. These we shall refer to in detail later but they include corn salad, endive, dandelion, beet tops, nasturtiums, chinese mustard and asparagus peas. Then there are many flowers which help to make salads more interesting: bergamot, calendula, rosemary and rose petals. Yellow and striped tomatoes also attract attention, while the very small fruiting varieties of various shapes are a little out of the ordinary but certainly tasty.

From the small patch given over to the herb garden there will always be supplies which can make so much difference to the taste and appearance of many dishes prepared in the kitchen.

It pays to buy seeds and plants from a reliable source and to depend on varieties known to be of high quality and yield.

Artichokes

There are at least three very different plants known as artichokes and which are of value both as vegetables and as attractive features of the general garden.

GLOBE ARTICHOKE *Cynara scolymus*

This is the species of which the buds are eaten. The flower is spectacular and the foliage ideal for floral arrangements. It is perennial and provides good ground cover. There are few plants which are so versatile.

In the past some confusion has existed concerning the origin of this plant. It was introduced into Britain from southern Europe about 1548 but is still not as popular here as on the Continent.

Of upright habit, the globe artichoke grows to a height of 1.20–1.80 m (4–6 ft). The well cut leaves are 60–90 cm (2–3 ft) long, greyish-green covered with white down on the undersides. The purple flowers produced in autumn are surrounded by an involucre of fleshy scales which with the central heart are the edible portion of the plant and are considered a great delicacy eaten hot with melted butter or cold with vinaigrette sauce. The flower heads should be cut with a short piece of stem, when young and tender, before opening, otherwise they become coarse.

Globe artichokes grow best in warmer districts. Weathered ashes, strawy manure and bracken are all useful for covering the crowns during late autumn and winter.

Move the ground deeply during the early winter, working in plenty of dung or good compost. Roots or suckers are planted from March to May. These will give a succession of heads from June to early October, especially if strong suckers are used. Plant firmly 75 cm (2½ ft) apart with 1.20 m (4 ft) between the rows. It is possible to intercrop with lettuce, carrots and turnips during the first season.

In good soil globe artichokes will remain productive for 5 or 6 years. An annual winter dressing of decayed farmyard manure will encourage good quality heads. Top dressings of an organic fertilizer in the spring are beneficial.

Always gather the heads at the bud stage. If it is not possible to use them immediately, the stems can be placed in water where they will keep fresh for some days. After the largest central heads have been cut, the side buds will develop. If plants due to be grubbed out are cut down to within a few inches of the ground early in July, new growths will form. The strongest of these can be blanched to provide chards. To do this draw the stems together and tie with raffia, putting straw or hay around the plants and earth them up. Blanching takes 5 or 6 weeks.

Varieties include 'Green Globe' and 'Purple Globe', the former being hardier and having fewer prickles. A particularly good well-flavoured French Variety is 'Gros Vert de Laon'.

JERUSALEM ARTICHOKE
Helianthus tuberosus

The word Jerusalem is believed to be a corruption of an Italian word *girasole* for *Helianthus annus*, the Sunflower to which this plant is related. The name artichoke was given to denote the similarity in the flavour of this root to the globe artichoke scales.

Although a hardy perennial plant, it is better to replant each year. The plants can be used as windbreaks, as a division or screen in the garden or for protecting tender crops, since they grow 1.80–2.10 m (6–7 ft) high.

They do best in enriched deeply dug, medium to light soil. Fish manure, well worked in, is most beneficial. On heavy ground the tubers are difficult to harvest and slugs may be attracted to them. A surface dressing of weathered ashes or sharp sand helps keep pests away.

Sometimes soil conditions make it possible to plant in February but March and early April are the usual times. Place tubers about the size of a pullet's egg 25–30 cm (10–12 ins) apart in drills or furrows about 15 cm (6 ins) deep. Cover lightly, and work in some fish manure or other organic fertilizer.

Allow 90 cm (3 ft) between rows. Once growth starts, draw up soil towards the plants. In exposed windy places, a stake at the end of each row connected with 2 or 3 strands of wire will keep the plants upright.

If the plants show signs of flowering, remove the buds so the plant's energy is devoted to the production of tubers. Towards the end of October cut off top growth within 30 cm (12 ins) of the soil.

The tubers are hardy and can be left in the ground and lifted as required. They have a better flavour freshly dug than stored, although it is possible to store the tubers in boxes of sand or soil or in clamps outdoors. When harvesting remove every tuber from the soil otherwise 'odd' plants become a nuisance the following season.

To prepare Jerusalem artichokes, scrub clean with a stiff vegetable-cleaning brush and drop each one into water to which a little lemon juice has been added to prevent discoloration. Cook by boiling in their skins. Drain and peel after 7 minutes.

RECOMMENDED VARIETIES: 'New White' is of excellent flavour and better than the purple-skinned sort. 'Fuseau' has smooth tubers which are easier to deal with in the kitchen.

Globe artichokes ready for cutting

CHINESE ARTICHOKE *Stachys affinis* (syn. *tubifera*)

Similar in appearance to the Jerusalem artichoke and in flavour to the true artichoke, this is not an artichoke at all. The spirally twisted tubers vary in length from 2.5–7.5 cm (1–3 ins). At their widest part they are about 2.5 cm (1 in) thick. It is a member of the family *Labiatae*; most *stachys* are grown for their attractive flowers.

It flourishes on a well cultivated light soil where the situation is sunny. On poor ground work in compost or organic fertilizer before planting in March and April. Place the tubers 10 cm (4 ins) deep and 23 cm (9 ins) apart with 38–45 cm (15–18 ins) between rows.

Use tubers of Jerusalem artichokes quickly after harvesting

During dry weather the rows should be watered to encourage even development. The tubers mature from November onwards and should be dug as required. Use them as soon as lifted. Never expose them to light or they will turn green and be inedible. If stored under cover for any length of time they may grow again and become flavourless.

ASPARAGUS *Asparagus officinalis*

The wild species grows in sandy coastal regions, which suggests that the plant has a preference for sand and salt, yet large quantities of cultivated asparagus grow in peaty or loamy soils. But whatever soil is used, it must be well-drained. Medium loam enriched with humus matter is ideal; heavy ground by itself is usually too cold for good growth. Applications of manure and other organic material not only assist drainage but make the soil warmer, and a warm soil and favourable aspect encourage an earlier crop. Frost pockets and low lying areas are not suitable for asparagus growing, because the young buds may be damaged by spring frosts.

Since this crop remains in position for many years – up to 20 years is not unusual – soil preparation must be thorough. To grow asparagus on dirty, weed-laden land means constant work in cleaning the site. Early soil preparation and enrichment is essential, and although planting is not done until the spring, manuring must be done in autumn.

There are two ways of obtaining a crop from seeds or plants. Obviously the latter will produce results before plants raised from seed. In a good seed bed, which should be firm and brought to a fine tilth, seed can be sown thinly from the end of April onwards, making the rows 38–45 cm (15–18 ins) apart. The drills should be made 2 cm ($\frac{3}{4}$ in) deep. Germination is always slow and it is a help to mix a little radish seed to mark the rows and facilitate early hoeing, since the radish germinates so quickly. Soaking the seed in water speeds germination. Firm the drills after sowing.

One-year-old crowns can be moved without much damage, but whatever their age at least a year, preferably three, are needed for

Left: Chinese artichokes. Right: Spears of asparagus 'Regal Select'

them to become established. Planting is best done towards the end of March or in early April when the soil is fit to work and warmed by the sun. Rake in a dusting of fish meal, 85 g per m^2 (3 oz per sq yd), before opening the trenches. It is important to spread out the roots at planting time. This applies whether the crowns are being grown on the ridge system, or on a flat bed. The central bud should be at least 8 cm (3 ins) below the surface. Never let the crowns dry out before being planted.

The plants should be set out in rows 60 cm (2 ft) apart, with 1.05 m (3$\frac{1}{2}$ ft) between rows. It is unwise to cut the spears until the plants are three years old, and even then, harvesting should cease quite early in June. Subsequently, the cutting season will be prolonged to the end of that month.

RECOMMENDED VARIETIES:
The question of strains and varieties is important and many specialist growers have their own selection. 'Argenteuil Early' is an old but widely grown variety, most valuable because it is the earliest open ground sort. 'Connover's Colossal' is the best known and always popular. 'Kidner's Variety' produces very large spears. Two lesser known American sorts 'Mary Washington' and 'Martha Washington' are resistant to rust disease, although not as heavy cropping as the English cultivars.

Male plants are preferable as they not only yield more heavily than the female, but

there are no infuriating seedlings appearing in spring, as there would be if females were grown and allowed to seed. Use special knives for cutting the crowns, severing them cleanly 8 cm (3 ins) below soil level.

Always leave some fern to develop to help build up the following season's crowns. Cut the fern down to about 15 cm (6 ins) of the surface soil in the autumn and do not allow the berries to ripen, since unwanted seedlings will result.

AUBERGINE *Solanum melongena* var *Ovigerum*

Often known as egg plants, aubergines are worth growing in a small way. Ideal for cultivating in the warm greenhouse, in warm districts they are often successful outdoors, once risk of frost has passed. Frames and cloches may also be used.

The soil, which must be prepared early, should be enriched with old manure and plenty of compost. Sow seed in late February or early March, using pots or boxes of sandy soil in a temperature of 15°C (60°F).

When they can be handled, the seedlings should be pricked out into 7.5 cm (3 ins) pots, or into soil blocks, using fairly rich compost. By the end of April they should be ready for 13 cm (5 in) pots. This will prevent any check from starvation. Spray with water daily to prevent red spider damage.

Towards the end of May, the plants can be put under frames or cloches, which should be kept closed for a few days, so the plants settle down quickly. When the plants are 15 cm (6 ins) high, take out the growing point.

When the resultant laterals have grown 10 cm (4 ins), they too should be stopped. Allow up to six fruits to develop on each plant removing all others which attempt to form. Keep on with the overhead sprayings to ensure that red spider does not gain a hold. Later crops can be sown directly into prepared sites under cloches.

The fruits are ready to gather from July to October. They should be handled with care since they bruise easily. To cook, the skins may be removed or left on. Slice and leave for 30 minutes after a dusting with salt. Pat dry and fry or bake in a casserole.

RECOMMENDED VARIETIES: usually offered simply as purple or white, 'Burpee Hybrid' is a fine dark violet sort and 'Blanche longue de la Chine', a good fleshy white cultivar.

Aubergines are best grown in pots under glass

Beans

There are several different vegetables of varying habits falling into this broad category.

BROAD BEAN *Vicia faba*

One of the oldest of cultivated vegetables having been grown in Britain for centuries, it is an annual with stiff quadrangular, hollow stems. The large seeds are white or green, according to variety. Broad beans will grow on almost any soil and while they like moisture, avoid badly drained ground liable to become waterlogged in winter and that which dries out in early summer.

A cool, deep, fertile soil, manured for previous crops is ideal and there should be no lack of humus. Lime too is necessary, although it should not be applied at the same time as farmyard manure. It is better to give a dusting of lime when the final surface preparations are being carried out. Broad beans like an open, but not exposed position, with plenty of light and spring sunshine, without being exposed to winds.

Sowings can be made outdoors in November or from mid-February to April, or under cloches from January onwards. Sowings after mid-April crop poorly and are subject to blackfly. Even for the November sowings some kind of glass covering is useful, since severe frosts will sometimes damage the plants. The plants will need uncovering in April, by which time they will be nearing the top of the glass. It is not worth making an autumn sowing in cold districts or where the soil is naturally very heavy and badly drained. Should weather conditions prevent an early outdoor sowing, sow the seed in February in boxes in a heated greenhouse for planting outdoors in April.

For the earliest sowings, the Longpod varieties should be used, since they are

Longpod broad beans at harvesting stage

good flavour; 'Red Epicure', a strong grower notable for its rich chestnut-crimson coloured beans of delicious flavour and 'Dreadnought', large pods of excellent quality.

WINDSOR VARIETIES: 'The Sutton', growing about 30 cm (1 ft) high and branching freely; 'Beck's Green Gem', an old but still reliable variety; 'Green Windsor', excellent flavour; 'Imperial White Windsor', long pods with large beans and 'Promotion' a high yielding variety.

HARICOT BEANS *Phaseolus vulgaris*

Very useful for winter eating, these are varieties of dwarf French beans specially grown for their dried seeds, not fresh pods. It is a pity haricot beans are not more widely cultivated. Sowing and culture are the same as for other French beans but the pods are left on the plants until they are ripe and are turning yellow. To give the plants an early start they can be sown under cloches at the beginning of April.

They can be gathered individually as they reach ripeness but it is easier to pull up the complete plants and hang them in bunches or in a sack in any airy place to allow them to become really dry.

When the pods are brittle the beans can be shelled or where large quantities are concerned, the pods can be carefully beaten with a stick which will knock out the seeds. These should be spread on paper or sacking in a cool greenhouse or other airy place, to complete drying, when the seed should be really hard and free from mildew. It is important that the seeds should be quite dry before they are stored in jars, tins or sacks. The storage place must always remain dry or the beans will be affected with mildew and will taste unpleasant.

RECOMMENDED VARIETIES: Varieties are now available which ripen satisfactorily in temperate climates. 'Brown Dutch', a well-known vigorous cultivar with yellowish-brown seeds. 'Comtesse de Chambord', strong growing variety, smallish white round seeds.

CLIMBING FRENCH BEANS
Phaseolus vulgaris

These varieties can be cultivated outdoors in warm districts but they are particularly

hardier and heavier yielding than the Windsor. The latter, however, are of better flavour. Sow the seed 5 cm (2 ins) deep in double rows, with 20 cm (8 ins) between the drills, 75 cm (2½ ft) being allowed between each of these double rows. Place the seeds zig-zag, 15 cm (6 ins) apart in double rows. Dwarf varieties can have rather closer spacing.

Particularly with autumn sowings, extra seeds should be sown at the end of the rows for filling up gaps. As the seedlings begin to push through the soil they should be slightly earthed up. This will give added protection as well as anchoring the plants better. The earliest sown plants can be protected with bracken, straw or cloches during severe weather. This covering should be removed when it is mild.

Keep down weeds by regular hoeing along the rows, which will also benefit the plants. Frequent inspection of the plants is advisable so that blackfly can be dealt with by spraying derris or a similar insecticide before the pests gain a hold.

Pinch out the top growth once the first trusses of flowers are in full bloom. This not only helps the pods to develop well, but discourages blackfly which like to settle there.

Broad beans should be gathered while they are young and before the skins become tough. Early picking will not only mean good flavoured tender beans, but a heavier and more prolonged cropping season. Side shoots should be removed too, although sometimes when the main growth has finished cropping, a secondary basal growth develops and will yield quite well. The top growth of finished plants can be cut off and the roots dug in.

LONGPOD VARIETIES: 'Major', early, producing long pods of white beans. 'Aquadulce Claudia', very early, excellent for autumn sowings; 'Longfellow' heavy cropper of suitable for growing in the greenhouse during the winter and early spring. For the earliest crops, the seeds should be sown during the first days of August.

A deep well drained soil containing a fair supply of organic matter is needed. Avoid the over use of nitrogen or the plants will become leafy at the expense of beans. Put one bean in each position where a plant is wanted, with a few extra seeds at the end of each row to gap up with or pull out as the case may be. For healthy growth before sowing or planting, a soil temperature of 12°C (55°F) is necessary.

Climbing French beans can be grown in greenhouses which are wired overhead for tomatoes and the rows can be the same distance apart as the tomato plants, that is, a double row 45 cm (18 ins) apart, then a space of 68 cm (27 ins) and then another double row 45 cm (18 ins) apart. The distance between the plants in the rows is 45 cm (18 ins). For supports, a stout peg to which is attached a T piece, is driven in at the end of the rows to carry a wire 10 cm (4 ins) from ground level exactly over the rows.

A single strand of soft stout string is tied to this wire and to the top tomato wire and the plants are trained up it. Never tie the string to the collar of the bean plant as is frequently done with tomatoes. A night temperature of 15°C (60°F) is required at all times for an early crop of beans. This can be increased by several degrees during the day.

A well-ventilated house is necessary and frequent overhead sprayings of water are desirable to keep down red spider and encourage quick growth.

Once the plants are climbing well and beginning to flower less overhead spraying is required. Careful feeding is needed, should it be decided upon at all, and it is best to use organic based liquid fertilizer. It is advisable to stop the laterals otherwise growth tends to become too crowded.

The cultivation of a spring crop of climbing beans can be gained by sowing seed in the middle of February, when the soil is warm. If the light is very poor bean plants will not climb.

For this sowing, it is best to use 20.5–23 cm (8–9 in) pots into which 6 seeds are sown when the compost is nicely moist so that watering is not needed again until after germination. Cover the pots with glass and paper, removing both when the seedlings appear.

The beans should be picked while young and tender and to ensure a continuous supply of fine-flavoured crops.

Once the crop is finished and the plants are removed, they can be followed by a planting of late tomatoes.

RECOMMENDED VARIETIES: 'Veitch's Climbing' also known as 'Guernsey Climbing' has flat 15 cm (6 ins) pods. 'Kentucky Wonder' forms clusters of round fleshy pods. 'Violet Podded Stringless' is of good flavour and has violet pods which turn deep green when cooked.

DWARF FRENCH BEANS
Phaseolus vulgaris

Although usually referred to as French beans, there is reason to believe they came from South America. They are sometimes known as kidney beans because of the shape of the seeds which can be eaten green or dried. In the United States stringless beans are referred to as snap beans or shell beans if grown for their seeds.

Dwarf French beans will grow on most soils that are reasonably warm and well drained. Early soil preparation is advisable, working in well-rotted manure or compost and raking the soil down fine. These beans make a good follow-on crop for ground that grew brassicas, including Brussels sprouts, for which the ground was well enriched with old manure. Bone meal or fish manure at 85 g per m² (3 oz per sq yd) provides phosphates, and 112 g (4 oz) per sq yd of lime should be given if the soil is sour.

In warm districts it is possible to sow seed at the end of April but usually it is best to

Dwarf French bean 'Remus'

wait until May. Take out double drills 5 cm (2 ins) deep, 22 cm (9 ins) wide with 75 cm (2½ ft) between the double rows. Stagger the seed 12–15 cm (5–6 ins) apart. To allow for possible failures, sow extra seeds at the end of the row. Gluts can be avoided by sowing small quantities at two or three weekly intervals until mid-July.

Bushy sticks placed at intervals along the rows will keep the plants upright and prevent the beans from trailing on the ground where they will be nibbled by slugs.

Pick the beans before they grow old and stringy. This not only ensures good, tender pods, but encourages the plants to keep on cropping. Under good cultivation one may reckon that a double row a metre (yard) long will produce about 2 kg (4 lbs) of pods.

Flageolet beans are the seeds of dwarf French beans, culled from pods gathered before they are fully ripe. The pods are discarded. Flageolet beans are widely used in France but as yet unfamiliar in English cookery. They have a deliciously delicate flavour, however, well worth trying, and are best prepared by steaming or minimal boiling in water before serving with butter and a sprinkling of herbs.

RECOMMENDED VARIETIES: 'Black Prince' of medium habit, pods up to 16 cm (6½ ins) long; 'Canadian Wonder', an old variety still good if a selected strain is sown; 'Masterpiece', excellent flavour, useful for cloche culture; 'Mont d'or', a golden podded or wax bean of dwarf, leafy habit; 'Pencil Pod Black Wax', bushy plants slightly curved medium sized pods; 'Tendergreen', stringless beans 15 cm (6 ins) long; 'The Prince', fleshy pods of splendid flavour.

RUNNER BEANS *Phaseolus multiflorus*

Usually treated as an annual, the runner bean is actually a perennial, forming tuberous roots which can be lifted in the autumn and stored for replanting the following spring. Excepting during times of seed shortages, there is no advantage in doing this, for the seeds sown in early spring give an abundant crop the same year. That most varieties produce scarlet flowers originally gave rise to the common name of Scarlet Runner, although some varieties have white, pink or red and white flowers.

Runner beans can be used effectively as attractive climbing plants as well as producing a heavy crop over a long period. They should be given a deep, cool root run, if possible, where the ground has been double dug with decayed manure, compost or other bulky material worked in. Apply a surface dressing of lime just before the seed is sown.

It is not advisable to sow outdoors until danger of frosts has passed. To make sure of an early crop, where a frame or a greenhouse is available, seed can be sown early in boxes about 13 cm (5 ins) deep, the seedlings being planted out after the frosts. Cloches can be used for standing over ground where the rows are to be made.

For kitchen use it is not the length of the beans that matters so much as straight brittle pods. For exhibition purposes it is a different matter for there is keen competition to secure really long, clean pods and good cultivation will bring rewards.

For the growing position a deep rich soil is best. On light, sandy soils it is helpful to take out trenches up to 20 cm (8 ins) deep and to place in them a really thick layer of compost, peat and other moisture retentive material with the addition of fish meal. Finish off the trench so there is a depression, for this will help to prevent the roots drying out during summer. On heavy land it is best not to make a trench but to dig the entire plot, otherwise the trench may become a sump for draining water.

Double rows 23–30 cm (9–12 ins) apart in the trenches makes it easy for staking and where a quantity of beans are being sown, the double rows should be 1.50–1.80 m (5–6 ft) apart. If possible, supports should be in position before the seed is sown 23 cm (9 ins) apart in the rows.

Hazel and ash poles are very suitable and

A white-flowered variety of runner beans with stringless pods

they can be placed upright or at an angle so the tops cross. Other poles placed through the tops of the crossed poles and fastened together, form a strong structure. Alternatively, string or bushy hazel sticks can be used or a group of poles or strings can be placed in a circle and connected to one central pole to form a tent-like structure. Alternatively, use proprietary bean support frameworks, or stout netting.

Once they begin to climb, the seedlings need some directing so they do not grow into each other. It is possible to grow runner beans without any support and for this purpose the growing points are pinched out when the plants are 25–30 cm (10–12 ins) high. The resultant shoots are also stopped and this leads to bushy growth, but heavier, more shapely beans and a cleaner crop undamaged by slugs are produced when supports are provided.

Frequent summer hoeings will keep down weeds and a mulch of leaf mould, peat or strawy manure in early summer will act as a weed smotherer and prevent the soil from drying out. Harvest the pods regularly,

Support systems: left, battens and strings; centre, rows of poles; right, netting stretched between posts

otherwise the production of pods will slow down. If the beans cannot be used fairly quickly after being picked the stem ends can be placed in shallow water where they will remain fresh for several days if kept cool.

Frequent overhead sprayings of water during summer will keep the foliage in good condition and encourage a good set. The dropping of buds and flowers before the pods develop is often due to a dry atmosphere and the absence of pollinating insects. Overhead sprayings help to distribute the pollen.

VARIETIES: Many varieties are available, including 'Achievement', 'Crusader', 'Enorma', 'Prize-winner', 'Scarlet Emperor', 'Streamline' and 'White Achievement'.

'Hammond's Dwarf' and its white form, are dwarf non-trailing 'runner' beans growing about 40 cm (16 ins) high. Extra early

'Streamline' is a reliable runner bean

and excellent for growing under cloches, they do not need staking and produce 20–23 cm (8–9 ins) pods continuously over a period of ten weeks or more if gathered regularly. Seed is sometimes difficult to obtain.

SOYA BEANS *Glycine hispida*

Although many rather extravagant claims have been made for the virtue of this bean, there is no doubt that it is a most valuable food crop which can be grown under widely varying conditions. Under ordinary good culture it produces a sizeable yield and since it has a high protein level, which is above that of other vegetables, as well as various vitamins, it is well worth growing. Even when the size of crop is limited because of adverse summer weather conditions, the

protein and vitamins content makes it a crop to grow. These beans have many uses in the kitchen and are sometimes used as a substitute for meat.

Growing 45–50 cm (18–20 ins) high, seeds can be sown in boxes in the same way as dwarf French beans, the seedlings being moved to their cropping sites in early June. Alternatively, seed can be sown in prepared positions in a sunny spot in the open ground at the end of May or early June. Growth is sometimes slow at first and the flowers are somewhat insignificant, but subsequently there is much vigour.

A soil containing plenty of humus matter and not lacking in moisture will provide the plants with the conditions they like.

BEETROOT *Beta vulgaris* var *esculenta*

A native of N. Africa and W. Asia, this crop is now widely distributed throughout the world. It is in great demand for salads although it can also be served hot. The roots should be used while young and tender before they become coarse and stringy.

A light deep soil is best for this crop, preferably one that was heavily manured with old compost or some other organic manure the previous season. A dusting of fish manure forked into the surface soil before seed is sown will do much good. The earliest sowings of globe varieties can be made in late April or early May according to soil conditions, with further globe sowings until late June. Maincrop varieties should be sown during the last half of May.

Space the rows 38 cm (15 ins) apart and 2.5 cm (1 in) deep. Each beetroot capsule is really a cluster of seeds so that sowing must be done very thinly. If two capsules are dropped in at stations 15 cm (6 ins) apart they can finally be thinned to the strongest plant per station. The second thinnings will be large enough to use.

Weeds should be kept down by careful hoeing which also aerates the soil surface. When pulling or lifting the roots for use, twist off the tops of red or crimson varieties – do not cut them or they may 'bleed' and lose colour.

Left in the ground too long, beetroot may be damaged by wet and frost, therefore lift and store early in November. Handle with care to avoid bruisings and store the roots in boxes of sandy soil or in clamps of small size to prevent heating. Heaps 1.20–1.50 m (4–5 ft) high and 1.20 m (4 ft) wide are

large enough. Provide a ventilation shaft of straw, or a drain pipe can be used to allow sufficient air to keep the roots firm. When dry, place the roots pointing inwards, in an orderly manner to form a compact heap.

RECOMMENDED VARIETIES: round or globe-shaped: 'Beethoven', 'Boltardy' and 'Detroit'; intermediate or oval; 'Formanova'; long; 'Cheltenham Green Top'.

A new variety known as 'Burpees Golden' 'Golden Beet' produces globe-shaped roots with golden skin and yellow flesh. It does not 'bleed' and can be cooked in the usual way while the leaves can be served like spinach.

BROCCOLI, SPROUTING
Brassica oleracea var *italica*

This is a hardy vegetable of good flavour which makes a pleasant change, especially as it matures when other green vegetables

are becoming scarce. The same soil preparation and cultural methods are required as for cauliflowers. Since the plants are fairly tall growing, they should not be placed where they are exposed to strong winds.

Seed need not be sown until April, but early soil preparation is necessary. Sow thinly and transplant early so the seedlings do not become drawn. Farmyard manure or a good substitute should be worked in. Alternatively choose a position well manured for a previous crop. Give a surface dusting of lime before planting out, if the soil is acid. Very rich soil leads to soft, sappy growth, liable to winter damage. Allow 75 cm ($2\frac{1}{2}$ ft) between the plants.

Sprouting broccoli is gathered when the flower heads are just beginning to form. If cut about two thirds of their length, more shoots will be produced from the base of the

stems. Do not cut off the leaves since these afford some protection to the sprouts, although they can eventually be used. As with other members of the brassica family, sprouting broccoli is much more palatable steamed than boiled.

RECOMMENDED VARIETIES: 'Early Purple Sprouting', at its best from February onwards; 'Late Purple Sprouting' matures from March onwards; 'White Sprouting' is hardy and ready from early March onwards.

'**Calabrese**' (green sprouting broccoli) is an excellent vegetable for late summer and autumn use which differs from the ordinary sprouting broccoli in that it first produces a good sized central head 15 cm (6 ins) or more in diameter. When this is cut, the plant produces from each joint, shoots or sprouts which should be gathered when they have a 10–12 cm (4–5 ins) stem.

Under good growing conditions 'Cala-

brese' is very productive, more so than the purple and white forms, probably because it makes most of its growth during the better weather conditions.

RECOMMENDED VARIETIES: There are now several strains including 'Atlantic', ready for cutting in the autumn from a spring sowing: 'Gem', F_1 hybrid, 'Corvet', is a F_1 hybrid which is particularly useful for deep freezing; 'Green Comet' is a F_1 hybrid giving a really large head, and 'Late Corona' a F_1 hybrid which is late maturing.

'Nine Star Perennial' provides heads rather like small cauliflowers. Since it is a perennial, the ground must be in really good condition at planting time.

Apart from farmyard and other bulky manures added when the soil is being prepared, a good dressing of fish manure or bone meal, say 85–112 g per m^2 (3–4 oz per sq yd) will encourage the production of the nine broccoli heads each year.

Sow seeds in April, first pricking out the seedlings to another bed so that they form plenty of roots and become sturdy specimens for planting 75 cm ($2\frac{1}{2}$ ft) apart each way in September. Cut the first heads in the following April or May.

A dressing of fish manure each spring is helpful and the plants should be replaced every three years.

BRUSSELS SPROUTS
Brassica oleracea var *bullata*

This most valuable and popular member of the large brassica family was derived through selection from the wild cabbage. Although it was not until towards the end of the last century that Brussels sprouts became widely grown in most European countries, they were known and cultivated in Belgium, particularly in areas around Brussels, more than 750 years ago. The sprouts are produced in the axils of the leaves in the first year of this biennial plant.

It is successfully cultivated in all soils, excepting those which are badly drained or very loose. The soil should be highly fertile. For best results the aim should be to provide an open, airy situation, with wide spacing to ensure good sprout development. A long season of growth is required.

Deep, early cultivation should be carried out, not only to allow the soil to become sweetened and well-weathered, but to give it time to settle. Good sized, tight sprouts cannot be obtained from hastily prepared, loose

Above: Round beet 'Detroit'; above right: 'Calabrese' green sprouting broccoli; below: the purple-sprouting variety

Brussels sprouts 'Early Half Tall' will be ready from October

soil. There is no hard and fast rule regarding the place in crop rotation of sprouts, although they follow potatoes or early turnips very well.

Sprouts do best where they follow a well manured and deeply cultivated crop, where the soil does not lack lime. Where such a position cannot be provided, farmyard manure and well-rotted compost, say a bucketful to a square metre, should be worked into the ground in late autumn or winter. A dressing of a good organic fertilizer such as fish manure, hoof and horn or bone meal is beneficial, and hoof and horn in particular supplies slow acting nitrogen. Alternatively, use a balanced compound fertilizer. Also give an occasional top dressing of organic based fertilizer when plants are in full growth, but not after the end of June, otherwise leafy growth will develop and the sprouts will be loose and of poor quality. Make sure there is potash in the soil for this encourages firmness.

Sowings can be made under cloches or in the cold frame during February. The resultant seedlings should be pricked out 8 cm (3 ins) apart in prepared beds under other cloches or frames but must not be coddled. Subsequently they can be moved to prepared open ground sites.

The main outdoor sowings for succession should not be attempted before April, following good weather in March. It is also possible to make open ground sowings in August or early September. In normal sea-

sons, these plants stand the weather well. Sowing at various times ensures a crop of sprouts over an extended period, although improved modern strains make autumn sowings unnecessary so long as early spring sowings are made. All outdoor sowings must be thinned out early, to ensure sturdy growth followed by firm sprouts.

Once the seedlings are 10–12 cm (4–5 ins) tall, which will usually be from early May onwards, they should be moved to their final positions. Choose a showery period for the job or water the plants in. Space the dwarf sorts 75 cm (2½ ft) apart and the tall, strong growing varieties 90 cm (3 ft) apart. This spacing allows for an early catch crop of lettuce, radish or spinach to be grown between the rows. Where a large number of plants are being grown, the growing points of some specimens can be pinched out when the buttons are beginning to form, to ensure that all the plants do not mature together. It also helps the buttons to develop firmly.

Since Brussels sprouts like firm root conditions, tread the soil if it is puffy, before planting. Weeds must be kept down and decayed leaves on the Brussels' stems removed to prevent grey mould from developing. Always use up loose, blown buttons first, but do not cut off the top of the plants until all the buttons have been picked. The head of the plant gives protection and helps in the growth of the buttons.

Picking will normally commence from late October onwards and provided suc-

cessional sowings of the right varieties have been made and it should be possible to gather sprouts well into April.

Apart from frost and wet damage which sometimes occur, one occasionally finds when cutting open a sprout that there is a dark streak of tissue in the middle. This is usually due to the plants growing in poor, wet, badly drained soils. Brussels sprouts are subject to the same diseases and pests as other members of the cabbage family but should not suffer unduly except from attacks of mealy cabbage aphid. Malathion may help but the pests are difficult to control.

RECOMMENDED VARIETIES: many improved cultivars have been introduced and among the best are the following F_1 hybrids. 'Achilles', producing long lasting tight sprouts; 'Citadel', maincrop; 'Peer Gynt', early; 'King Arthur', prolific; and 'Focus', extra good flavour. Other reliable varieties include 'Irish Elegance', 'Roodnerf Stiekema Early' and 'Roodnerf Stabilo', late cropping.

CABBAGE *Brassica oleracea* var *capitata*

Wild cabbages can still be found growing in many Mediterranean regions and parts of England and Ireland. Breeding over many years has given us the varieties we now know so well.

Cabbages contain a fair amount of vita-

'Hispi' is a reliable summer cabbage

min C, with smaller quantities of vitamins A and B and also calcium and iron. They are usually divided or classified as 1 spring cabbage, 2 summer and autumn cabbages, 3 winter varieties, including savoys. Botanically the savoy is *Brassica oleracea* var *bullata* and originated in Savoy, France; they are described below.

Sow cabbages in prepared seed beds in drills about 18 mm ($\frac{1}{2}$ ins) deep and 15 cm (6 ins) apart. As a precaution against club root, sprinkle calomel dust along each drill. Where cabbage rootfly has been a problem use Bromophos insecticide. This applies to all the cabbage family. Lightly firm the soil after sowing to assist germination. Do not leave the plants too long in the seed bed or they may become thin and drawn, with a poor root system.

Where possible spring maturing sorts should be given light ground, since this warms up quickly and encourages rapid development. If cabbages follow a well manured crop such as peas or beans there will be sufficient bulk in the soil. If humus is not present it will pay to work in decayed manure, compost or similar material. In the absence of any of these bulky types of manures peat or leaf mould can be used, plus a good dressing of fish manure. Lime is needed by all brassicas and if the soil is acid a dusting of garden lime should be applied as a top dressing before planting out.

To provide cabbages throughout the year means sowing seeds at different times. Cabbages to mature in late spring or early

Round-headed cabbages of the Dutch type mature from October to February

summer should be sown in late July, when they can follow early potatoes or peas. Transplant in September or October making the rows 45 cm (18 ins) apart with 22–30 cm (9–12 ins) between the plants. If, in April, the plants are growing slowly, an application of nitro chalk 28–43 g per m^2 (1–1$\frac{1}{2}$ oz per sq yd) will encourage growth.

Summer and autumn maturing cabbages are sown from February onwards under glass and outdoors from March onwards. Sow these little and often to ensure that all the plants do not mature together.

A sowing of the summer sorts can also be made in January or February in the cool greenhouse or frame. Plants from these sowings are planted outdoors in March.

Sow winter cabbages from the end of April to late May, the seedlings being planted out when the soil is moist. They need wider spacing than the earlier sorts. Make the rows up to 60 cm (2 ft) apart with 38–45 cm (15–18 ins) between plants. As soon as they can be handled thin the seedlings 5 cm (2 ins) apart. When they are about 15 cm (6 ins) transfer them to their final quarters.

Late cabbages may need extra phosphate and more potash to enable them to stand winter weather. Spring cabbages can be helped by applying a dusting of nitro chalk along the rows. Any spring cabbages which fail to heart may be used as spring greens.

Red cabbages are usually grown for pickling. but are very useful as an unusual winter vegetable cooked with onions, apple and a little spice, or chopped raw as a colourful variation on coleslaw. Sow in March, eventually spacing the plants 45 cm (18 ins) apart. They are better after they have been touched by frost. A distinct type of very hardy winter cabbage, it will stand quite severe frosts without harm. Savoys have deeply crinkled leaves and this seems to be the reason why some people do not grow them, preferring, instead, the smooth leaves of the cabbage. Properly cooked, savoys are tasty and especially valuable in northern areas and other cold districts.

They grow in ordinary soil which has been well cultivated and can be used to follow early potatoes or peas. The ground will probably have been manured for these crops, so that all that needs doing is to fork over the surface and, if the soil is acid, give a dusting of lime. On poor land compost or fish manure can be worked in. Make the ground firm before planting.

Seed is sown in April, the plants being moved to their final positions in July, preferably during showery weather, otherwise the ground should be watered. Allow 60 cm (2 ft) each way for the bigger-growing sorts and 46 cm (18 ins) for the smaller kinds.

RECOMMENDED VARIETIES: spring maturing varieties: 'April', 'Durham Early', 'Hispi', 'Offenham Flower of Spring', 'Wheeler's Imperial'; summer maturing: 'Extra Earlihead', 'Greyhound', 'Golden Acre', 'Hidena',

Cardoons tied up for blanching

'Derby Day' is a good summer cabbage

'Vienna', 'Winnigstadt'; autumn and winter maturing: 'Christmas Drumhead', 'Winter White'. Savoys: in order of maturing, from October to April: 'Dwarf Green Curled', 'Best of All', 'January King', 'Ormskirk Late', and 'Alexander's No. 1'. Red cabbage: 'Niggerhead', 'Ruby Ball'.

Savoy cabbages like 'Best of All' are very hardy

CARDOON *Cynara cardunculus*

A near relative of the globe artichoke, this handsome plant has silvery, fern-like foliage. It is grown for its blanched stalks, which are not unlike the chards produced by globe artichokes. These are used in the same way as celery, both subjects requiring similar culture.

Cardoons like a rich, moist soil and succeed in trenches about 30 cm (1 ft) deep and 20 cm (8 ins) wide, where there is rotted manure or decayed compost at the bottom.

Plants can sometimes be bought but usually, they are raised from seed sown from March onwards, keeping the roots moist throughout summer. Occasional applications of liquid manure will encourage good, tender growth.

From mid-September the plants will be ready for blanching. One method is to tie all the leaves together and then earth up as for celery, or corrugated tubes can be placed over the plants. Alternatively, bracken or straw can be used for a covering. The blanching process takes eight or nine weeks. The stems should be dry before starting the blanching, or they may rot when earthed up. The balanced stalks and inner leaves that are used in salads, soups and stews.

RECOMMENDED VARIETIES: there are two types – the French cardoon, often listed as Tours, has long stems with prickles which makes it difficult to work with. The spineless Spanish cardoon has less flavour and the plants apt to run to seed.

CARROT *Daucus carota* var *sativus*

The carrot is probably unequalled by any other vegetable as a source of vitamin A, and the roots also contain quantities of vitamin B and C.

Although there are white and yellow carrots, it is the orange and orange-red varieties which are usually grown. Colour is important, since it is directly related to the carotin content, which is found in the outer layer of the root. Heavy foliage indicates a thick core, although it is necessary for the foliage to be strong enough to allow for easy pulling.

This crop likes a deep soil where the moisture content can be maintained at a good level. Drought conditions affect the size and texture of the roots. Plenty of organic matter should be in the soil, but where manure is not well rotted, the roots become forked.

Sowing time extends over a long period, and in favourable seasons drilling can start in February, using a stump-rooted variety such as 'Nantes'. Cloches can be used to secure a very early crop. To facilitate even,

thin sowing, seed should be mixed with sand and some gardeners make this moist, to encourage quick germination. The drills should be about 6–13 mm ($\frac{1}{4}$–$\frac{1}{2}$ in) deep and 30–38 cm (12–15 ins) apart, the surface being lightly firmed after sowing.

Carrotfly can be a menace, and is best controlled by thin sowing and disturbing the foliage as little as possible, and dusting drills with Bromophos.

Late sowings can be made in July, with early or quick maturing varieties. These will provide tender young roots in autumn and early winter. These normally escape the carrotfly.

Although shorthorn varieties are excellent for growing under cloches or early outdoor sowings, they do not produce the weight of crop yielded by the intermediate and long rooted type.

The intermediate varieties are best for most soils, since they do not need such a great depth of soil and there is less difficulty in storing than the long varieties.

RECOMMENDED VARIETIES: earlies 'Early Horn', 'Nantes', 'Parisian Rondo'; intermediate: 'Ormskirk Market', 'Chantenay', 'James Scarlet', 'Amsterdam Forcing'; long: 'St Valery', 'Vita Longa'.

CAULIFLOWER (winter type)
Brassica oleracea var *botrytis*

Once known as heading broccoli winter cauliflower. Most winter varieties fold their leaves protectively over the curd. Summer cauliflower leaves tend to grow upright.

Winter cauliflowers grow on many types of soil so long as they are fertile. An open, but not exposed position is needed, and one not likely to become a frost pocket. Freshly manured ground is not required. Winter cauliflowers are best planted after early potatoes, beans, peas or lettuce. An application of lime is recommended. A dusting of superphosphate and sulphate of potash worked into the seed bed provides the phosphates young cauliflowers need. Avoid fertilizers rich in nitrogen for these encourage quick growth of plants that are easily damaged by frosts.

Bring the seed bed to a fine tilth for even germination and lumpy soil gives cover to flea-beetles. Sowing time is from late March onwards according to soil, weather and variety. Make the drills 13 mm ($\frac{1}{2}$ in) deep and 23 cm (9 in) apart. Sow thinly and after dusting the drills with calomel powder as a

Early carrot 'Nantes' is of French origin

precaution against club root lightly firm the soil after covering the seed. Keep the bed weed-free by frequent light hoeings or hand pullings. Ground reserved for cauliflowers should be well-cultivated making the surface firm but not hard. Do not leave the plants in the seed bed too long or they will

'St Valery' is one of the most popular long carrots

become thin and lanky and never produce good heads.

Discard coarse, poorly shaped, badly coloured plants and any without growing points. Ideal seedlings have short sturdy stems, plenty of fibrous roots and four or five good coloured leaves. This should be the size if you have to buy plants. Dull, showery weather is the best time to move the plants but if it becomes necessary to transplant during dry periods water the seedlings in. The old practice was to 'puddle' the plants. It consists of mixing soil, cow dung and water in a bucket and putting the roots in it. This mixture clings to the roots and supplies moisture for some time.

Do not plant cauliflowers too closely. Smaller growing sorts, which include the increasingly popular Australian varieties, should be placed 45 cm (18 ins) apart with 60 cm (2 ft) between the rows, but most varieties need to be 60 cm (2 ft) apart with 67–75 cm (27–30 ins) from row to row. Close spacing prevents plants from developing fully and makes it easy for disease to

gain a hold. Plant firmly and keep the hoe moving, particularly until the plants are established. Draw the soil towards the plant stems for this anchors the plants more firmly, giving protection and preventing moisture settling round the stems.

Cut the heads as they mature. Left too long they continue to grow and the good tight head of curds will open out and turn a poor colour and become 'ricey'. Early morning sun can damage the curds. To prevent this, heel over the plants in November so that the heads face the north. This is done by taking some soil away from the north side of the plants and pulling them over, then place the soil on the opposite side from where it was taken, making it nicely firm.

If heads mature faster than needed, they can be kept back a bit by bending a leaf or two over the centre of the plants, which also gives protection from frost. If the entire plant is pulled up and hung in a dry, airy place the curds will remain in a good condition for seven to fourteen days.

RECOMMENDED VARIETIES: autumn and winter use: 'Veitch's Self Protecting' (August, September); 'Snow's Superb Winter White' (November onwards); 'St Agnes' (December–January). Australian varieties include: 'Boomerang Bondi' (September); 'Kangaroo' (August–October); 'Barrier Reef' (late October); 'Canberra' (October–November) and 'Snowcap' (November–December).

For spring use: 'Leamington' (March–April); 'Markanta' (April–May).

For summer use: 'Royal Oak' (May–June); 'Asmer June' and 'Asmer Midsummer' (June).

CELERIAC *Apium graveolens* var *rapaceum*

This is the delicious turnip-rooted or knob celery with a nutty flavour not found in other vegetables. Splendid for winter use, it can be grown where celery has proved difficult to cultivate. It is at its best from mid-October onwards. The roots can be peeled and boiled or grated and used in salads.

Since celeriac is planted on the flat it means less work than is needed for celery. Best results come where an open sunny position is provided. Dig the ground deeply during the winter adding farmyard manure

or compost. Leave the surface rough for the weather to break down, and apply a dusting of lime.

Sow the seeds in a pot or box of light compost in March in a cool greenhouse or closed frame where the temperature is not less than 15°C (60°F). Keep the compost moist to prevent a check to growth. Harden off the seedlings in a cold frame before planting out in May.

It is helpful if mature compost or peat is worked into the bed. Alternatively balanced fertilizer at 85–112 g per m² (3–4 oz per sq yd) will be beneficial. Space the plants 30–38 cm (12–15 ins) apart with 45 cm (18 ins) between rows. Plant so that the little bulbous-like roots just rest on the top of the soil. Remove all side-shoots and make sure there is no shortage of moisture.

Excepting in cold districts where the roots should be stored in boxes of sand in a shed, lift roots as required. During the winter a covering of straw or bracken will be helpful. At the end of October, lightly earth up the plants as a protection against frosts.

RECOMMENDED VARIETIES: 'Giant Prague', hardy; 'Early Erfurt', a smaller, earlier variety and 'Globus' of good flavour and cooking qualities.

CELERY *Apium graveolens*

Celery was originally cultivated for its medicinal qualities, but is now widely grown as a vegetable. It was derived from the wild plant sometimes known as 'smallage' which grows in moist places in many parts of the world. A biennial plant, it is eaten raw or cooked, while considerable quantities are now canned for use.

Moisture loving, celery does best in peaty or similar soils where there is a high water-table, but this does not mean a water-logged position. Acid soil suits this plant better than chalky soil.

Celery is often grown on the 'flat', blanching being done by covering the stems with 'collars' or even drainpipes. For finest results trenches are best. Make them 38 cm (15 ins) wide for single rows and 45 cm (18 ins) or more where double rows are being grown. Dig them 45–60 cm (12–18 ins) deep and throw the soil equally on both sides of the trench, where it can, if required, be used to grow a catch crop such as lettuce or radishes. When growing a double row, the plants should be placed side by side and not zig-zag as is usually done with a double row. This makes it easier for blanching. If more

than one double row is grown, allow at least 90 cm (3 ft) between them. Better plants are secured from single rows. Should side shoots develop, pull them off.

For the earliest sticks, sow seed from the third week in February into early March. Make the main sowings during March and April. The later sowings are less likely to produce plants which 'bolt' – especially likely with self-blanching types sown too early. Sow very thinly in boxes or pots of seed compost. Give a light covering of seed compost, firm the surface and apply a sprinkling of water. Cover with glass and paper and keep in a temperature of 15°C (60°F) until growth is seen. Then remove the covering and when the seedlings can be handled easily, prick them off into other boxes. After ten days or so, remove them to a frame or cloches for hardening off. As far as possible, lift the plants from the seed box with plenty of soil on their roots. This will lessen the check. Unless it is showery, give the soil a good watering after planting firmly during late May. Frequent sprayings of clear water will prove beneficial during spells of dry weather. Once established, the plants revel in plenty of moisture, while good growth can be encouraged by applying a dried blood solution or a well balanced fertilizer. Keep side shoots and decayed leaves removed. A sprinkling of weathered soot over the leaves deters celery fly.

Blanching is done by earthing up, a process which must be carried out gradually. It is usually possible to add at least 15 cm (6 ins) of soil at each operation, which will have to be repeated at least three times at 14 day intervals. The roots should be moist and the leaves dry when this job is done. Tie the stems with raffia or the corrugated paper round them so that the soil does not enter the centre of the plants. The leaves should be left exposed and the soil made smooth and steep, so that rain is deflected.

The blanching process takes seven or eight weeks. During severe frosts celery plants should be protected by straw, bracken or similar material, removing it when mild conditions return. Blanching can also be achieved by wrapping brown or corrugated paper around the plants, tying it with raffia so that water does not remain inside.

RECOMMENDED VARIETIES: white: 'Giant White', 'Invincible', and 'Wareings Dwarf White'; Pink or red: 'Giant Red'.

Celery grown in trenches is generally superior in flavour

Celery, Self Blanching. Most useful where space is limited or where the gardener does not wish to make trenches. It is not difficult to cultivate this crop, which requires soil rich in organic matter. Farmyard manure worked into the ground some months before planting will be beneficial. Failing manure, use bulky organic material such as ripe compost, peat or leaf mould with a good sprinkling of bone meal.

Apart from open ground culture, self-blanching celery can be grown where a modified form of French gardening is practiced. On suitable, well-manured soils hot bed frames can be used effectively for this celery which can follow early carrots or globe beet. All that is needed is to dig and clean the ground, adding a good sprinkling of balanced organic fertilizer, or hoof and horn meal.

Of the white and cream varieties, 'Golden Self Blanching' is the most popular, while 'American Green' is crisp and tender. The fine seeds should not be sown until early March, earlier sowings being liable to run to seed. It is a mistake to sow deeply and the lightest possible covering of finely sifted soil is sufficient. Afterwards, water with a fine rosed can. Germination is often slow, largely depending on the temperature.

Once growth is seen, ventilation should be given and early pricking out 5–8 cm (2–3 ins) apart is essential. Later move them to the open ground or frames allowing 23 cm (9 ins) each way.

The basic cultural operations are hoeing, weeding, watering, and leafspot control. The close planting suggested leads to blanched stems but additional help can be given by placing clean, dry straw between the rows ten days before the crop is gathered, which it must be prior to severe frosts.

Self-blanching celery is available from the end of August onwards, before ordinary celery is ready. Generally speaking the flavour of self-blanching celery is not as good as trenched celery.

RECOMMENDED VARIETIES: 'American Green' selections include 'Greensnap' and 'Utah Green'; 'Golden Self Blanching' selections, include 'Golden Elite' and 'Monarch Self Blanching'; 'Lathom Self Blanching'.

CELTUCE *Lactuca sativa*

Coming from China, this unusual vegetable is quite easy to grow, although it has never become really popular. It should be sown

'Solid-White' celery is an old favourite

Right: Forcing chicory in pots. Cut off top of roots above crown. Trim ends if necessary. Place 5 roots to a 22.5-cm (9-in) pot and cover completely with another pot to exclude light. Keep in a warm place (10°C/50°F min) for 4 weeks before harvesting blanched chicons with sharp knife

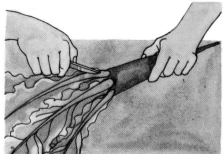

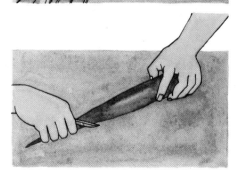

from the end of April onwards, covering the seeds with 12 mm ($\frac{1}{2}$ in) of fine soil and allowing 30 cm (12 ins) between the rows. It is advisable to sow little and often and to thin the plants so they finally stand 23–25 cm (9–10 ins) apart.

Celtuce is sometimes referred to as the 'two in one' vegetable, since the leaves, which have a high vitamin content, can be used as lettuce, whilst the heart or crisp central stem is often eaten raw in salads or cooked in the same way as celery.

CHICORY *Cichorium intybus*

This crop is grown for the thick stalks and ribs of its leaves which, when blanched, are eaten in salads or boiled. The Brussels Witloof chicory particularly, should be grown for providing a delicious salading in winter and spring. This becomes available when lettuce and endive are usually scarce and expensive to buy. It can also be eaten like celery, with cheese, and can be stewed and served with melted butter in the same way as seakale. It is the Magdeburg chicory which, after drying, roasting and grinding the roots, is used for mixing with coffee.

Sow seed from late May onwards, in rows 45 cm (18 ins) apart, thinning the seedlings to 30 cm (1 ft) apart. Select a well-worked soil, plentifully supplied with organic matter which does not dry out. A dressing of fish manure 85 g per m² (3 oz per sq yd) will be helpful.

In October, forcing begins in succession when roots are lifted from the open ground. The best roots for forcing are about 5 cm (2 ins) in diameter. Chicory can be forced in sheds, but a cool or cold greenhouse is better. A forcing pit with a temperature of not less than 10°C (50°F) is ideal for growing chicory or a special place can be reserved at one end of the greenhouse.

The procedure is simple. Make a trench 30 cm (1 ft) deep and 60 cm (2 ft) wide, fork the bottom and place the roots upright and close together. Water in when the trench is full of roots. Soil from the second trench can

be used to cover the roots in the first trench and watered to wash the soil around the roots. Then place the remainder of the soil over the roots to a depth of 23–25 cm (9–10 ins). The last soil covering must be dry to ensure clean, healthy heads. Chicory is ready for cutting when the sprouting shoots, known as chicons, show through the soil. Keep them out of the light or they will turn green and become bitter and useless.

Another method is to cut off the leaves to within an inch of the crown at the end of September. Then earth up as for celery. Supplies of delicious heads will then be available from December onwards.

RECOMMENDED VARIETIES: A fairly new variety, 'Sugar Loaf' (Pain de Sucre) can be strongly recommended. This has the appearance of a well grown cos lettuce with a long standing solid head, most useful for salading. 'Red Verona', is another good variety which when forced, produces a compact red head. Both these varieties should be cultivated as for endive and are excellent salad vegetables.

CHINESE CABBAGE (Chinese Leaves) *Brassica cernua*

More like a cos lettuce than a cabbage, with green leaves forming an oval or oblong head. This crop has for many centuries been widely used in China. It is only in this century that it has attracted attention elsewhere, firstly in the United States. Chinese cabbage is now becoming increasingly popular, since it has many uses and, after picking, keeps in the refrigerator more satisfactorily than lettuce.

The plants are rapid growing and must be used immediately they mature otherwise they throw up flower heads and become useless. Frosts will spoil the plants. If the soil becomes dry in hot weather the leaves are inclined to wilt badly and lose their freshness.

Sow at intervals from mid-June to early August, making the drills 60 cm (2 ft) apart and 2 cm (½ in) deep, thinning the seedlings

Chinese cabbage is easy to grow and can be cooked or used in salads

so there is 23 cm (9 in) between them. Chinese cabbages do not transplant well and are at their best during a damp season. They should be watered generously during dry spells.

As the elongated heads develop, a tie or two of raffia should be placed around the outer leaves to ensure the formation of a good blanched head. The heads are cut complete as with cabbage. The leaves can be used as a substitute for lettuce or steamed or boiled. They should be cooked very quickly. There is no unpleasant cabbage smell when they are cooked.

RECOMMENDED VARIETIES: 'Chili', tender, crisp, spicy flavour; 'Pe tsai', pure white, cos lettuce-like heads when blanched; 'Michili', growing 38–45 cm (15–18 ins) tall, and up to 7–10 cm (3–4 ins) in diameter; 'Wong Bok', large, tender juicy heads; 'Sampan', large squat heads.

CHINESE MUSTARD *Brassica juncea*

Widely used in the United States and parts of North America and sometimes in tins or cans in this country, Chinese mustard is not unlike the better known Chinese cabbage, with its loose distinctive, rather open habit of growth. It is hardy and can resist hot, dry weather when many other forms of green stuff fail to grow well and are in short supply.

Growing about 60 cm (2 ft) high, it has several common names including mustard greens, mustard spinach and tender greens, and it is sometimes used as a substitute for spinach. The flavour is quite strong.

Seed can be sown from April to August. Make the rows 38 cm (15 ins) apart and thin the seedlings so there is about 15 cm (6 ins) between them. In fairly rich, moist soil, growth is rapid and it is often possible to gather a useful picking of leaves within seven or eight weeks of sowing. If the ground is on the poor side, it should be enriched before planting and when in growth, the plants can be encouraged to make more leaves by applying a nitrogenous fertilizer.

Plants left unused will quickly run to seed, so it is advisable to cut down the entire plant at ground level rather than picking off individual leaves as is done with spinach or with leaf lettuce.

CORN SALAD *Valerianella locusta*

This is also known as Lamb's Lettuce and there are several good forms. Eat the leaves raw or cooked. Easily grown, it is a useful substitute for lettuce during the winter. This crop can follow early potatoes, peas or broccoli. Make the drills 19 mm ($\frac{3}{4}$ in) deep and 30 cm (1 ft) apart.

Sowings can be made at intervals from the end of July until the end of September

Corn salad is a useful winter crop

The succulent leaves of Chinese Mustard 'Pak-Choi' grow up to 50 cm (20 in) long

to provide supplies from autumn until spring. The young plants should be thinned out so there is 15 cm (6 ins) between them. They make an excellent cloche crop.

Cress

Several distinct plants fall into this group, but all are eaten raw in salads.

CRESS *Ledpidium sativum*

This is the plain leaved or common cress which is easy to grow in trays or pots or on the greenhouse bench in beds of finely sifted soil. The curled or double cress is preferred by some gardeners although there is no difference in flavour. Known in Britain for over 400 years, cress was at one time valued for the medicinal properties in the seed. It is useful for its food value since it contains vitamins C and B1 while it is beneficial when used for green manuring.

White mustard is a member of the cabbage family and best known for its part in 'mustard and cress'. An annual plant, it is a native of Britain, and other European countries. Black or brown mustard is not really suitable for salad purposes since the leaves are so hot and unpalatable. *Brassica napus* or agricultural rape is often used instead of white mustard for salad purposes. Its leaves maintain their colour well and do not decay as quickly as mustard.

Seed can be sown under glass during the autumn and winter, when it will provide valuable salad material. It is also in demand throughout the spring and summer. If both crops are to mature together sow cress four days before mustard. A minimum temperature of 10°C (50°F) is suitable and a fine, fairly rich, nicely moist compost should be used. The seeds need only be pressed in and not covered with soil. After sowing place damp paper or hessian over the receptacles or seed beds, removing it as soon as growth is seen. This prevents the surface soil from drying out and encourages germination.

Bulb bowls filled with bulb fibre will grow excellent crops and where small quantities are required seeds can be sown directly into small punnets or pots. Keep them in the dark for a few days until long stems have been made; then bring them into light so the leaves become green.

Seed can also be sown outdoors on slightly raised beds.

Sufficient moisture must always be available. If the compost is nicely damp at sowing time no further watering need be carried out until the seedlings have established themselves and are growing well.

LAND CRESS (American Cress)

In spite of its name this plant is hardly known in America. An excellent substitute for watercress, the tender young leafy shoots are used in salads. It does not require water in the same way as the normal watercress and is much easier to manage. The plants appreciate semi-shade and do well in a north border, succeeding in town gardens and in damp situations that other crops will not tolerate.

Make the first sowings in late March to give pickings from late June onwards. Prepare a seed bed with plenty of organic material. Bring the surface to a fine tilth and sow in drills 20–23 cm (8–9 ins) apart and 13 mm ($\frac{1}{2}$ in) deep. Alternatively, broadcast the seed thinly and rake it into the surface. Cloches or frames encourage quicker growth. Do not thin the seedlings; leave them to grow like well-spaced mustard and cress. The soil should be kept moist for continued production.

Seed of American or Belle Isle perennial cress can also be sown in August and wintered under a well-ventilated frame for early spring pickings. Protection may be necessary during severe weather. Keep the soil just moist or the plants may rot. There is a less common variety known as Australian cress, which has pointed leaves of a mild agreeable flavour.

Mustard and cress are easy to grow

Land Cress, a hybrid form, is less susceptible to frost than other cresses

WATERCRESS *Nasturtium officinale*

This nutritious crop is available over a long period when other salad ingredients are scarce. It has a higher mineral content than lettuce and salad onions, and contains useful quantities of vitamins C and B1.

One reason why some people say they dislike watercress is that they so often see it sold as a bundle of discoloured, wizened, leafy stalks.

Henslow, in his book on 'The Use of British Plants' says the Latin name is derived from *nasus* – the nose, and *tortus* – twisted, from the pungent sensation. It was familiar to the Ancient Greeks as *kardomon*, and was used in salads. It was also valued for its medicinal virtues. Its nutritive value is attributed to its aromatic oil and exceptionally high mineral content.

Watercress is divided into two main groups, the green which is available in summer, and the more popular brown or winter strains. The green form produces long shoots which do not always branch well. This is a drawback if the growing area is limited. In addition, the plants seem only to flourish where the temperature of the water rises appreciably during spring and summer. This has the advantage of making them suitable for growing in streams and other shallow water. The depth of colour seems to depend on both climatic conditions and water temperature.

Phillip Miller in 1754 records 'that many people preferred these herbs for their

Clear streams are the natural habitat of watercress

agreeable warm, bitter taste; and being accounted an excellent remedy for the scurvy and to cleanse the blood'.

Watercress can be propagated from seed or cuttings. With the former, sow from mid-June to mid-August on an almost dry seed bed.

Sprinkle the seed thinly over the soil, then water lightly to encourage germination which normally takes a week. The little plants soon form a tap root. The seed bed should then be pressed down to firm the soil to encourage a mat of roots to form at the bottom of the bed.

Anyone who has a constant supply of water can grow cress in specially constructed beds. Water from natural springs is warmer in winter than that of streams.

While running water is ideal for growing watercress, a crop can be grown without it. Select a shaded position where the soil is rich and moist in summer. If the site is naturally on the dry side make trenches up to 20 cm (8 ins) deep and filled with vegetable compost, covering this with 5 cm (2 ins) of soil, so the surface is a little below the surrounding soil.

If you already have watercress plants it will be easy to strike cuttings from the sturdy shoots. Do this in May and June for autumn and winter cropping, and in September and October for spring and summer cutting; the brown variety is best for later cutting.

Watercress is rarely, if ever, attacked by diseases, and if the beds are kept free from rubbish, slugs will not be a nuisance.

CUCUMBER & GHERKIN *Cucumis sativus*

Indoor Good greenhouse or frame grown cucumbers cannot be bettered for flavour, but they do require rather more care in their cultivation than many other less fussy vegetables.

Preparation of the growing area is important, and there is nothing better than good clean straw, horse manure and turfy loam which has not been stacked too long. Old loam will have lost a good deal of its fibre and will be inclined to dry out frequently. Tests have shown that two parts of loam to one of strawy manure is about right. Bone meal and hoof and horn can be mixed either separately with the loam or when it has been mixed with the manure. An 8 cm (3 in) potful of chalk to each barrow load of loam will boost sturdy growth.

Sow seed in standard 35 × 25 cm (14 × 9 ins) seed boxes or in pans, filling them with compost made from good clean fibrous loam and well-rotted horse manure, to within 13 mm (½ in) of the top. Use a fairly gritty, not too fine a soil mixture.

Cover the boxes with glass and paper and place them on the staging in a temperature of at least 18°C (65°F). Rapid germination is required and this usually takes place within three days. The glass is then removed.

From this time on a moist atmosphere is needed. Take care not to damage the roots of the seedlings when they are being moved. (Some gardeners prefer to sow directly into small pots to avoid this transplanting). The seedlings will need more root room within a fortnight of sowing and as further growth proceeds repot into 13 cm (5 in) and then into 15 cm (6 in) pots. Maintain night temperature of at least 18°C (65°F). A continuous humid atmosphere is necessary but the roots must not lie wet.

When the plants are well-established (about a month after sowing) they will be ready for their final positions. Make the holes in the bed large enough to drop in the ball of soil and roots, and carefully firm the soil around the little stems. Allow at least 60 cm (2 ft) between the plants each way. Place a stake near each plant so they can climb up to the horizontal wires.

Keep on training the growths up the wires and regularly take out the growing points. Allow the main stem to grow to the top of the wire, when it should be stopped.

Two cucumber plants in a greenhouse will be enough for a family's needs

This encourages fruiting and the development of side shoots which in turn will need to be stopped at the second joint and tied in. Developing sub-laterals must be stopped at the first joint, this process continuing until growth slows down and energy concentrated on the remaining shoots.

Most plants have male and female flowers and the males should be removed, as they are not needed for fertilization. The female flowers are easily distinguished by the swollen 'bulb' (embryonic fruit) behind the petals. You will find that if the flowers are fertilized, not only is the cropping capacity of the plants lessened, but also that the fruits have a bitter taste.

Several varieties producing all female flowers are available, such as 'Fertila' and 'Femdan', which crop heavily and produce fruit free from bitterness.

Cutting must be done regularly once the plants come into bearing. The time taken for fruit to develop depends on the season. January sowings do not usually mature until late March, but from spring sowings cutting should be possible in about seven or eight weeks.

Some years ago, as a result of various trials, cordon training systems were developed. Such plants are exceptional for the sustained vigour and first class fruits which are produced within six weeks of sowing. The individual fruits are straight and attractive in appearance. The weight and quality of the crop depends entirely upon the skill of the individual grower. It is customary to wind the plants up strings as is done with tomatoes.

Sow the seeds in trays or pots covering them with a 6 mm (¼ in) layer of moist soil. Once germination occurs, gradually bring the seedlings to full light and pot them on about the third day, before they straighten up. From then on, keep the compost moist. The first stopping of the growing point causes shoots to break out rapidly from the base. These should be rubbed out the moment they are seen.

Fruits begin to appear in clusters of five to seven at the base of the rough leaves, and provided the plants are in good condition all should be allowed to mature; they are soon ready for cutting. Care is needed with the first fruits. If possible they should be spaced equally around the stem and should not touch the soil, otherwise they will become mis-shapen. Following the pinching at the second rough leaf, shoots are nipped back again at the next leaf and this stopping at the leaf joints continues as long as there is vigorous upward growth.

Fruit clusters result from each stopping.

After the first fruits have matured and are harvested, a second crop of larger clusters will emerge from the joints, and these usually need thinning to get good shaped high quality fruits.

An oddity I have grown is the so-called Serpent Cucumber, the fruit of which curl round like a snake, and are 90–120 cm (3–4 ft) long. Grow it in the same way as ordinary cucumbers.

Outdoor or ridge These cucumbers should be grown in fairly rich soil, avoiding fresh manure. Plant them on little mounds, with well rotted manure being placed at the bottom of the hole. Seed is sown in the warm greenhouse or frame in April and once the first leaves have developed, pot plants singly into 7 cm ($2\frac{1}{2}$ ins) pots, where they can remain until planted outdoors at the end of May. Alternatively, sow outdoors in early May, placing two seeds at each station.

Allow 45–60 cm ($1\frac{1}{2}$–2 ft) between the plants, spacing the rows 60–75 cm (2–$2\frac{1}{2}$ ft) apart. It is wise to nip out the growing point when the stems are about 38 cm (15 ins) long. This encourages branching and each lateral shoot is then stopped one leaf beyond the first fruit. Plenty of moisture is needed during dry weather.

RECOMMENDED VARIETIES: 'Bedfordshire Prize' and 'Nadir' an F_1 hybrid producing long fruit of outstanding quality. Less common is 'Crystal Apple' producing round creamy-white fruit the shape of a good sized apple.

There are several F_1 Burpless hybrids, all of which are valuable since they are not indigestible. Remarkable long-fruited Japanese varieties include 'Chinese Long Green', smooth skinned fruits up to 60 cm (2 ft) in length and 38 mm ($1\frac{1}{2}$ ins) in diameter. 'Greenline' is specially good for cloche culture.

'Patio-Pik' is a compact grower which crops heavily, while 'Victory' is a vigorous F_1 hybrid producing only female flowers, and has shapely green fruits 19–20 cm ($7\frac{1}{2}$–8 ins) long.

Above: 'Kyoto' is a Japanese variety of cucumber that can be grown outdoors. Below: Gherkins are ridge cucumbers picked at 10 cm (4 in) long

Gherkin The gherkin proper, *C. anguria*, is a weed, native to the U.S.A., whose immature fruits are used for pickling. In Europe the vegetable used in this way is the immature fruit of the ridge cucumber. If grown for pickling, the aim should be to produce succulent fruits up to 10 cm (4 ins) long. To ensure this, gather them before they become large and coarse.

General culture is the same as for cucumbers, the main difference being that plants rarely transplant satisfactorily. It is therefore best to sow seeds where they are to remain. Do this in early summer on well prepared and enriched sites. Bulky manure or compost encourages a good root system. Place the seeds 2.5 cm (1 in) deep and if two are put in stations 60 cm (2 ft) apart the weakest seedling can be removed when the plants are growing well.

RECOMMENDED VARIETIES: 'Boston Pickling' is one of the finest, producing good coloured juicy fruit. 'Parisian Pickling' and the American 'Ohio' are reliable.

65

ENDIVE *Cichorium endivia*

This salad plant is not grown as much as it deserves. An annual, belonging to the chicory family, it has been cultivated in Britain since the sixteenth century. Endive resembles lettuce, although the plants have to be blanched before use, otherwise they will have a bitter taste. Now that lettuces are expensive in winter, there is good reason for growing endive, which is in season from November to April.

This crop prefers a well drained, sandy loam with a dry sub-soil. The ground need not be freshly manured or very rich, but the plants do best in soils with a high humus

Blanching improves the flavour of endive

content. Work in a good general fertilizer, preferably of organic origin, such as fish meal at 85 g per m² (3 oz per sq yd) before sowing seed.

The earliest sowings should be made in March on a hot bed, in heated frames or under cloches. Plant out the resultant seedlings from mid-May onwards. Outdoors, successional sowings may be made from late May until early September. Space the drills 38 (15 ins) apart, and gradually thin out the seedlings, so that there is about 30 cm (1 ft) between them.

The plants will be ready for blanching about 12 weeks after sowing. This can be done by tying them with raffia or covering with slates, boards, inverted flower pots with the drainage holes blocked, or with rough hay or litter. Blanching takes six or seven days and it is best to cover a few plants at a time. Make sure they are dry at the time, or the leaves will rot. Excepting in warm, south-western districts, move the later sowings to frames or cloches for blanching to be carried out.

RECOMMENDED VARIETIES: There are two distinct types of endive, curled and plain leaved. Of the former, 'Ruffec' and 'Meaux' are first class. The plain leaved sort, such as 'Batavian Green', is best for winter work, being hardier than the curled types.

FLORENCE FENNEL *Foeniculum vulgare* var *dulce*

Though related to the herb common fennel, Florence fennel differs in that it is grown as an annual, is smaller, and is cultivated for the bulbous stem rather than the foliage.

Both the bulbs and foliage of fennel can be used in cooking

Raw sliced fennel goes well in salads. Cooked, it goes well with pork and chicken or in fish dishes. The flavour is anise-like.

Florence fennel needs a warm summer to do well. Sow seeds outside in April after working a light dressing of all-purpose fertilizer into the soil. Sow in shallow drills 45 cm (20 ins) apart, thinning the seedlings to 22–30 cm (9–12 ins) apart in the rows. Keep adequately watered. Earth the bulbs up as they begin to swell in order to blanch them. Harvest ripe bulbs as required from September. The leaves may be used as those of common fennel for flavouring. There are no named varieties of Florence fennel.

GOOD KING HENRY
Chenopodium bonus—henricus

Sometimes known as Mercury or All Good. While dormant, this hardy plant carries a number of crowns which in early spring open to produce small green leaves, followed by light green fleshy shoots which bear clusters of green leaves at their growing points. These should be gathered and eaten in the same way as spinach which they resemble in flavour and for which they can be used as a substitute.

Good King Henry is an old-fashioned plant worth reviving

When young, these shoots are useful for including raw in salads. The more mature leaves should be cooked and eaten as spinach. Six or twelve shoots can be tied in bundles and gently cooked with just enough water to cover. The thick fleshy roots can be cooked and served with hot melted butter.

Seed is sown in the spring, the plants being finally spaced about 30 cm (1 ft) apart. Unlike asparagus, the plants can be cut the first year after planting. This subject is valued because it is rich in iron and other health giving properties.

These plants respond to an early spring mulching of decayed manure or compost. The top growth must not be covered.

HAMBURG PARSLEY *Petroselinum crispum* var *tuberosum*

This is a dual-purpose vegetable, the roots being used like parsnips or carrots and the tops as parsley. Perhaps this is not so surprising when it is remembered that parsley belongs to the same family as the carrot. As the name suggests, this crop is much used in Germany.

The soil should be prepared as is done for parsnips and seed is sown in deeply cultivated ground from late March onwards. Make the drills 6 mm ($\frac{1}{4}$ ins) deep and 38 cm (15 ins) apart. Thin out the plants so that there is 15–20 cm (6–8 ins) between them. They like plenty of moisture during the growing season and should be kept free from weeds.

The foliage usually remains abundant in winter and can be used for flavouring. The roots can be used from early October onwards. They are hardy and can be lifted as required, or taken up and stored in boxes of moist sand. Well grown, the roots will be 15–17 cm (6–7 ins) long and about 7–8 cm (3 ins) thick, and look much like parsnips.

KALE *Brassica oleracea* var *acephala*

This is a member of the large cabbage family and is sometimes known as borecole. One particular variety of kale was once eaten by Dutch peasants or Boers and became known as Boer's kale. Plain-leaved kales have the strongest flavour and are generally grown for feeding livestock though perfectly edible. The curly-leaved varieties are best for human consumption.

Kales are hardy and withstand severe weather conditions. Since they mature from February to April, they are valuable when there is little other greenstuff about. Soil containing organic matter leads to the heaviest yields. Lime should be present and badly drained positions and frost pockets avoided.

This is a crop which can follow early potatoes, peas or broad beans for which the

Kale is one of the hardiest cabbage plants

Roots and leaves of Hamburg Parsley

land was well-prepared. Where this is being done, it is not necessary to re-dig the ground, simply remove weeds and debris. Sow seed from late April onwards, a little earlier in northern districts. Most kales can be sown in beds for transplanting in the usual way, but 'Hungry Gap' is best sown where it is to grow.

Planting distances vary according to habit of growth. For the majority, allow 45 cm (18 ins) between plants with rows 60 cm (2 ft) apart. For Hungry Gap allow 38 cm (15 ins) each way. If the central or growing point is removed in January it will encourage the side shoots. Kale should not be used too early but kept until spring when greenstuff is scarce.

RECOMMENDED VARIETIES include: 'Asparagus' kale which is now difficult to obtain. It produces in spring long thin shoots resembling asparagus which can be cooked in bundles in the same way.

'Cottagers' 75 cm (2$\frac{1}{2}$ ft) high has crinkled leaves on strong stems and is not particularly good flavoured. The 'Dwarf Green Curled' and 'Tall Green Curled' are hardy; the top part of the plant is first out to provide 'greens' and then the stem produces short shoots which are gathered in the same way as sprouting broccoli.

'Hungry Gap' is a hybrid sown in summer for cropping the following spring when greenstuff is scarce. It is extremely hardy and withstands drought, wet and frost.

'Pentland Brig' is a fairly new kale bred in Scotland. Very hardy, it produces an abundant crop of shoots from February to April.

Ornamental kales with purple or silver-variegated leaves are very decorative. The leaves turn green when cooked.

Despite its name, kohl rabi 'Purple Vienna' has white flesh

KOHL RABI *Brassica oleracea* var *gongyloides*

This is a crop which must be grown quickly, otherwise it becomes tough. It should be used when the 'bulbs' are the size of a cricket ball. On light soils it is a good substitute for turnips which are liable to fail, and it has a distinct nutty flavour.

Sown from early March onwards, either broadcast or in drills 38 cm (15 ins) apart, the 'bulbs' will be ready from mid-August. Thin the seedlings so there is 15–17 cm (6–7 ins) between them.

Kohl rabi is not particular as to soil so long as it contains plenty of humus matter and is well-drained. This hardy plant will usually come through the winter without harm but the roots will not keep for any length of time when stored.

Kohl rabi is not particularly susceptible to attacks by pests. The only disease likely to cause problems is club root. This is a member of the cabbage family, which is prone to this disease. Crop rotations will prevent a build-up.

RECOMMENDED VARIETIES: Although seedsmen normally offer the seeds simply as kohl rabi, there are several forms, including 'White Vienna' and 'Purple Vienna'.

LEEKS *Allium porrum*

Provided the ground has been deeply worked, leeks will grow in almost all moisture-retentive soils that drain well. The best position is one well-manured for a previous crop such as early cabbages or peas, which will be cleared from the ground in time to make room for leeks. Make sure the site selected does not lack lime.

Although the crop can be cultivated on the flat, the best method is to grow the plants in trenches. These should be taken out 25–30 cm (10–12 ins) deep, and 30 cm (1 ft) wide, for a single row, or 45 cm (18 ins) wide where a double row is being grown. Work decayed manure, compost or other organic matter into the bottom of the trench, on top of which place a layer of fine soil, to bring the depth of the trench to 15 cm (6 ins). Where bulky manure is not available, fish manure or bone meal can be used at 50–75 g per m² (2–3 oz per sq yd).

For the earliest crop a sowing can be made in January under glass in a temperature of 15–18°C (60–65°F) using trays or pans of seed compost. As soon as the seedlings can be handled prick them out into other boxes keeping them in full light near the glass in a temperature of around 12°C (54°F). Toward the end of March, move the plants to the cold frame for hardening off before planting outdoors in April and May.

Alternatively leeks can be raised under cloches from the end of February onwards. Make the rows 23 cm (9 ins) apart, and by the end of March or early April, the young plants can be left uncovered. Once they are 20–23 cm (8–9 ins) high they should be moved to their final positions.

When growing leeks on the flat make 15 cm (6 ins) deep dibber holes 20–30 cm (8–12 ins) apart, and drop the seedlings into them. Do not fill the holes with soil, instead, pour a little water into each hole. This will wash some soil over the roots which can be filled up as growth develops, although they often become full naturally. If the foliage droops or the tips of the leaves wilt or lie on the soil the plants should be cut back or worms may pull these drooping leaves and upset the plants. In prolonged dry weather the leeks should have their roots and leaves trimmed before planting. All leeks should be in their final positions by early July.

Once the plants are growing well they can be helped by dusting a good organic fertilizer along the rows at about 50 g per m² (1½–2 oz per sq yd) run. An application of liquid manure at 14-day intervals from mid-August to the end of October, will help further in producing really thick stems. Keep down weeds and remove any flower stems that appear.

When grown in trenches the earthing up process will normally begin about a month after planting, soil being drawn up at intervals of 3 to 4 weeks. The soil used should be fine so that the plant stems are covered evenly. Some gardeners place rings of corrugated paper around the stems before earthing up. This stops the soil from falling between the leaves and prevents grittiness when the leeks are cooked.

Leeks can be lifted as required throughout the autumn and winter. Any left in the ground at the end of April should be moved and heeled in near a north wall or hedge in order to release the ground for another crop.

For exhibition purposes, leeks will require extra cultural attention. Special leek shows are still held, particularly in the northern parts of the country. The standard there is very high and 14 cm (5½ ins) or more should be the length of the perfectly straight blanched portion of stem. Measurement tables are often used and competition is keen.

Leeks should be thoroughly cleaned under cold running water before cooking to make sure they are completely free of grit.

An excellent main crop variety of leek is 'Royal Favourite'

RECOMMENDED VARIETIES: 'Winter Reuzen', a winter hardy variety producing well-blanched white stems. 'Musselburgh', an old hardy, reliable variety with long thick stems; 'Lyon', also old, large growing and good for late lifting; 'Prizetaker', hardy and splendid for exhibition; 'Marble Pillar', a fairly new sort producing solid white stems usually much longer than other varieties; 'Walton Mammoth', one of the best varieties with medium green foliage and long thick, solid stems, valuable for exhibition; 'Malabar', a quick growing variety for autumn use and 'North Pole', a really winter hardy sort.

LETTUCE *Lactuca sativa*

Lettuce is the most popular salad plant, valued as much for its green leaves as the blanched heart.

Lettuce are classified in several ways. There are two main divisions between the cabbage (crisphead or butterhead) types, and cos: they may be classified further as summer and winter varieties, and those suitable for frame or greenhouse cultivation.

The cabbage section is the largest group, taking in varieties which are quite small, such as 'Tom Thumb', and the really large so-called butterheads which have soft, smooth light green leaves. There are others having quite brittle leaves. These are not often obtainable in shops since they do not market or travel well but they are first class for the gardener who can use them straight from the garden.

Summer lettuce should be sown in March, where they are to mature, although it is best to delay sowings in very cold districts or when the soil is wet. To ensure succession it is better to sow a little seed at frequent intervals, say, once a fortnight, rather than large quantities at once.

'Webb's Wonderful' is the best-known crisphead lettuce

Make the drills about 13 mm ($\frac{1}{2}$ in) deep, and 30 cm (12 ins) apart and cover the seed with fine soil. Thin sowing should be practised, so that there is little necessity for thinning the rows. Use some of the plants before they grow too large for this prevents overcrowding, which, because of root competition can sometimes lead to bolting.

Winter lettuce can be sown in light well-drained soil. If the plants follow a crop which was well-manured this should encourage steady growth. Here again, if some good organic fertilizer is worked into the surface soil, at the rate of 75 g per m² (3 oz per sq yd) it will be helpful.

Winter lettuce should be sown about the second week in September, making the rows 30 cm (1 ft) apart, and thinning the plants out early so that there is about 13 cm (6 ins) between them. Thin the rows, later removing alternate plants. Although these thinnings have no hearts they can still be used in the kitchen. Winter lettuce can also be sown in pots or boxes and this may be necessary in cold and northern districts. Seedlings raised in this way will be ready for planting out from the third week in October onwards, according to soil, situation and district. It is possible to leave the plants in the seed bed to over-winter, then planting them out in March. They will be ready for use from the middle of May onwards.

Where heat is available lettuce is a really rewarding crop. Certain varieties have been bred for production under glass in winter. With these, plenty of light is essential and this is one reason why it is necessary to keep the glass clean. Use John Innes compost No 1 to avoid trouble from botrytis infection.

Sow the seed in standard-size seed boxes. If carefully done, 150 seeds will be sufficient for each box. Move the seedlings into their final cropping places as soon as the first pair of true leaves are showing well.

They should not be left to become large before being transplanted. Final spacing varies according to variety, some sorts growing larger than others. Even the largest varieties should not need more than 23 cm (9 ins) each way, and many are placed in rows 18–20 cm (7–8 ins) apart, with 18 cm (7 ins) between plants.

Once the greenhouse or frames are planted it is a good plan to water the seedlings well straight away, and to maintain a temperature of just over 15°C (60°F). After about ten days the temperature can be lowered to 10°C (50°F) or so. Little more

Cos lettuce 'Lobjoit's Green' is firm and flavourful

water will be necessary until January after which time it will need to be given more frequently.

When planting out seedlings, whether in the open ground or in greenhouses, make sure the tap root goes straight down and is not turned up in the hole.

Lettuces sometimes bolt or run to seed prematurely. This condition is caused by high temperatures and long days. With summer transplanting, especially during a dry spell, seedlings will often throw up a seed head even when the roots are moist. The flavour will then be impaired by an unpleasant bitterness and the plants should be consigned to the compost heap.

Leaf lettuce 'Salad Bowl' is a good choice for growing-bag cultivation

Lettuce are ready for cutting as soon as the heart is nicely firm. Once growth begins to push up from the centre it is a sign that the plants are beginning to run to seed and they should therefore be eaten as soon as possible. If it is not possible to use them immediately they can be pulled up complete with roots and placed in a cool shaded position in vessels of very shallow water. A special watch must be kept for aphis attacks.

The majority of the best modern varieties of cos lettuces are self-folding and need no help by tying. Even so, during spells of dry weather they may not heart up well, and it is therefore a good plan to give a light tying with raffia or soft string.

There are some varieties of lettuces, chiefly of American origin, which do not heart, and in these cases individual leaves can be pulled off and used as required. Notable among these is 'Salad Bowl', which is shaped like a rosette, about 30 cm (1 ft) across, with curled and lobed leaves.

RECOMMENDED VARIETIES: Although as a result of comparison trials the number of lettuce varieties in cultivation has recently been reduced, there are still many sorts offered in seedsmen's catalogues. It is possible to obtain a mixture of cos and cabbage varieties which mature at different dates, thus extending the cutting period. Too high a temperature at seed sowing time will inhibit germination, however, especially with butterhead types. Lettuce are usually grouped under separate headings which give some indication of their type. They include the following:

Cabbage Crisphead: 'Pennlake', 'Avoncrisp', 'Great Lakes', 'Iceberg', 'Webb's Wonderful'.
Butterhead: 'Avondefiance', 'Buttercrunch', 'Tom Thumb', 'All the Year Round', 'Hilde'.
Loosehead or leaf varieties: 'Grand Rapids', 'Salad Bowl'.
Cos: 'Little Gem', 'Paris White', 'Lobjoit's Green Cos'.
Hardy winter lettuce for sowing in the open ground in autumn: 'Arctic King', 'Imperial Winter', 'Valdor', 'Winter Density'.
Forcing varieties: 'Kordaat', 'Kloek', 'Kwiek', 'May Queen', 'Premier' – all are excellent for sowing under glass from September onwards.

MARROW & COURGETTE
Cucurbita pepo ovifera

The marrow, more properly known as the vegetable marrow, and the courgette, which is a baby marrow, belong to the same family as cucumbers and melons. All have a high water content, and some vitamin A, and all have either a trailing or climbing habit of growth.

Cultivation Sow seeds into pots in April. Allow two seeds for each pot and when the seedlings have established themselves discard the weaker one and transfer the healthy seedling to a permanent growing position in a frame. To ensure germination, lay the required number of seeds on a sheet of damp blotting paper in a warm place for 2 days before planting. Make up beds by digging sites of 30 cm (1 ft) or more deep, and filling them with well-rotted manure which should be trodden in and covered with soil. Make a small planting hole with a trowel and put the plants in firmly. Water as necessary and keep the frame lights closed until danger of frost has passed. Toward the end of May remove the glass and give a boost to growth by watering in a dressing of dried blood. Outdoor crops are fertilized by bees and other insects but for early fruits it is advisable to pollinate the female flowers on each plant by hand using a camel hair brush. This is best done about mid-day, preferably when it is sunny and the flowers are dry. The female flower is easily recognized by the embryo fruit present at the back of the petals. Once the flowers have set and the fruit is developing, regular watering and occasional feeds of

Courgettes are small, sweet tender marrows and are easy to grow

liquid manure are essential. The earliest fruit may be ready for cutting by mid-June.

The first outdoor sowings should not be made until the middle of May into prepared planting sites. These outdoor plants will produce fruit from July until the end of September. Planting distances for bush types is 1.20 m (4 ft) square and for trailing varieties 1.80 m (6 ft) square.

RECOMMENDED VARIETIES: 'Long Green Bush' and 'Long Green Trailing'; 'Marco', F_1 green courgettes, bush; 'Tender and True', round marrow fruits, bush; 'Table Dainty', short striped fruits, trailing; 'Zucchini', F_1 prolific green courgettes, bush.

MELON *Cucumis melo*

These plants, which can be cultivated in a similar manner to cucumbers, have been grown for centuries. They are easy to manage when grown in favourable positions and where they have the maximum amount of sunshine.

Seed can be sown in a propagator in April, or on hotbeds of about 22°C (72°F)

in pots or boxes. Use a mixture of loam and peat to which a little wood ash and old mortar rubble has been added, or a proprietary loam- or peat-based seed compost.

Place the seed edgeways 13 mm (½ in) deep, and keep the propagator closed until germination occurs. Then give ventilation and water as necessary. When the seedlings have two leaves, move them to the frame or Dutch light, where a bed has been prepared by incorporating plenty of well-rotted manure. Handle them with care and give some shade until they are established.

Plant on slightly raised soil to prevent moisture collecting round the base of the stem at soil level, to avoid collar rot. Shade from direct sunshine and regular ventilation are important factors.

Frequent syringings of water will help in providing a moist atmosphere. When the plants have formed three leaves pinch out the leading shoot, preferably when it is sunny for quick healing of the wound, to encourage laterals to form. Once the laterals have formed four leaves, they too are stopped above the third leaf and it is on the sub-laterals that the fruit is borne.

Male and female flowers are produced,

the latter being larger and recognized by a small swelling at the base. Pollen is usually transferred to the female flower by bees and other insects but early in the season and with frame plants, it is advisable to hand pollinate. This is done by picking the male flowers and lightly rubbing the pollen on to the stigma in the centre of the female flower. Wait until four or five flowers are open together, so the fruits develop evenly.

If possible, do this job between 12 noon and 2 pm, preferably when it is sunny and the flowers fully open and dry. After a few days, the swelling at the back of each female flower will begin to enlarge.

Plants can also be placed in the cold frame or under cloches from the middle to the end of April. Prepare a good hole for each plant, filling it with well-rotted manure. Plant the melon on a little ridge to avoid the roots becoming waterlogged. Cutting begins in August. Signs of ripening are a crack on

'Ha-ogen' melons ripening in the greenhouse

the fruit near the stalk, deep colour and a rich honey smell.

Water melons can be grown where a little heat is available. Sow the seeds in April in pots of peaty compost standing them in the cold frame. When the seedlings are ready for their fruiting positions select sandy soil, well-mulched with good compost. Set the plants on little mounds about 75 cm (2½ ft) apart remembering that the plants will not be bushy specimens but will be kept to one main stem growing 1.50 m (5 ft) or more. Make sure water does not settle round the plants or stem rot will develop.

Shallow furrows can be made both sides of the plants as necessary during the summer or clay pots can be sunk in the soil near the plants and these can be frequently filled with water. After the fruits have set, carefully place them on pieces of wood or slate to prevent slug or other pest damage.

RECOMMENDED VARIETIES. The group known as Canteloupe melons are the easiest to manage and include 'Dutch Net' and 'No Name'. For growing with little or no heat, also the F₁ 'Burpee Hybrid', which has rounded golden, netted fruit and thick juicy, orange flesh. 'Sweetheart' is another splendid hybrid with salmon-pink flesh. It does well in frames or under cloches. 'Charentais' is a small delicious variety with scented flesh. Of the varieties of melons needing heated or warm greenhouse treatment, 'Hero of Lockinge', 'Superlative' and the green fleshed 'Emerald Gem' are most reliable. Water melon 'Florida Favourite' produces oval fruits of 2.7 kg (6 lb) or more with green skin and pink flesh.

MUSHROOM *Psalliota campestris*

Mushrooms require a precisely controlled environment in cellars or in boxes under the staging of a greenhouse. Wherever you choose to grow mushrooms, the site must be clean, draught-free but well-ventilated, dimly lit or dark, and capable of maintaining a temperature between 10 and 13°C (50−55°F). Mushroom spawn needs a particular compost in which to thrive. Ready-made mushroom compost is available and should be used if you are unable to prepare suitable compost in your own garden. To do this, use only wheat-straw-based horse manure. Make a broad heap and leave for a week or ten days to generate heat. Turn the outside of the heap to the inside three or four times over the following month, watering it as necessary; the process is complete when no smell is given off and the texture of the compost is friable. Pack the compost firmly into the chosen growing site about

30 cm (1 ft) deep. The temperature will rise and then fall to 24°C (75°F), at which point put lumps of spawn about the size of a golf ball 1 cm (2½ ins) below the surface 30 cm (1 ft) apart each way. Ten days later cover the compost with a damp layer of 'casing' (50:50 peat and chalk). About a month later the mushrooms will appear. Harvest regularly to maintain productivity and mushrooms will keep coming through for up to two months. Never use spent compost for a second crop of mushrooms.

ONION *Allium cepa*

One of the most widely grown and valued of all vegetables, the onion has been known and grown for thousands of years. There are numerous varieties, some suitable for Autumn sowing, some best sown in Spring, others which are valued as salad or spring onions, while a number are useful for producing small bulbs for pickling.

Onions are a crop which responds well to generous cultural treatment and it is advisable to select a good site.

Both the bulb and salad or spring onions prefer a medium to light soil. Onions used to be grown on the same patch year after year, but this is not generally recommended because of the possibility of disease building up. Good drainage is important although the soil must not dry out. The best crop is produced on medium loams which have been deeply cultivated and enriched with compost or generous amounts of farmyard manure. The site should be free from perennial weeds and away from buildings or trees which would cast shadows and one where there is free air circulation and exposure to full sun.

'Button' mushrooms appear about a month after spawning

Many gardeners have their own ways of making an onion bed. Some prefer to prepare the ground by digging deeply and placing a layer of decayed vegetable matter at the bottom of the trench, following this with a layer of soil then a generous sprinkling of sulphate of potash and bone meal. More soil is then applied covering the bed, with wood ash lightly pricked into the surface soil. Do this as early as possible – October is not too soon. Then before sowing the seed, apply a dusting of hydrated lime to ensure that the soil is not acid.

If the ground is inclined to be loose it should be firmed by treading lightly or a light roller can be used. For the earliest and largest bulb onions, seed should be sown in the open in late August or early September. Sow thinly in rows 30–38 cm (12–15 ins) apart. The seedlings should be transplanted in March and April 15 cm (6 ins) apart in rows 30 cm (1 ft) apart. One disadvantage with autumn sowing is that if the winter is very mild the seedlings may make too much soft growth and some may run to seed prematurely.

When transplanting the seedlings take care not to break the roots. Use a fork to prise up the soil along the rows. Plant firmly so that the bases of the seedlings are just settled in the soil. They must not be buried deeply but be well embedded in the soil.

According to soil and weather conditions spring sowings can be made from late February onwards although the bed should have been prepared well before that time. Never attempt to sow while the soil is sticky. Sow shallowly in rows 25–30 cm (10–12 ins) apart after making the soil firm. A 7 g ($\frac{1}{4}$ oz) packet of seed will sow a row about 15 m (50 ft). Thin the seedlings gradually using the thinnings in salads, leaving the plants finally to stand at least 10 cm (4 ins) apart. Take care not to bruise the seedlings otherwise the scent emitted may attract the onion fly. Always firm the soil along the rows after thinning out has been done.

Seed of salad onions is usually sown early in September. This will supply pullings from early March onwards. A second sowing should be made in late February or March as soon as soil conditions are suitable. Make further successional sowings until June.

Make the rows 20–30 cm (8–12 ins) apart and sow fairly sparingly. There is no need to thin the seedlings which can be used as needed. 'White Lisbon' is the most widely grown and easily obtained variety.

The so-called Welsh or 'ever-ready' onion, A. fistulosum, is a hardy perennial

Onions have the same soil requirements as beans and peas

producing spring onion-like growths quite closely together. Available throughout the year they are a reliable standby when the usual spring onions are not available.

They can be propagated by division of the clumps in early spring or autumn; any good well drained soil is suitable. Seed is occasionally available and can be sown in June or July.

If you want to grow large exhibition onions seed should be sown under glass early in January. Use trays of John Innes seed compost making it firm before sowing thinly. Cover the seed with compost, make the surface firm and level. Then give a sprinkling of water and place the trays on the greenhouse staging where the temperature is around 18°C (65°F) and cover with a sheet of glass and brown paper. Once germination is seen remove glass and paper and keep the trays on the staging in the

light. After three or four weeks the seedlings can be moved to the frame for hardening off preparatory to planting outdoors in April.

RECOMMENDED VARIETIES: Many varieties are available and among the best are the following: 'Ailsa Craig', one of the most useful of all purpose varieties which can be sown in spring or autumn. 'Bedfordshire Champion' makes large globular bulbs much like 'Ailsa Craig' and is excellent for exhibiting. 'Reliance', an extra fine vigorous growing variety and a wonderful cropper; best results come from autumn sowing. 'White Spanish', very large bulbs which keep sound a long time.

'Barletta Barla' is probably the best for pickling having pure white globe-shaped bulbs. 'The Queen' is another particularly good pickler with silver skin, while 'Giant Zittau' has long been used for this purpose.

'Amber Express' is one of the new Japanese onions and should be sown in October

The Welsh onion is a useful perennial

For spring onions 'White Lisbon' is wholly dependable. slender-shaped with white skin.

A new race known as Japanese onions has been developed to give early maturity. Seed must be sown in the autumn, the bulbs maturing and being ready for lifting in July. They are heavy croppers. Varieties include 'Express Yellow' and 'Extra Early Kaizuka' making flattish bulbs while 'Imai Early Yellow' forms globe shaped bulbs.

Onion sets These are favoured by gardeners who have had trouble from onion fly or who do not wish to make a seed bed or plant out seedlings in spring. Sets are small onions which have been arrested in their development and dried off and stored during the winter. They are generally sold by weight, 225 g (8 oz) being enough for the average garden.

Culture is simple: treat the soil as advised for seed sowing. Plant the sets shallowly from early March onwards according to soil conditions. Allow 10–15 cm (4–6 ins) between the bulbs with 30–40 cm (12–15 ins) from row to row. Check the rows in the weeks following planting to make sure the small onions are still in place.

Several varieties are available and 'Sturon' is a distinct type making large solid keeping onions which very rarely bolt. It is of attractive appearance with rich golden-yellow skin and keeps well. 'Stuttgart Giant' is semi-flat with a clear amber skin.

There is also a strain of 'Ailsa Craig' sets which are prepared for exhibition by special heat process. Start the bulbs in pots during March and April or plant in the open ground towards the end of April.

74

ORACHE *Atriplex hortensis*

Sometimes known as Mountain Spinach, there are three forms of this annual: green, white or red, all growing about 1.20 m (4 ft) high. The red variety is not out of place in the ornamental garden, but it should not be allowed to flower there, since it seeds itself freely and can become a nuisance.

The young leaves are excellent in salads, while the older ones are cooked like spinach.

Orache is an ornamental food plant

People who find ordinary spinach indigestible can eat this type without discomfort. Seed can be sown thinly in moisture-retentive ground from the end of March to the end of July. Plant rows 45 cm (18 ins) apart and thin the seedlings early so that there is 38 cm (15 ins) between them. It is best to gather some leaves from each plant rather than stripping individual plants.

PARSNIP *Pastinaca sativa*

A native of Great Britain, the parsnip is a nutritious vegetable containing vitamin C with traces of B1 and A, iron and calcium. A useful vegetable, it may well be that the reason it is not used more widely is because it is not always cooked properly. Parsnips steamed or baked are delicious.

It is one of the easiest vegetables to grow and thrives in a deep, light to medium soil

'Avon resister' is a reliable variety of parsnip

where there are few or no stones. Parsnips can also be grown on shallow ground so long as the fairly new stumprooted varieties are used. On thin, gravelly, chalky soil the roots tend to fork. It is best to select a site which was generously manured for a previous crop. If soil is very poor and it is not possible to obtain bulky organic manure, a complete fertilizer can be used at the rate of

113 g per m² (4 oz per sq yd).

This crop occupies the ground for a long time, which is one reason why it is not popular in small gardens. It is one of the first crops to be sown, usually at the end of February or early in March. Seed is sown in drills in the usual way, or a few seeds can be placed at stations 15 cm (6 ins) apart, or if extra large roots are required an even wider spacing can be allowed.

Individual holes can be made up to 60 cm (2 ft) deep with 7.5–10 cm (3–4 ins) diameter at the top. These holes can be filled with a compost of three parts clean garden soil and one part of good compost or rotted manure. Pass this through a 6 mm (¼ in) sieve. Sow three seeds in each hole and thin the seedlings down to the strongest one. The rows should be 30 cm (12 ins) apart.

Seed is liable to be slow in germinating and it is quite a good plan to sow radish or lettuce seed along the rows. The quick germination of these will show where the rows are, and prevent loss when the ground is being cultivated. Thinning must be done early, the best time being when the first two true leaves have developed. After this, cultivation consists of keeping down weeds.

Parsnips are hardy and can be left in the soil throughout the winter and dug as required. Since the roots are needed when the soil is liable to become frozen hard, it is a good plan to use straw or other protective material for placing around some roots, making it easier to lift them. Alternatively, some roots can be lifted and stored in sand, although this is not recommended since the roots tend to go soft.

There are very few diseases or pests likely to attack parsnips, except canker fungus which may be troublesome. This may be seen as cracks and brown areas chiefly around the top, and other places. Fungi and a physiological disorder are the culprits and often appear in badly drained soil; if too much nitrogen was given; or if the roots were damaged by the hoe.

RECOMMENDED VARIETIES: 'Avonresister', needs less space than other varieties and it is most resistant to canker; 'Hollow Crown Improved' heavy cropping, well shaped, broad shoulders; 'Offenham', intermediate size with broad shoulders, useful for shallow soils; 'Tender and True', medium size, extra tender flesh; 'The Student', well shaped roots of fine flavour; 'White Gem', a medium sized broad shouldered variety with smooth skin; 'Lisbonnais', one of the largest and longest varieties.

PEA *Pisum sativum*

The garden pea has been cultivated for centuries. Its food value is good, for among other properties it contains vitamins A, B and C and calcium and iron in small quantities. Peas are grouped as either round or wrinkled. The former are hardier and are widely used for autumn sowing. Wrinkled peas are generally of superior flavour since they have more sugar than starch.

The average family of four requires about 1 kg (2¼ lb) of shelled peas to make a decent dish. Good medium soil is necessary. Peas occupy the ground for a long time so it is important that the land should be in good condition. Move the soil fairly deeply working in good compost or rotted manure, while a dusting of fish manure at 85–113 g per m² (3–4 oz per sq yd) well raked in before sowing, will provide all the feeding

Above: 'Onward', the most popular second-early pea. Below: Ripe pods of 'Kelvedon Wonder', a first-early variety

matter the plants will need. Once the soil has been worked into a fine, friable condition, it will be ready for sowing. Flat bottomed or V shaped drills should be drawn out 8 cm (3 ins) deep. The distance apart of the drills depends on variety, but as a guide, the dwarf sorts growing 30 cm (1 ft) high, should be spaced 38 cm (15 ins) apart. Those growing 60–90 cm (2–3 ft) high should be allowed 60–90 cm (2–3 ft) between rows and for the taller sorts allow about the same distance between the rows as the height of the variety.

Autumn sowings can be made from the end of October onwards using the round seeded varieties. Spring sowings can commence in mid-March, these being made more thickly, and 43 cc (¾ pint) of seed will sow a

75

row 15 m (16 yds) long. For the later sowings 28 cc ($\frac{1}{2}$ pint) is sufficient for the same length row. It is best to go back to the earliest wrinkled varieties for the latest July sowings.

Birds often attack pea seedlings as they come through the ground. It is a good plan to place pea guards or to stretch strands of black cotton along the rows. Twiggy sticks should be inserted as soon as the seedlings can be seen, as they keep them from blowing about and from falling on the ground where they become a prey to soil pests. Use pea sticks or netting for the final supports. A mulch of peat drawn towards the plants will prevent the soil drying out and ensure an even supply of moisture to the roots.

The earliest varieties will be ready from June onwards and successional sowings will give pickings into late September.

RECOMMENDED VARIETIES: good first early round seeded varieties include: 'Meteor', 45 cm ($1\frac{1}{2}$ ft); 'Superb' 60 cm (2 ft), and 'Pilot', 45 cm ($1\frac{1}{2}$ ft).

First early wrinkle-seeded: 'Hurst Beagle', 45 cm ($1\frac{1}{2}$ ft); 'Kelvedon Wonder', 45 cm ($1\frac{1}{2}$ ft) and 'Early Onward', 60 cm (2 ft).

Second early and main crop wrinkle-seeded: 'Histon Kingsize', 1.05 m ($3\frac{1}{2}$ ft); 'Hurst Green Shaft', 75 cm ($2\frac{1}{2}$ ft); 'Onward', 75 cm ($2\frac{1}{2}$ ft) and 'Miracle' 1.35 m ($4\frac{1}{2}$ ft).

Late wrinkle-seeded varieties: 'Lord Chancellor', 90 cm (3 ft); 'Senator', 90 cm (3 ft); 'Victory Freezer', 75 cm ($2\frac{1}{2}$ ft);

'Recette' 60 cm (2 ft), is an interesting variant – it produces three pods at almost every stem joint.

Sugar or Mangetout peas Provided they are gathered when young these peas are a real delicacy. The entire pods are eaten, and all the preparation they need is topping and tailing, as required for French beans. Seed is sown in the ordinary way. Since birds find the young pods attractive, it is wise to cotton the rows. Slugs too, may attack the plants and young pods if they are allowed to fall

Above: 'Mange-tout' and (below) asparagus peas are delicacies with a fine flavour

over and touch the ground. This is why they should be given supports at an early stage. 'Carouby de Maussane' and 'Dwarf Sweet Green' are recommended varieties. A fairly new sugar pea known as 'Sweetpod', bears light green, succulent pods of sweet flavour.

The Carlin pea These are peas grown chiefly in the north of England, being used especially on mid-Lent Sunday, which was once widely known as Carlin Sunday. The seeds, now seldom offered by seedsmen, are very distinct, being darker than any other variety and resembling lentils.

The cultivation for the Carlin pea is the same as for the ordinary types, the seed being sown in April. Choose a well-limed patch of soil and work 85 g per m² (3 oz per sq yd) of fish manure into the site before sowing.

Plants grow more than 2 m (6 ft) high, and must be provided with suitable supports. Neither birds nor mice are interested in these peas, which are rarely if ever, attacked by mildews, and other troubles associated with the normal sorts.

The plants produce a prolific crop of short pods, particularly during July and August. They should be left until fully ripe when the entire plants can be pulled up and the pods shelled. It is essential to allow the seeds to dry well, after which store them in a cool, dry place for winter and spring use. The dried seeds should be soaked for some hours before being cooked until tender. If sprinkled with sugar and rum, the flavour is superb.

Asparagus pea *Tetragonolobus purpureus* In spite of its common name this is not an ordinary garden pea and it is only because of its flavour that asparagus comes into the name at all. It has deep brownish-red flowers.

Not fully hardy, it is best to raise plants in gentle heat, sowing in April, gradually hardening the seedlings for planting out towards the end of May onwards. A sunny situation should be provided and the soil should be on the light side. Pick the pods while small – not more than an inch long and cook them whole. Left to grow large they become stringy.

Petit Pois This is reckoned by epicures to be the best of all. Very popular in France, it has a delicious sugary flavour. Seed should be sown in April, making the drills 25 mm (1 in) deep. Allow 10–15 cm (4–6 ins) between the seeds, with the rows about 1.06 m

(3 ft 6 ins) apart. Since the plants grow 90 cm–1.20 m (3–4 ft) high it is an advantage to provide supports.

Gather the pods immediately they are filled, and if they are steamed without delay, the peas will readily fall out of the pods and the full flavour will be there too! 'Gullivert' is the variety most usually grown.

The Purple Podded pea This is a little grown type of pea, which has deep green foliage but flowers and pods of a purple colour. It needs normal culture for peas and is hardy. Growing about 1.35 m (4½ ft) high or more and it succeeds in most soils. The peas which are green, may be used fresh in the ordinary way or can be dried for winter use. In either case they have a most pleasing flavour.

PEPPER *Capsicum annuum*

Sweet Peppers are not cultivated as much as they deserve. This is probably because they are often thought to be hot. If they are properly grown and cooked, they are a real delicacy. Some success is being achieved in breeding self stopping (those which branch freely) varieties which have a more compact habit.

Plants can be raised in exactly the same way as aubergines, spacing the seeds 2.5 cm (1 in) apart in pots or trays of seed compost. Do this in February or March in a temperature of about 15°C (60°F). Prick off seedlings as soon as they are big enough to handle moving them to small pots when they reach 15–18 cm (6–7 ins). Keep them in full light and spray with water frequently to keep off red spider.

If the plants are to be grown in a sunny, sheltered position outdoors, they can be pricked off into soil blocks or peat pots of John Innes No. 1 compost. Plants are also grown under cloches or frames. It is best to plant in shallow trenches and to raise the glass when necessary keeping the plants covered throughout growth.

The plants grow 60–75 cm (2–2½ ft) tall, and bear white flowers that are followed by fruit which colours according to variety. If plants fail to produce side shoots, pinch out the growing points. Once the fruit begins to swell, liquid fertilizer will prove beneficial.

Capsicums vary in length from 10–13 cm (4–5 ins) although in the case of the bull-nosed types, they are only 5–8 cm (2–3 in) long but much thicker and irregularly shaped. Chilli peppers are very hot and only used for flavouring and pickles.

RECOMMENDED VARIETIES: Green peppers are the red and yellow sorts before they turn colour. Good varieties include: 'Canape' with sweet mild flesh; 'Bell Boy' F_1, 'Burpee Hybrid' and 'New Ace', a heavy cropper for glass culture.

POTATO *Solanum tuberosum*

We eat more potatoes than any other vegetable. This crop is grown where ground needs to be cleared of weeds before other crops are planted. Potatoes will grow on all types of soil, although a deep, well-drained medium loam is best. Soil has a great influence on flavour. Plenty of light and air are required, for under stagnant, close conditions blight may spoil the crop. Heavy clay and peaty soils are said to produce 'waxy' or 'soapy' tubers, but this is not always so.

Early soil preparation is helpful. Farm-yard manure, seaweed or compost can be worked in when digging the ground during the winter. Then leave the surface ridged if the land is heavy, so that it breaks down easily at planting time. At planting time, rotted manure or compost spread along the rows underneath the tubers, makes the roots more active. For the maincrop and even the second early sorts, manure can be supplemented with a good fertilizer such as bone meal or hoof and horn.

Medium sized tubers the size of a hen's egg and weighing about 56 g (2 oz) are best, the most usual size being those which have passed through a 6 cm (2¼ ins) riddle but will remain on a 3 cm (1¼ ins) one.

Buy fresh, certified seed every year to be sure of a healthy crop. Very large tubers can be cut. This should be done lengthways, so each portion has at least two strong sprouts. Cover the cut portions with a damp cloth until they can be planted.

Green peppers are best grown in the greenhouse

'Desirée' is a new potato cultivar

Harvest potatoes carefully to avoid damaging the tubers

When planting, take out flat bottomed trenches about 15 cm (6 ins) deep, deeper on light land. A layer of leaf mould or peat sprinkled along the opened trench helps to ensure that the tubers retain good skins.

The earliest tubers can be spaced 25–30 cm (10–12 ins) apart with 45–52 cm (18–21 ins) between rows. Second earlies can be spaced 38 cm (15 ins) apart with 68 cm (2¼ ft) between rows. Maincrops need to be 45 cm (18 ins) apart with the rows 75 cm (2½ ft) apart.

The earthing up of potatoes keeps the haulm upright, and prevents the new tubers from becoming exposed and turning green, when they become useless for eating. The extra covering of soil also protects the tubers from blight.

Earthing up is done gradually and can be started when the stems are 20–23 cm (8–9 ins) high. The ridges made should have fairly sharp, sloping sides. This allows

Rows of potatoes earthed up

heavy rains to drain off.

Potatoes can be grown successfully under black polythene without earthing up. The ground is prepared in the usual way, the tubers being pressed lightly into the surface. A sheet of polythene is then laid over the rows, a cross cut about 8 cm (3 ins) long, like a plus sign being made over each tuber. Fix the edges of the polythene by taking out a little furrow 5–8 cm (2–3 ins) deep. Cover the edges with soil, making it firm by treading.

This leads to quick growth, supression of weeds, and the retention of moisture. Scatter slug bait over the ground, under the polythene, for the dark, cool shelter this cover gives makes an ideal hiding and breeding place for slugs.

Early potatoes are ready for lifting when the flowers begin to wither; main crops when the leaves turn yellow. The earliest crop is usually ready at the beginning of July. To ensure that tubers are really ready for lifting, it is a good plan to scrape away the soil and remove one or two tubers. Then light rub the skins. If they remain firm the tubers are ready for harvesting.

New potatoes in the autumn can be obtained by following on with another planting of early potatoes, on ground from which the first crop has just been lifted. From the first lifting, select sound shapely tubers about the size of a Victoria plum, weighing between 42–57 g (1½–2 oz).

Expose the chosen tubers to the light and sun for two or three days and then replant. Choose a favourable sheltered site. Turn over the soil fairly deeply, working in a good dressing of an organic fertilizer. Then make a trench 13–15 cm (5–6 ins) deep and place the tubers 25–30 cm (10–12 ins) apart with 52 cm (21 ins) between rows.

RECOMMENDED VARIETIES: *First earlies:* 'Arran Pilot', white kidney, floury, heavy cropper; 'Home Guard', medium sized, oval; 'Ulster Chieftain', white, oval; 'Ulster Prince', white, kidney, crops well under dry conditions; 'Epicure', a good cropping variety, white, round; 'Stormont Dawn', white, floury, good flavoured.
Second earlies: 'Craig's Alliance', white flesh; 'Craig's Royal', creamy fleshed kidney; 'Dunbar Rover', white fleshed, floury; 'Great Scot', white round. 'Maris Peer', white oval, shows some resistance to scab. *Maincrop:* 'Arran Peak', white flesh, keeps well; 'Dr. McIntosh', white kidney, grand for exhibition; 'Majestic', white kidney, waxy, irregular shape. 'King Edward', large tubers, heavy cropper; 'Maris Piper', new cultivar.

PUMPKIN & SQUASH *Cucurbita maxima, C. moschata*

Pumpkins and squashes are two more members of the interesting family *Cucur-*

'Hundredweight' Pumpkin grows to proportions worthy of a harvest festival

'Golf Nugget' squash is highly decorative

bitaceae, which includes vegetable marrows and courgettes, cucumbers and melons. Cultivation techniques are similar to those described for marrows (q.v.). The planting site should be prepared by digging in a generous quantity of farmyard manure at 30 cm (1 ft) deep and covering with soil to make a mound on which the plant can be generously watered without becoming waterlogged. All members of this family are composed of about 90 per cent water and must be kept well supplied with water throughout their season of growth. Construct a 'moat' around the growing mound and keep this full of water rather than watering the plants directly.

The culinary uses of pumpkin are few: pumpkin pie is a great American favourite, and slices of pumpkin roasted with pork to soak up the flavoursome juices is an idea worth experimenting with.

Squashes are divided somewhat confusingly into two groups, summer and winter: in fact cultivars from each group can be grown at various times of the year. The proper winter squashes, known in America as Hubbard squashes, are eaten when they are ripe (unlike vegetable marrows, which are eaten when they are immature) and in fact keep in store for up to 4 months in a cool but frost-free place. They contain considerably more nutrients than marrows, cooked cabbage, or summer squash, and far less water.

Vegetable spaghetti is a newly developed variety which is grown in the same way, harvested when about 20 cm (8 ins) long and then cooked whole. When cut in half the flesh is eaten in strands just like spaghetti and is very good with butter and freshly ground black pepper.

All the members of this family have attractive bright orange flowers which can be eaten if dipped in batter and quick fried.

The custard marrow, or scalloped summer squash, has not been very widely grown in this country, although it has been known for about 400 years.

Perhaps one of the most popular reasons for growing members of this family is that, as well as being edible, they are very decorative plants, both in their trailing or climbing habit of growth and in their beautifully coloured fruits. One plant can occupy a surprising amount of ground and cover it generously with its broad-leaved foliage.

RECOMMENDED VARIETIES: 'Baby Crookneck', yellow squash, with a neck like an umbrella handle, bush; 'Custard White', flat white with scalloped edge, bush; 'Gold Nugget', round yellow fruit, bush, winter keeping; 'Golden Delicious', top-shaped orange fruit, trailing, winter keeping; 'Hubbard's Golden Squash', orange-yellow pumpkin, trailing, winter keeping; 'Little Gem', orange-sized, round squash, trailing, winter keeping; 'Mammoth', probably the best-known pumpkin, trailing, winter keeping; 'Sweet Dumpling', delicious squash, looks like a melon, trailing, winter keeping; 'Vegetable Spaghetti', yellow strings of flesh when cooked, trailing.

PURSLANE *Portulaca oleracea*

This is a plant which is much valued in Eastern countries, although it has also been grown for centuries in Europe. An annual with succulent foliage, it thrives in light soil, and likes the sun. The young leaves can be cooked or used raw in salads and sandwiches and give a delicious flavour to soups. To ensure succession, sow the seeds in small batches from April onwards. The rows should be 23 cm (9 ins) apart and the seedlings are thinned to 15 cm (6 ins) in the row. They transplant well but should never lack moisture.

Purslane is an attractive addition to salads

RADISH *Raphanus sativus*

This easy crop can be cultivated in the open ground, the cold frame and the cool green-house. An excellent catch crop, it can be grown on the sides of celery or leek trenches or between rows of lettuce or other salad plants. There are red, white and red and white varieties, varying in shape from round or globe to half-long and fully long with a broad top. The newer varieties have dispelled

Quick-growing radish 'French Breakfast'

the belief that radishes are hot and cause indigestion.

Although radishes do not need deep soil, the ground should be well prepared and stay moist, for quick growth is required for crisp, succulent roots. Soil containing plenty of organic manure is ideal. Dry soil induces leafy growth with little or no bulb development.

Do not sow too thickly. While it is quite usual to spread (broadcast) the seed, it is best to sow in drills 15 cm (6 ins) apart and about 13 mm ($\frac{1}{2}$ in) deep. Make the soil firm after sowing for loose soil rarely produces firm roots. A half ounce of seed will sow two rows 4.50 m (15 ft) long. Thin the seedlings early so that all have an opportunity to develop properly and if flea beetles are troublesome dust the drills with Sevin or BHC powder before the seed is sown. Pull the roots as soon as they are usable.

RECOMMENDED VARIETIES for early maturing outdoors: 'Flamenco', 'French Breakfast', 'Cherry Belle', 'Saxa', also known as 'Red Forcing', 'Red Prince', 'Icicle' white, 'Wood's Frame' a long variety deep pink in colour, and 'Sparkler' half-red and half-white.

Winter radishes These can be sown from July onwards, although in warmer areas, wait until August. Make the drills 23 cm (9 ins) apart, thinning the plants to 15 cm (6 ins) in the rows. The roots can be left in the ground to be dug as required or they can be lifted in November or December and stored in boxes of sand, sandy soil or peat. Winter radishes can also be grown in boxes although these should be at least 20–23 cm (8–9 ins) deep. For good results the roots require plenty of moisture in the growing season, otherwise they become stringy and very hot.

RECOMMENDED VARIETIES of winter radish: The variety 'China Rose' is one of the best, being similar to a very large 'French Breakfast'. The skin is cerise-red, the flesh white and crisp. 'Black Spanish' has black skin and white flesh and comes in round or long rooted forms. 'Mino Early' is a fat sausage-shaped variety with a very mild flavour. All need slicing and are not eaten whole.

The Bavarian radish is a most unusual variety, forming roots the size of large turnips, the top growth reaching 75–90 cm ($2\frac{1}{2}$–3 ft). This is a variety which is served in Bavarian beer halls where it is cut into spiral pieces or grated and served in salads. The decorative seed pods are an added attraction especially since they make a useful sandwich filling if cut and used while green.

Although an easy crop to grow, gardeners often find there is plenty of top growth but the roots are small and stringy. This is usually because the soil is 'thin' and lacking in phosphates vital for good root development. Overcome it by dressing the soil with 113 g per m² (4 oz) per sq yd of superphosphate before sowing.

RHUBARB *Rheum rhaponticum*

An easy plant to grow, rhubarb will remain productive for many years. Sadly it is often grown in positions which are badly drained or where the soil is poor.

Although its food value is not great, rhubarb is much appreciated early in the year before fresh fruit becomes available. This ancient plant has medicinal value and was originally used solely for this purpose. The leaves are poisonous since they contain oxalic acid.

Dig the soil deeply since the plants make thick branching roots. If stable, farmyard

Tender shoots of forced rhubarb. Bins or boxes can replace the traditional terra-cotta pots

manure or compost is worked in it will provide feeding material over a long period. Bone meal and wood ashes are also beneficial. For earliest outdoor rhubarb, a fairly sheltered position is required.

Plant in November, or February and March, when the soil is workable. Allow 90 cm (3 ft) between the crowns, for they increase in size and need ample room. Spread the roots fully, planting firmly, covering the crowns with 5 cm (2 ins) of soil. Do not pull any stalks the first season and in subsequent years always leave some stalks on each plant.

It is best not to pull after early July excepting in the case of stalks needed for jam or wine making. Rhubarb should not be cut but gripped at the base of the stem and pulled with a jerking movement. Flower heads should always be removed. To keep the plants productive, give a dressing of manure annually. Inverted pots or boxes placed over some of the plants will provide earlier outdoor pullings.

Rhubarb is generally trouble free. If plants show signs of rotting at the crown, dig them up and burn them.

raised to 10°C (50°F) and after a further eight to ten days to 15–18°C (60–65°F).

RECOMMENDED VARIETIES include: 'Prince Albert', 'Linnaeus' and 'Victoria'. If one or more of these are grown it will provide a natural succession of sticks for pulling from April onwards. For forcing, 'Champagne' and 'Dawes Champion' are good. It is possible to raise rhubarb from seed. 'Glaskin's Perpetual' and 'Holstein Bloodred' which mature quickly are the best for this purpose.

SALAD SPROUTS

For centuries the Chinese and Japanese have eaten sprouted seeds, knowing that they contain valuable proteins as well as other health promoting qualities. Seeds for sprouting are now offered by several seed firms and apart from Alfalfa and Mung beans, Adzuki, Fenugreek and Triticale are now available, as well as a mixture of Salad Sprouts.

The simplest way of growing them is to place the seeds in a jam jar indoors and fix muslin over the top with an elastic band. Fill the jar with water and shake well. Do this morning and evening until sprouting occurs. The time will vary from three to seven days and the sprouted seed can be eaten raw or cooked.

The Mung Bean, *Phaseolus aureus* is now becoming popular because of its high food value. It has a high protein content and contains vitamin E. The tasty sprouts are served in Chinese restaurants, frequently being added to rice dishes. All they need is to be cooked for a few minutes in boiling water containing a little salt.

They are as easy to grow as mustard and cress and are most useful for persons living in a flat or otherwise without a garden. Simply sow the beans on the surface of damp peat or flannel in a dish or bowl, cover the containers with polythene and place them in a cupboard or other dark moderately warm place. They will soon germinate and produce their succulent blanched top growth which will be ready for use within a few days. Cut the shoots when about 5 cm (2 ins) long and cook as soon as possible, when they will be crisp and nutty. Remember to keep the material moist at all times. It is best to sow small quantities at frequent intervals, rather than fewer large sowings. These beans cannot be grown outdoors.

Salad sprouts are ready within a few days of germinating

Forcing rhubarb While it is usual to force three year old plants, rather younger specimens can be used, provided they are strong and healthy. Plants to be forced should not be pulled during the summer. This means that the energy of the plants will have been directed entirely to building up strong crowns for producing a good crop when forced.

The simplest way to force rhubarb is in boxed soil under the heated greenhouse staging. If sacks or hessian are draped in front of the staging this will provide the necessary darkness. Should hot water pipes be under the staging, it is best to stand a sheet of asbestos or some boards in front, to screen plants from the heat.

Timing is important. If the aim is to produce sticks for Christmas, forcing should commence in mid-November. To maintain a succession, bring in batches of crowns at fourteen-day intervals. Make sure that the soil is nicely moist before planting.

Pack the crowns closely together, filling in the spaces between them with sandy loam, fine peat or leaf mould so that there are no air pockets. Once planted, the crowns should be given a good soaking with water. To begin with, a temperature of 8°C (45°F) is adequate, but a week later it should be

SALSIFY *Tragopogon porrifolius*

This is a biennial plant, often known as the vegetable oyster because of its flavour. It is not widely grown in this country, but is much used as a winter vegetable in France and Italy. It likes a deep, light, moisture retentive soil, preferably enriched with decayed manure or compost the previous season.

Sow seed in mid-April in drills 25 mm (1 in) deep and 30 cm (1 ft) apart, and thin the seedlings to 15—18 cm (6—7 ins) apart. The roots are ready for use from October onwards and may be lifted as required, being treated like parsnips. Take care not to damage them or they will 'bleed' and loose their nutty flavour.

If some plants are left in the ground during winter young top growth, which has an asparagus flavour, can be cut and cooked in spring. The cream coloured roots should be 15—23 cm (6—9 ins) long, and 5 cm (2 ins) thick. They can be steamed or boiled in their skins, which are rubbed off, before being served with white sauce. The variety usually grown is 'Sandwich Island'.

SCORZONERA *Scorzonera hispanica*

Very similar to salsify, this is preferred by many because of its flavour and its help in various forms of indigestion. Fertile soil, free from clods or stones, ensures straight roots. Sow seed from April onwards in drills 25 mm (1 in) deep and 38 cm (15 ins) apart. Thin the seedlings early, leaving strong plants 15 cm (6 ins) apart. The plants are perfectly hardy and while roots can be stored in boxes of sand, it is better to lift as required and cook without delay.

Boil or steam the roots before peeling. The black skin is not easy to remove, the best way being to rub them in a cloth while the roots are hot.

Left in the ground for the second year the plants often produce flowers. In ancient cookery books, we read that if flower buds are gathered, washed and dried, they can be cooked in butter until they are brown and then mixed with eggs for making omelettes.

'Russian Giant' is the variety usually offered.

Left: Salsify and (below) scorzonera

SEAKALE *Crambe maritima*

This native of Britain and other European countries may be found growing wild in coastal districts. Best results come from good sandy loam which holds moisture without becoming waterlogged. Cultivate the ground in autumn, working in bulky manure. When final soil preparations are being carried out in the spring, fork in a light dressing of an organic fertilizer such as fish manure at 57—85 g per m² (2—3 oz per sq yd).

Seakale stalks have a delicate nutty taste

Plants can be raised from seed, although a couple of years elapse before forcing crowns are produced. Sow seed in prepared beds early in April, the rows being 38—45 cm (15—18 ins) apart and 25 mm (1 in) deep. Thin the seedlings early so that they stand 13—15 cm (5—6 ins) apart, and take out any flower heads that develop.

A quicker method of propagation is by root cuttings, usually known as thongs. They should be straight and clean, 15 cm (6 ins) long and pencil thick. Cut them horizontally at the top and sloping at the bottom.

These cuttings are prepared when lifting plants for forcing. Tie them in bundles and bury in sandy soil, either in the frame or a sheltered position outdoors until planting time in spring. While they are buried each root normally produces several buds, but only the strongest one should be retained. The best time for planting is during March when the soil is workable. Make the rows 45 cm (18 ins) apart, with 30 cm (1 ft) between the plants.

Seakale needs forcing, and this can be done in the open by covering the plants with pots or boxes, around which old manure should be heaped. It is also possible to blanch seakale where it is growing, by earthing up the plants, using soil that is dry, fine and friable. Best results come when the roots are taken into cellars, frames or are placed under the greenhouse staging. Stand to encourage plenty of young tender leaves to develop. This crop will go on until the winter when some roots can be forced indoors to extend the supply.

Seakale is prepared in the same way as asparagus, by boiling or steaming and served with melted butter.

SHALLOTS *Allium cepa* var *ascalonicum*

Shallots are easy to cultivate and require much the same growing conditions as onions. Largely used for pickling, they are also useful for grating into salads. In addition, some of the fresh young shoots can be cut and used as spring onions.

They will grow in a wide variety of soils, although they dislike heavy clay. Freshly manured land is best avoided but well rotted compost or manure dug in during the autumn is beneficial, particularly where exhibition bulbs are required. Fish manure at 57–85 g per m² (2–3 oz per sq yd) will also be helpful.

It is possible to raise shallots from seed but the resultant plants are liable to bolt. Normally, small bulbs are planted from early February onwards. At one time gardeners reckoned to plant shallots on the shortest day and harvest them on the longest day, but this is neither necessary nor practical, because of bad weather usually experienced at that time of the year.

The soil should be nicely firm at planting time. Loose skins and dead tops should be taken off before the bulbs are pressed into the soil about half their depth. Space them 12–15 cm (5–6 ins) apart with 30 cm (1 ft) between rows. Birds sometimes force them up. It is advisable to inspect the rows from time to time after planting, so that the bulbs can be pushed back into position again, although they do not like to be buried deeply. Take care not to damage the growing plants when hoeing or otherwise cleaning the ground.

Once the leaves begin to yellow during the summer, draw the soil away from the bulbs to encourage ripening, then lift and dry thoroughly before storing in a cool dry, airy place. The red or common shallot is the most widely grown although some gardeners like the yellow variety. For exhibition purposes, 'Hative de Noir' is greatly favoured.

Shallots have a wide range of culinary uses

Make successional sowings of summer spinach for a constant supply

SPINACH *Spinacea oleracea*

Of Persian origin, this plant was once grown almost solely for medical purposes. There are various kinds, and by sowing successively it is possible to have spinach available throughout the year. While not everyone's favourite green vegetable, it is undoubtedly full of goodness. Flavour will be better if little water is used in cooking.

Summer spinach tends to run to seed quickly on light soils so it is advisable to work into the ground, bulky moisture holding material such as decayed manure or compost. Quick growth is needed and it is beneficial if liquid manure is applied along the rows once the plants are growing well.

Summer spinach should be sown in early March, in drills 20 mm (¾ in) deep and 30 cm (1 ft) apart. Cover and firm in the seeds with the head of a rake. Thin the seedlings early using the thinnings for salads. Further sowings can be made at fourteen day intervals and if the weather is very dry, first soak the seed in water for about twelve hours. If plants begin to run to seed they are best pulled up.

Winter spinach should be sown from mid-August to mid-September, preferably on beds raised about 8 cm (3 ins) to provide good drainage. Thin the plants early so they stand 13–15 cm (5–6 ins) apart. If left too close they are liable to bolt.

While summer spinach can be picked quite hard, winter spinach must not be overworked. Pick the outer leaves only, rather than stripping individual specimens.

This will ensure a regular supply of fresh, young tender leaves. In colder areas the plants should be protected by continuous cloches or straw, bracken, etc. placed between the rows.

RECOMMENDED VARIETIES:
Summer: 'Viroflay' is a fine round seeded variety with smooth round leaves. 'Victoria Long standing', produces thick, dark green foliage; 'Nobel' is a heavy cropper with large, fleshy leaves. *Winter:* 'Broad leaved Prickly', a hardy abundant cropper and its selection 'Standwell' produce hardy, large succulent leaves over a long period; 'Greenmarket' is slow to run to seed and resistant to disease.

Spinach, Perpetual; Spinach Beet *Beta vulgaris* var *cycla* This is a perennial beet, and an excellent substitute for the true spinach. It produces green leaves but no typical beet root. The leaves are larger and more fleshy than those of summer spinach and are easier to gather and cook. One sowing in April and another in late August will usually ensure a year-round supply. On fairly rich soil, make the drills 13 mm (1 in) deep and 38 cm (15 ins) apart and thin the seedlings so there is 15—20 cm (6—8 ins) between them. Make sure the roots do not dry out in summer. Always keep the young leaves picked even if you cannot use them immediately. Left to grow old, production slows down with loss of quality. Remove the flower heads too.

Spinach, New Zealand *Tetragona expansa* While not a true spinach this plant has similar leaves and can be used as a substitute for summer spinach. It grows well on light, dryish soils, tolerates heat and does not run to seed like the ordinary spinach.

It has a different habit of growth too, since it grows rather flat and spreads rapidly over the ground. The plants do not bolt and if the growing tips are pinched out, an abundance of leaves will be produced forming a ground cover, stifling almost all weeds.

Sow seed under glass in March, first soaking it in water overnight. Move the plants to their final positions in mid-May. Open ground sowings should not be made until towards the end of May. Space the plants 60 cm (2 ft) apart with 75—90 cm ($2\frac{1}{2}$—3 ft) between rows and do not allow them to become overcrowded. While this spinach will grow well in dry soils, the leaves will be all the more succulent if plenty of water is given during dry weather. Alternatively, sow under cloches *in situ* in April. Harvesting normally continues from early July until frost kills the plants.

SWEDE *Brassica rutabaga*

Giant turnips, which are known as swedes, originated in Sweden more than 180 years ago. They are hybrids between a turnip and wild cabbage. Purple, white or yellow varieties are available, all with yellow flesh. Hardier than turnips, garden swedes are sweeter but slower growing. They rarely become woody. Sowing time is early May for northern districts and mid-May or early June elsewhere.

Swedes prefer well-drained soil, rich in organic matter and early preparation is advisable, working in farmyard manure or compost. Sow the seed in 25 mm (1 in) deep drills, 45 cm (18 ins) apart, and subsequently thin the seedlings so that there is 30 cm (1 ft) between them. Roots can be left in the ground for use as required in winter. They are very rarely damaged by frost. If a few roots are lifted and packed in boxes of soil, taken into the cool greenhouse and kept in the dark, blanched top growth will develop. This can be cut and boiled, providing a tasty winter dish.

Above left: Spinach beet is very hardy while New Zealand spinach (above right) resists drought.

Below: 'Jubilee' is a bronze-top swede

SWEET CORN *Zea mays*

This is a distinct type of maize with a sugary fruit reserve. It is used as a vegetable and should not be confused with starchy types of maize used for fodder.

Plant sweet corn in blocks to aid wind-pollination

This crop is unsuited to high altitudes and places exposed to sea winds. Medium and light soils are best, ideally manured for a previous crop. When growing in really light soil, work in manure before the crop goes in, while a general fertilizer can be raked in before sowing.

Where small quantities of seed are involved, they can be sown in 7 cm (3 in) pots from the second week in May. Don't sow earlier or the roots may become pot bound and growth will be stunted. Sowing in boxes cannot be recommended because of damage to the roots when transplanting.

Seed can be sown in cold frames where the plants can be left to mature, or cloches are useful for covering direct outdoor sowings.

For uncovered sowings from the third week in May onwards, 5 cm (2 ins) deep furrows are drawn out in a fine tilth. Two seeds are dropped in at 38 cm (15 ins) intervals or singly 23–30 cm (9–12 ins) apart. Make the rows 52–60 cm (21–24 ins) apart, the greater distance for the varieties which mature later.

Thinning is done at the five leaf stage discarding all unhealthy or insect damaged plants. Sweet corn is wind and insect pollinated and carries male and female flowers on the same plant. The best crops are secured where the plants are grown in blocks, because the pollen can easily reach other plants instead of being lost which nearly always happens when the plants are grown in single rows.

The grains set after fertilization and become the edible 'cob'. Proper harvesting influences the yield and it is necessary to gather them carefully so that only fully developed cobs are cut or picked. Once the green husks are pulled aside, the way is open for earwigs to enter. It is therefore, most unwise to strip off the husk to find out if the 'corn' is ready.

According to season, picking begins about the third week of August. If a creamy solution springs from the grains when pressed with a finger nail, they are ripe. The cobs are trimmed by removing untidy 'silks' or broken outer husks. Keep the cobs in the cool until they are used.

RECOMMENDED VARIETIES: 'Golden Bantam', early sweet and tender; 'Prima', fourteen days earlier than 'Golden Bantam'; 'Golden Standard', tall, heavy cropper; 'Kelvedon Glory' and 'Northern Belle', two reliable F_1 hybrids of good flavour.

TOMATOES *Solanum lycopersicum*

Records show that the tomato has been known for many centuries. Natives of South America, these plants came to Britain in the sixteenth century when they were cultivated as ornamental subjects under the name of Love Apples.

The fruit contains vitamin C, although less than that found in the juice of black currants, strawberries or oranges. Vitamin B1 is also present, but it is their vitamin A content that makes tomatoes so valuable.

Whether grown outdoors or under glass, the plants are raised the same way. Since the seeds are large and can be handled individually, they should be spaced 13 mm ($\frac{1}{2}$ in), 6 mm ($\frac{1}{4}$ in) deep, apart in boxes or pans of a clean seed sowing compost. Cover the seeds, then place glass and paper over the boxes to exclude light.

For quickest results, keep the receptacles in a temperature of 18–20°C (65–68°F). After a few days growth will be seen and the covering can be removed. Once the seed leaves open, transfer each seedling separately into a small pot or soil blocks.

When they have settled in the pots, the temperature can be reduced a little with free ventilation. Pot up only first class seedlings. Plants with fern-like leaves are known as rogues or 'jacks' and should be discarded.

Really strong plants can be produced by maintaining a fairly even temperature. When the heat varies, growth is irregular. Sturdy, short jointed plants of a deep green colour are likely to be the most fruitful. Avoid long-jointed, wiry-stemmed plants.

The majority of gardeners sow seed in a heated greenhouse from early February onwards in order to obtain fruit throughout the summer and autumn.

Tomatoes thrive in the warm greenhouse where there is an absence of draughts, good ventilation and a minimum night temperature of around 12°C (55°F). For preference, use a greenhouse glazed to ground level if the plants are to be grown in the 'floor' or border. Otherwise, the beds will have to be raised or made up on the staging. Alternatively, grow the plants in large pots or deep boxes, or growing bags.

It is unwise to put tomatoes outdoors until danger of cold weather has passed. Allow 38–45 cm (15–18 ins) between the plants. If more than one row is planted have rows 90 cm (3 ft) apart. Bush types need wide spacing, say 60 cm (2 ft) between the plants and 90 cm (3 ft) between rows. Stake and

85

tie immediately after planting, further ties being made as growth proceeds.

Disturb the roots as little as possible. Pot grown plants are easy to knock out. Those raised in boxes should be carefully removed, with plenty of soil adhering to the roots. Transplant them firmly so there is 13 mm ($\frac{1}{2}$ in) of soil above the roots.

Standard varieties are usually grown on a single stem, all side shoots being removed while they are small. They can also be grown on double or treble stems depending on their strength. It is rarely worthwhile allowing outdoor plants to carry more than four trusses of fruit for there is insufficient time for more fruit to ripen. Pinch out growing points in late summer, even if they have only formed three trusses.

When buying plants choose a named variety from a known source. Plants from street barrows or other draughty places have often suffered a check from which they may never fully recover. Well grown specimens, ready for planting, should be 18–20 cm (7–8 ins) high, stocky, short jointed with dark green foliage.

Whether outdoors or indoors, tomatoes like fairly rich root conditions. Strawy horse manure is ideal but difficult to obtain. Among good substitutes used by growers are moist wheat straw, well dusted with hoof

'Kirdford Cross' is a disease-resistant variety

and horn manure, ripe compost, well decayed seaweed or spent hops. Peat or leaf mould helps to increase the humus content and provide bulk which encourages plenty of roots. Add lime if the soil is acid and sour.

At planting time, make sure the sub-soil is moist. Beds on the greenhouse staging can be made up with the same soil mixture. First place asbestos or a similar covering over the slats, followed by drainage material. Boards 23–25 cm (9–10 ins) wide, should be fixed to the front and back of the staging, to get the proper root depth when the compost is added. This need only be 13 cm (5 ins) deep at first. Add more compost as growth proceeds, so the soil level comes to within 25 mm (1 in) of the top of the board.

Liquid manure should be given at ten day intervals once the first truss of fruit has set. For plants in pots or boxes, a simple soil mixture on the basis of the John Innes No 2 can be used.

Side shoots should be removed cleanly and as early as possible, and if the dwarf or bush varieties make too many stems, it is best to reduce their number.

Tomatoes can be grown successfully in frames of various kinds, and barn cloches are also suitable. Place these structures in a fairly open, yet sheltered position, preferably running north and south, to encourage

Pinching out side shoots from tomato plants

good growth.

Planting is usually done about mid-April. A bed of fairly rich soil should be made up, adding moist peat to encourage a good root system. Good supports will be needed. Keep the glass on the frames until June, ventilating freely whenever the weather is favourable. Plants under tall frames can be supported by wire or string and canes.

Cloches should be placed on a sunny site sheltered from winds. Take out a trench 20 cm (8 ins) deep and 30 cm (12 ins) wide at the top. tapering to the bottom. Apply a good organic fertilizer and plenty of peat at the base, to provide proper growing conditions.

Planting outdoors Tomatoes are most accommodating plants but it is essential to make a good start for complete success.

Since plants are frost tender, weather conditions and the state of the soil must be such that growth continues unchecked once the plants have been set outdoors – usually very early in June.

On deep well-prepared land, artificial Many gardeners now use hormone setting sprays when atmospheric conditions are unsuitable for natural fertilization, or where growth is rank and flowers fail to set fruit. With good culture these aids should not be necessary, but it is important to get the bottom truss of fruit to set, for this encourages even, healthy growth and improves both the quality and setting tendency of later trusses.

Intermittent drying out and heavy watering lead to irregular growth as well as cracked fruit. A surface mulch of peat, leaf mould, or similar material will help to maintain a cool root run enjoyed by the plants, as well as preventing the surface from drying out.

On deep well-prepared land, artificial

'Gardener's Delight' is a sweet-flavoured tomato

watering should be less necessary. If it can be avoided so much the better, for continued light watering in hot weather tends to bring the roots near the surface, where they suffer from dryness much more than when they are deep in the soil.

If the soil has been well prepared and enriched, it should be unnecessary to give extra feeding. Should growth become luxuriant and rank, a dressing of seaweed manure scattered round the plants and watered in, will help to steady growth.

Outdoors, it should easily be possible to bring three trusses of fruit to maturity. If the position is warm and sheltered and the weather good, a fourth truss can sometimes be allowed. There is no point in allowing plants to waste their strength on growth and flowers from which it is impossible to secure fruit. When the chosen number of trusses has been selected, the plants should be stopped at one leaf beyond the top truss and from that time, one or two side shoots can be allowed to develop.

This will keep the sap flowing and discourage fruit splitting which sometimes occurs once the plants have been stopped. The excess of sap is absorbed by the fruit which cannot expand fast enough and the skin cracks, particularly if heavy rains follow a period of dry weather. Old and discoloured leaves should be removed to improve air circulation as well as lessen the possibility of blight infection.

Gather the fruit as soon as it is well coloured. In some districts birds will peck the fruit once it begins to colour. Often they are only seeking moisture, so it is helpful to place shallow containers of water near the plants. This applies to other crops, both vegetables and flowers, which birds sometimes attack, particularly during spells of hot, dry weather.

If in autumn, some fruit is still unripe, complete trusses should be cut off and hung up in the warm greenhouse or living room. Alternatively, fruits can be gathered individually and wrapped in paper and placed in a drawer or box, where they will ripen in the warmth and darkness. Ripening fruit will be available over a period of weeks.

Autumn and winter fruiting By careful planning, ripe fruit will be available from the greenhouse from autumn onwards – a time when fresh fruit is appreciated. For autumn fruiting, seed should be sown towards the end of May using boxes of good compost, with a layer of peat at the bottom. For a winter crop, sow in the greenhouse in summer. Space the seed at least 5 cm (2 ins) apart and cover the boxes with paper to prevent them drying out. Remove the covering once germination occurs. This spacing results in the minimum root disturbance at pricking off time.

It also means that seedlings can be moved straight from the seed boxes to small 60 size pots, 7 cm (2¾ ins). Repot into larger pots as growth develops. By the time 20–30 cm (8–9 ins) pots are reached the plants should be sturdy and in full growth. Keep them in the cool for a week or two. Then stand outdoors in a sheltered place for a

couple of months.

For the final potting, provide a good layer of drainage crocks and use a soil mixture of four parts turfy loam, one part strawy horse manure, and a good sprinkling of hoof and horn meal, or wood ash. Alternatively, use John Innes potting compost No. 3. While outside, feed the plants with liquid manure. This encourages short, stocky growth and strong fruit trusses. Fish meal can be lightly worked into the soil in the pots and watered in. Take the plants into the greenhouse towards the end of summer. Air and light are essential, with a night temperature of 10°C (50°F). The ripening process will be slow, but the fruit colours up evenly.

RECOMMENDED VARIETIES: Although some tomato varieties have been in cultivation for many years, new varieties are introduced annually. This does not mean that all of them are better than the older kinds. The following are among the leading sorts and can be relied upon to crop and grow well:
'Ailsa Craig', good shape, heavy cropper, splendid flavour;
'Alicante', for outdoor and indoor cultivation, free from greenback;
'Big Boy', an F_1 hybrid for greenhouse cultivation, producing extremely large fruits with meaty flesh and fine flavour;

A plum-shaped Italian tomato – 'Roma'

'Eurocross BB', an outstanding variety of excellent quality;

'French Cross', of superb flavour, producing round fruits of uniform shape;

'Gardener's Delight', an outdoor variety with small fruits of sweet flavour;

'Growers Pride', a heavy cropping, reliable indoor variety;

'Kirdford Cross', a compact growing, leaf-mould disease resistant variety;

'Marmande', large, irregularly shaped fruit, an outdoor variety;

'Moneymaker', a popular, heavy cropping variety, medium sized fruits;

'Outdoor Girl', a heavy cropping outdoor sort;

'Ronaclave', an early outdoor hybrid with large, non-greenback fruit;

'Supercross', a variety tolerant to virus and cladosporium (leaf-mould disease);

'Super Marmande' produces large ribbed fleshy fruit with a good flavour. Ideal for slicing. Suitable for growing outdoors or under glass.

'Tangella', similar to 'Ailsa Craig' but an intense tangerine colour;

'The Amateur'; 'Sleaford Abundance'; two of the most popular bush tomatoes, heavy cropping.

There are one or two yellow fruiting varieties, such as:

'Golden Sunrise' and 'Golden Boy' which have thin skins and excellent flavour.

'Tigerella' has fruit striped yellow and red. Flavour is the same as red varieties.

Tomatoes are ideal subjects for growing-bags

Ring Culture The culture of tomatoes in bottomless rings is a method which provides controlled conditions of nourishment and water supply.

Rings of different materials can be used. Stand the rings on weathered ashes, small grade clinkers, sand, crushed ballast or peat. Gravel or stone chippings can be used but are not so moisture retentive. The depth of the aggregate should not be less than 10 cm (4 ins). About 15 cm (6 ins) deep is suitable.

While it is not essential to lay polythene before putting down the aggregate it is an effective way of isolating the aggregate layer from the greenhouse soil if in the past there has been trouble from disease or eelworm. In this case some provision must be made for the escape of surplus water. The aggregate must be kept constantly moist so that the roots probing it stay nicely damp.

Where there is sufficient height, tomatoes can be grown in rings on greenhouse benches and provided shade is given the plants can be trained to the roof. There is no problem in growing tomatoes in rings in the open ground. Select a south facing site, and raise the aggregate layer a little above the surrounding soil to prevent compost washing into or over the aggregate. John Innes No 3 compost is suitable for ring culture.

It is possible to buy bituminized cardboard rings for this method of culture. A good size is 20 cm (8 ins) deep with a top diameter of 23 cm (9 ins). Having made a 5–7.5 cm (2½–3 ins) layer of compost firm on the bottom of the ring, over the aggre-

Ring culture of greenhouse tomatoes

gate, the tomato plants should be planted firmly. Top up the soil to within 4 cm (1½ ins) of the top of the ring. Leave this space for initial waterings and for feeding.

Give a good watering so the roots settle and after ten days, apply water close to the plant stem (ball watering). Keep the aggregate wet at all times. About a month later the roots will penetrate the aggregate and ball watering should cease, all moisture will then be drawn through the secondary root system in the aggregate, and feeding can start into the rings at 7 day intervals.

Do not water into the rings after feeding until it is evident the compost is becoming dry. It is best to use a diluted liquid fertilizer, since this will be carried to the fibrous roots more quickly.

The fertilizer first used on tomatoes grown in rings was known as 667 from the analysis of 6% each of nitrogen and phosphoric acid and 7% potash. It also provides the necessary magnesium for good colour. Several good proprietary tomato fertilizers made to a similar analysis are readily available. Once the first truss has set, give liquid fertilizer at 7-day intervals.

Plants in rings require more feeding than those in the border in order to give quantities of good fruit. The removal of side shoots and general attention for tomatoes in rings is the same as that required by conventionally grown plants.

Outdoors, ring culture is carried out in the same way as with the greenhouse plants, although it is helpful if the side of the aggregate layer is protected by boards of bricks to keep it in position. Supports should be given at planting stage.

Growing Bags A most successful method of growing tomatoes is by the system of growing bags. The bags used contain tomato compost which is specially formulated to produce the right type of good firm, close jointed growth, with broad dark green leaves and well-developed flower trusses. This tomato compost contains all the necessary plant foods, both in rapidly available and slow release forms, to give the plants a good start and encourage the development of a high quality sound firm fruit. For a long term crop in a heated greenhouse, three plants can be grown in each standard bag which is usually 1.10 m (42 ins) long, 38 cm (15 ins) wide and 15 cm (6 ins) deep. Five plants can be accommodated for short term or cold house growing allowing five or six trusses.

Raise the tomatoes in the usual way and before planting 38 cm (15 ins) apart, shake the compost evenly along the bag which should be placed level, and square up the sides. To form a single row, lay the bags end to end and cut out the panels along the dotted lines to form a mini-trough, leaving the cross-bands to support the sides.

Plant the young plants with the minimum of firming. Water throughly to moisten *all* the compost in the bag. For supports string the plants (with a non-slip loop, tied around the stem below the first leaf) to the overhead wire, and twist plants round the string in a clockwise direction. Canes should not be driven through the bags. Tie the canes to horizontal wires at 30 cm (1 ft) apart. Well-fed plants carry heavy crops and must be properly supported.

After about a week when the growing bags have settled into their final shape, three drainage holes can be pierced in each side of the bag, about 13 mm ($\frac{1}{2}$ in) above ground level. If you are going on holiday, you will need to find someone to water the bags regularly.

Keep the compost adequately moist at all times and avoid extremes of feeding and watering, especially when the plants are carrying a heavy weight of fruit. Once established, daily watering will probably be required but this will depend on the situation of the plants. It should always be possible to squeeze water easily out of the compost. A vigorous plant of 90 cm (3 ft) or more growing under good conditions should be watered daily from May to August.

Tomatoes are gross feeders, and feeding should commence once the first truss of fruit has formed. This should be continued until the last truss is half developed.

TURNIPS *Brassica rapa*

Many people think of turnips as no more than a dull vegetable useful when others are in short supply. When well-grown and properly cooked, however, they are delicious. Choose small young specimens and cook them quickly. Turnips are an excellent accompaniment to rich meats and poultry such as roast duck.

There are now many smaller growing, tender, tasty varieties and by careful selection roots can be dug over a long period; you can also force them in frames.

Turnips like fertile, moist loam on the light side. Heavy soil can be improved by working in well-rotted compost. This will encourage good drainage, while still holding moisture. Plants will quickly run to seed on dry ground. Limy soil discourages club root disease. A position well-manured for a previous crop is very suitable, and a dressing of fish manure at 57 g per m^2 (2 oz per sq yd) applied just before sowing, is an excellent stimulant.

The earliest sowings can be made under frames, over mild hot beds, or in soil heated frames or cloches, from January onwards.

Adequate ventilation and water are required for good results. Seed can be broadcast so long as it is well covered, or it can be sown at 10 cm (4 in) intervals and thinned out to one plant at each station.

The first outdoor sowing can be made on a sheltered, warm border from mid-March onwards, followed by sowings at 14-day intervals until the end of May. A further sowing from late July to late August, will provide maincrop or winter turnips, these being thinned to stand 23 cm (9 ins) apart, and pulled as required, although in exposed or Northern districts they should be lifted and clamped. Sowings can be made in September for turnip tops, a useful source of winter greens. This time, allow 38–45 cm (15–18 ins) between rows, or broadcast the seed. No thinning is necessary, although weeds must be kept down.

For the best tasting, tender roots, quick growth is necessary. This requires cool, moist conditions, with no check and pulling should be possible within six to eight weeks of sowing, while they are young and fresh. Left in the ground a long time, the roots become coarse and woody.

Flea beetle is sometimes troublesome and the row should be dusted with Gammexane as soon as the seedlings appear.

RECOMMENDED VARIETIES:

Frames and cloches: 'Milan White', 'Jersey Navet'. Early outdoor sorts: 'Snowball', 'Golden Ball', 'Golden Perfection'.
For winter storing: 'Manchester Market', 'Veitch's Red Globe'.
'Tokyo Cross' is a new F$_1$ hybrid which can be sown in succession in frames or outdoors from February to October. Under the right culture it produces superb little tasty turnips in 5 to 6 weeks which retain their flavour when left to grow larger.

Pick turnip 'Early Snowball' when young for the best flavour

A-Z Guide to Herbs &Spices

Herbs cannot be omitted from any plans drawn up for growing vegetables. Apart from their aroma, they possess undeniable health giving properties. Spices too, can be used with herbs in tasty meals and snacks.

Many people obtain their herbs dried in jars or packets. Although in an average sized garden it is not possible to grow all the herbs needed for the kitchen, it should not be difficult to find a place for a useful selection. While parsley, mint, sage and thyme are indispensable, others of great culinary worth are just as easy to cultivate.

The herb garden may be considered an adjunct to the vegetable garden and a minimum of labour is needed for its upkeep. Keep a watchful eye on rampant growers and cut them back or divide them before they smother less vigorous kinds.

If a choice of site is available select one which faces west and slopes slightly, to receive maximum sunshine. Since the garden will be more or less permanent, the ground should be deeply trenched and enriched with a generous supply of manure or compost and a scattering of bone meal. Sharp sand, bonfire ash or leaf mould will lighten heavy, clingy soils.

With perennial and biennial herbs, a top dressing of loamy soil applied each spring as growth commences, will promote steady growth. Keep the bed in a healthy vigorous condition by lifting, dividing and replanting young portions of the perennial kinds about every four years.

Spices have been grown and used for centuries and although there is rarely any shortage of these, how many of these will grow if seeds or roots are planted in pots or in the open ground? Unfortunately, many are treated and dried so throughly that all life has gone from them when you buy them in the shops.

Capsicums or chillies are grown chiefly for their edible pods, but they are also very colourful, and make attractive greenhouse and living room plants. Culture is simple in

this country, even though these plants are natives of East Africa, the West Indies and India. Seed is readily available and is sown in trays or pots in February or March, in light, rich soil, in a temperature of 15°C (60°F). Move the seedlings singly into small pots and give them more room as they increase in size. The first move can be avoided if seed is sown individually in the small thumb pots. By the time the plants reach 50–60 cm (20–24 ins) high, they are usually laden with fruit.

To ensure herbs are available throughout winter they need to be dried. This is best done just before the plants come into flower for the flavour is then at its peak. Ideally gather the leaves when the dew has just dried and before strong sun reaches them, but do not pick them when they are limp through being in strong sunshine or wind-blown. It is best to tie the cut stems into small bunches, for it is difficult for air to circulate around a large bunch and this could lead to lack of flavour and mildew.

While you can hang small bunches in a cool airy shed or outhouse the ideal place is a dry warm room where the air is moving slightly. Another method is to spread the herbs on a bench or table in a cool dry place. In very wet seasons, small quantities can be dried gently in a very cool oven. They can also be dried in paper bags but holes should be punched in them to let air in and moisture out.

Herbs to dry in trays include chervil, lovage, parsley, thyme and rosemary. When dry, it is easy to rub the leaves of many herbs into a powder which can be put into jars or other containers and sealed tightly to use as required. Keep them in a cool dark place and use within six months.

Herb and spice seeds to dry, include coriander, cumin, caraway, dill and fennel. For these, cut the whole plant and place it head down in paper bags to catch the seeds as they fall.

The following herbs are among the most useful and can be cultivated in gardens.

ALECOST (Costmary) *Balsamita major*

This is a pleasant herb with a scent of mint. The roundish leaves are greyish-green, the button-like flowers are yellow. Growing 45—120 cm (1½—4 ft) the plants flourish in a sunny position in rich soil. Finely chopped leaves add zest to salads, soups and stuffings. At one time an ointment was made from the leaves and used for soothing burns and bruises.

ANGELICA *Angelica Archangel*

Angelica leaf and flowerhead

There are several forms of this plant to be found growing wild in Britain. The true angelica of confectionery is a native of parts of Russia and Germany, although it grows in most European countries.

Growing 90 cm—1.50 m (3—5 ft) high, it is either a biennial, dying after flowering, or a short lived perennial. It prefers partial shade and a cool moist, but not wet, root run. The broad umbels of white flowers appear in May and June and if they are removed before they develop, the plant is more likely to survive the winter.

It is best to sow seed in spring, although it can also be sown in early autumn. Angelica has sculptured foliage of stately appearance and this makes it valuable as a feature plant. The thick hollow stems possess an aromatic scent which is retained when they are candied. The young stems are greatly valued when cut up and used in tarts with rhubarb, as well as in jams. A leaf added to salads imparts a pleasing taste, while both foliage and roots have certain medicinal qualities. A tale connected with this plant says that it holds powers against evil spirits.

BALM (Lemon Balm) *Melissa officinalis*

Growing in any soil, this plant reaches 90 cm—1.2 m (3—4 ft) high, has lemon scented leaves and small white flowers in summer. Propagation is easy: by division of roots in spring or autumn or seed sown in boxes in May. Thin the seedlings early and finally move them to their permanent places 60 cm (2 ft) apart. Although of little commercial value, the dried leaves retain the refreshing lemon flavour which makes them useful for stuffing poultry. A leaf or two placed in the tea pot with the tea provides a pleasant drink. A useful bee plant, it was also once used to soothe the nerves and 'drive away melancholy'.

Above: Alecost in flower
Below: Balm is a perennial herb

Above: Basil has many culinary uses
Below: A bay tree enhances any garden

BASIL *Ocimum basilicum*

Widely grown in Britain and treated as a half-hardy annual, basil is a perennial in warm countries. Seed is sown under glass in late March/early April in a temperature of 15°C (60°F) and the plants are moved to the garden in early June. Alternatively, sow outdoors in sandy soil in May. Germination is usually erratic. The irregularly shaped leaves have a pleasant clove-like flavour, useful to adding either fresh to tomato salad or dried to soups and stews. Flowers are white or purple-tinged. Basil has been cultivated for centuries and is said to 'procure a merrie heart'. At one time it was infused with water used for washing.

BAY *Laurus nobilis*

This evergreen laurel-like shrub should be grown either in the open ground or in tubs in a sunny sheltered place. It is valued for its leaves, either fresh or dried. The flavour is potent so use the leaves sparingly. The yellow flowers in May are often followed by purplish berries. It is best to buy new plants in pots since transplanting from the open ground is not always successful.

RED BERGAMOT *Monarda didyma*

Summer blooms of bergamot

Known also as Bee Balm and Oswego tea, this is a perennial growing up to 90 cm (3 ft) high. The plants like a cool root run and should never lack moisture in summer. Both leaves and flowers can be included in salads and the leaves may be used fresh or dry to impart an aromatic flavour to the usual Indian or China tea. A few leaves chopped fine are delicious in salads and fragrant in pot pourris.

BORAGE *Borago officinalis*

This most decorative plant is worthy of a place in any garden. It was Gerard who said that borage can be used 'for the comfort of the heart, to make the mind glad, and drive away sorrow'.

It is an excellent bee-plant, while the leaves and stalks are frequently used by herbalists to remedy chest and throat complaints. The leaves and flowers are useful in pot pourri while the blue flowers brighten a salad dish. The leaves and peeled stalk should be used sparingly, since they impart

93

Borage is an attractive plant which is easy to grow

an acquired flavour to salads.

An infusion of the leaves makes a cooling drink welcomed in hot weather. Lemonade and cider can be improved by the addition of a few borage flowers.

Borage grows 45–60 cm (1½–2 ft) **high** and can be raised from seed sown in the open from late April onwards. Usually grown as an annual, the plants will sometimes come through the winter in rosette form and flower in early spring. It seeds freely so that new plants appear annually. The grey-green foliage and the somewhat drooping flowers on upright stems are effective plants for raised beds where the blooms can be viewed from below.

There are taller growing perennial members of the family producing showy blue flowers. These however, are not herb plants.

BURNET *Poterium sanguisorba*

This hardy perennial growing 45–50 cm (18–20 ins) high, is sometimes found growing wild. The greenish flowers have red stigmas. Keep removing the blooms to encourage more leaves to form. The foliage has a cucumber-like flavour with a nutty undertone, making it useful in salads and soups and cooling drinks. Seed should be sown in prepared beds in May and the plants moved to their final positions in any good garden soil in October.

CARAWAY *Carum carvi*

A biennial plant about 75 cm (2½ ft) high. Seed is sown in well-drained soil in May, the flower umbels appear the following spring and the seeds ripening in June and July. The seeds are easily lost if the heads are left too long, so cut them as soon as they ripen. Hang them to dry over paper so that the seeds are caught as they ripen and fall.

Caraway seeds are frequently used in cakes or sprinkled on bread as well as for flavouring soups and cheese dishes. The flavour is very distinctive.

Burnet is a decorative plant

CHERVIL *Anthriscus cerefolium*

An annual growing to 30–45 cm (12–18 ins). Select a fairly rich moist soil and sow from early May onwards. Allow 15–18 cm (6–7 ins) between the plants. Chervil is included in mixed herbs for improving soups and salads.

Above: Chervil; below: Caraway

CHIVES *Allium schoenoprasum*

Usually bought as plants, although seed is sometimes available. These make a useful edging to a border and even a very few of these perennials will ensure that onion flavouring is always available. They are easy to grow even in fairly dry soil.

Growing about 15–18 cm (6–7 ins) high, they produce lots of thin, reedy stems and once established they can easily be propagated by division in spring, placing the separate portions 23 cm (9 ins) apart. It is advisable to lift and divide plants every three or four years to maintain a healthy stock.

The green stems or 'grass' should be regularly cut whether or not they are required in the kitchen. This will ensure the continued production of young tender shoots. Never let chives run to seed or they will deteriorate and lose their subtle flavouring.

94

DILL *Pendedanum graveolens*

Dill has a pungent, aromatic yet slightly sweet flavour. It has a long history and it is believed that the Romans brought this plant to Britain. A couple of hundred years ago dill seeds were taken to church, to be nibbled during long dry sermons and to prevent the congregation from becoming hungry. A tisane made from the seed is said to alleviate persistent hiccups.

The plants grow up to 90 cm (3 ft) high, and the dark green, erect stems are hollow. The white and green flowers are produced in umbels.

Dill is an annual and is propagated by seed sown in the spring. Germination is sometimes erratic. It is best to sow in succession from early April until early July. Draw the drills up to 30 cm (1 ft) apart. Make sure to water the seedlings in times of drought. Space the plants so they do not touch in full growth, or they may harbour greenfly.

The plants can be grown in pots although there they will not grow as tall but this makes them useful where space is limited. Dill grows quickly and the aroma is best just before flowering. Whole or ground dill seeds are useful for adding to vegetable dishes and the attractive feathery leaves make a garnish suitable for salads and open sandwiches.

Below: Chives in flower

FENNEL *Foeniculum vulgara*

This very ancient plant is found growing wild in many parts of the world including Europe, China, South Africa, America, Russia and New Zealand. It will succeed in greatly varying positions. All parts of the plant can be used. One cultivated variety has bronze or coppery foliage, which many gardeners believe is hardier, longer living and of better flavour.

Growing 90 cm–1.80 m (3–6 ft) high, the stems are blue-green, smooth and glossy; the leaves are bright green and feathery.

The form Florence fennel, also referred to as finocchio, has an enlarged leaf base which is cooked as a vegetable.

Fennel was used by country people long before the introduction of synthetic drugs, and one of Culpepper's famous remarks

Above: Use the leaves and flowers of dill

Fennel has decorative foliage

about this plant is 'that it is used in drinks to make people more lean that are too fat'. Certainly the leaves have a pleasantly acid taste that goes well with various sauces. It is also used in the making of herbal teas and syrups and it is of value in dispersing flatulence. The association of fennel with cooked fish is well known.

Propagation is by seed sown in a sunny situation in April or May. Germination is often slow, but once started the plants grow well. The bright yellow flowers are produced in umbels. As the seeds approach the ripening stage, cut the stems and tie them in bundles. Then lay them on some kind of sheeting so that the ripe dry seed can be properly harvested.

GARLIC *Allium sativum*

This first came to Britain and other European countries via the returning Crusaders of the Middle Ages. They brought it from Ascalon from which the name of our shallot is derived. For long widely used in continental cooking, it is only fairly recently that British gardeners have taken a real interest in garlic, which is now gaining popularity. Though hardy, it does best in sunny, fairly sheltered positions. A light, well-drained soil produces the best crops. Ground manured for a previous crop should be chosen, for garlic should not be grown on freshly manured soil. Wood ash and weathered soot are beneficial if raked into the surface soil just before planting.

Garlic forms a number of bulblets or cloves, as they are known, being grouped together in a whitish outer skin. A well developed bulb often consists of up to two

95

dozen individual cloves and specimens about 12 mm ($\frac{1}{2}$ in) in diameter are best for planting. Planting is usually done in March, but in warm districts in light well drained soil, an October and November planting gives good results.

On wet soils garlic should be grown in raised beds. Space the cloves 20–23 cm (8–9 ins) apart with 25–30 cm (10–12 ins) between each row and plant 5 cm (2 ins) deep. During July or August the leaves will wither and this is a sign that the crop is ready for lifting and drying.

Garlic ready for use

Always lift with a fork. If the cloves are pulled out by the stem there will be injury to the neck and an easy entry for disease spores. Dry garlic thoroughly before storing in a frostproof, airy shed or larder, then it will keep well for many months.

A tiny quantity of garlic in salads improves the flavour of the other ingredients and it is widely believed that garlic eaten in moderation contributes to good health.

'Jumbo' garlic, a comparatively new strain of mild flavour, can be raised from seed sown in a temperature of 16°C. Use boxes of seed compost and eventually plant the seedlings 30 cm (1 ft) apart in the open ground. Keep the flower heads pinched out.

HORSERADISH *Armoracia rusticana*

This is a native of south-east Europe, and now naturalized in parts of Britain.

To secure good thick roots, it is advisable to grow it on well-prepared, deeply dug and manured ground, where lime is not lacking. To prevent the roots spreading, which is a drawback of this crop, the base of the site where the plants are to be grown should be made very firm.

Not more than a dozen roots will be required for the average household. Good strong thongs about 20 cm (8 ins) long, and of pencil thickness are best. Reduce the buds to one. In early March, holes should be made 25 cm (10 ins) apart and the roots or thongs dropped into them so that about 10 cm (4 ins) of soil covers the top.

To prevent horseradish from becoming a nuisance, lift annually and replant each spring. Lifted roots can be stored in moist sand where they will remain firm.

HYSSOP *Hyssopus officinalis*

A native of southern Europe, hyssop likes light soil and plenty of sunshine. An old-fashioned shrubby perennial plant, it makes a nice low hedge of 60–75 cm (2–2$\frac{1}{2}$ ft) high. It can be clipped annually to retain its shape but too much cutting back will reduce the show of gentian-blue flowers. Forms having pink or purplish flowers are sometimes available and seedlings from these often exhibit intermediate colourings.

Propagation is by seed sown under glass in March or in the open ground in May or June. Take cuttings of strong shoots in summer. Hyssop is not much used as a herb since the flavour is rather strong. Very few finely chopped leaves are sufficient to include with mixed herbs or in the salad bowl. Hyssop tea made from the dried flowers and used with honey is of value for chest troubles, while an infusion of the green tops relieves coughs and catarrh.

Below: Horseradish should be lifted annually. Right: Lemon Scented Verbena

Choose young delicate leaves of hyssop

LEMON SCENTED VERBENA
Aloysia triphylla

A native of Chile, this plant has been in cultivation for almost a hundred years. It is sometimes known as *Aloysia citriodora* or *Lippia citriodora*. The leaves smell and taste of lemon and make a fragrant tea. They also flavour fruit drinks, jams and jellies, and are used in finger bowls.

It grows in any good garden soil. Do not use fresh manure or growth will be soft and weak. A sheltered position is necessary as it is susceptible to frost damage. Outdoors, mulch the roots with leaf mould to protect them during the winter.

Lemon scented verbena makes an excellent plant for the living room and greenhouse. Propagation is from cuttings in spring. Both leaves and flowers can be harvested in August although leaves can be plucked off at any time.

LOVAGE *Ligusticum scoticum*

This hardy perennial has handsome polished foliage and the scent of the whole plant is reminiscent of celery or parsnips, with an extra sweetness. A native of Mediterranean areas, it has been grown in Britain for centuries, and was probably introduced by the Romans.

The plants thrive in semi-shade or sun, in rich moist soil, and reach a height of 1.20 m (4 ft). The umbels of yellowish flowers open in July and August. Propagation is by seed

sown in spring or division in spring or autumn. Lovage was once greatly favoured as a tisane for fever and colic. It can be used as a substitute for celery and is normally available fresh or dry.

MARIGOLD *Calendula officinalis*

The old fashioned marigold, usually single flowered, has long been used in salads and mixed herbs. While not so showy as the modern cultivars it was once greatly valued for its medicinal qualities and culinary purposes. The whole plant was used to make an ointment to help heal ulcers and other wounds. In salads the flowers add colour and a distinctive flavour when dried and they can be added to soups and broth.

MARJORAM *Origanum* species

There are several species of marjoram invaluable for culinary flavourings.

Origanum onites is the French or pot marjoram, a hardy perennial growing 30 cm (1 ft) high, with rich green aromatic leaves and pinkish-mauve flowers.

Origanum majorana, a native of Portugal, is the Italian, sweet or 'knotted' marjoram. It has smallish grey leaves which have a particularly pleasing scent and flavour. A half-hardy perennial, it is frequently grown as an annual, the seed being sown in March under glass and the plants transferred to their growing positions from late May onwards. It can be grown in pots in the cold or cool greenhouse where it will remain productive for several seasons. It is the grey-green bracts surrounding the tiny flowers that give rise to the common name of 'knotted'.

Marjoram is used in bouquets garnis

Above: Lovage grows in any ordinary soil.
Below: Use the dried flowers of marigolds

Origanum vulgare, wild marjoram, is a native European plant. In Britain it flourishes on the Chalk Downs. The south European plants have more flavour than the British and provided the herb, oregano. Growing 30–75 cm (1–2½ ft) high, the flowers produced vary from pinkish-mauve to purple, while occasionally a white form appears.

Origanum vulgare 'Aureum', is the golden marjoram, a variety with golden, sweetly perfumed foliage, and soft pink flowers. This species too, can be grown in the cool greenhouse and should be propagated by division in spring or autumn. All the others are usually raised from seed sown in boxes in spring in the cool greenhouse or frame. Alternatively sow shallowly in the open ground in May, protecting the young seedlings from drying winds and drought.

Grow the plants in good soil adding plenty of compost to sandy ground, which should be kept free of weeds. The fresh or dried leaves add a delightful flavour to many dishes, and are used in stuffings and salads.

MINT *Mentha* species

Of the many known mint species *Mentha spicata* or *M. viridis* is most popular. Usually known as spearmint, mackerel, pea, potato or green lamb mint, its aromatic taste peps up new potatoes and peas. This species often grows to 90 cm (3 ft) high and is distinguished by its pointed, glossy, dark green leaves. Of invasive habit, it should be divided frequently or propagated from cuttings. Grow it in a sunken bucket punched with drainage holes, to confine its invasive root system.

Mentha suaveolens (syn. *M. rotundifolia*) often known as the apple or round-leaved mint, is fairly strong growing with large leaves. It is excellent for mint sauce and for flavouring jellies. Less susceptible to 'rust' than other species, it can be grown where the fungus is troublesome. Some dislike it because of its rather hairy or woolly leaves.

Mentha piperita, peppermint, seldom grown in gardens, is enormously important commercially for oil of peppermint distilled from the purple flower heads.

There are several mints which are not suitable for eating but which have for centuries been cherished for their aroma in sachets and for keeping moths out of stored linen. Particularly good is *M. piperita citrata*, the Eau de Cologne mint, which when rubbed gives off the odour from which it gets its name. Other mints have a ginger scent and there is one with variegated foliage which has a penetrating scent not unlike pineapple. It was much used with lavender and rosemary in posies carried by Victorian ladies. Old herbals recommend mint infusions for stomach troubles and head colds.

Mint is easy to propagate by dividing established plants in spring or autumn. Quite small pieces of root will produce sturdy plants in a short time. Young succulent growths can be obtained during winter if roots are placed in boxes or pots of ordinary soil and kept in the warm greenhouse, in full light in the living room, or on the kitchen windowsill.

NASTURTIUM *Tropaeolum majus*

Very well known as a flowering annual, nasturtium is a valuable salad plant. Use the young and clean leaves to provide a piquant flavouring. The seeds can also be included in the salad bowl, although they are rather hot. The flowers, too, can be eaten and provide a bright and appetizing display.

Nasturtiums flower best in poor soil. In rich soil they are apt to produce leafy growth at the expense of flowers. The large seeds can be sown individually 13 mm ($\frac{1}{2}$ in) deep. Watch the plants for aphids since these pests can soon cripple growth. Control aphids with a derris or pyrethrum based insecticide.

There are many varieties and it is best to depend on the dwarfer bushy strains rather than the trailing or climbing forms, unless one wishes to use the plants for ground cover or to hide a fence.

Left: Peppermint is grown not for its fresh leaves but the oil of peppermint it exudes

Below left: Round leaved or apple mint has a good flavour

Below: Nasturtium leaves have a slight peppery taste

PARSLEY *Petroselinum crispum*

This biennial plant has been grown for well over 500 years. It has many health giving properties as well as improving the flavour of food.

Parsley rivals mint for popularity in the kitchen. There are several types although

an improvement with tightly curled deep green leaves resistant to bad weather.

ROSEMARY *Rosmarinus officinalis*

An excellent bee plant, this is one of the best known herbs, around which there are many legends. It is the shrub of remembrance and friendship, as the phrase 'rosemary for remembrance' indicates. Rosemary is eulogized in old books. One states that 'it comforteth the heart and maketh merry and lively'.

Its leaves impart a powerful flavour and one or two are sufficient to enhance a soup or stew. Rosemary has a number of other uses: it is an ingredient of a shampoo, and

Above left: Parsley is the most useful herb

Above: Rosemary is a shrubby plant

Left: Rue 'Jackman's Blue'

sugar and the dried leaves are used in pot pourris. The narrow dark green leaves are silvery beneath, the pretty blue flowers appearing in spring. The species grows about 90—180 cm (3—6 ft) high and with regular clipping, keeps shapely for many years. After flowering cut the shrubs back to encourage new shoots. Sun and good drainage suit these plants. There is a rare variegated form. Another, known as 'Miss Jessops' Upright', has an upright habit and is often grown as a hedge 1.20—1.50 m (4—5 ft) high.

RUE *Ruta graveolens*

There are many legends about this well known shrubby plant. One is that it is a symbol of 'repentance and regret'. It was

the chief kinds now grown are either the numerous curled-leaved varieties or the broad or plain leaved kinds. Freshly gathered parsley is infinitely preferable to dried.

Using cloches and cold frames, it is possible to have sprigs for cutting all year round. Parsley is usually sown for succession, starting in February.

Where the intention is to grow parsley for drying, seeds should be sown early. For summer use, April and early May sowings are the most useful while for plants to stand the winter, July is the time.

There are numerous superstitions in connection with parsley, many arising from the time it takes to germinate, which may be up to seven or eight weeks. If seed is sown in a layer of really moist peat it usually germinates quickly. Little is gained by soaking the seed. Some gardeners believe that parsley keeps away onion fly if a few plants are set in the onion rows.

Early thinning is essential to secure first rate parsley. If flower stalks develop they should be cut down to ground level. As a rule the plants are of little value after the

second year and are best discarded. A fresh sowing should be made annually.

This crop succeeds in any good cultivated soil well supplied with humus. The rows should be 38—45 cm (15—18 ins) apart, and the seedlings thinned to 15 cm (6 ins) apart.

Parsley sauce is in great demand. Finely chopped parsley is added to mixed salads and in soups and stews.

The 'Moss Curled' variety is the most widely used but a newer sort, 'Bravour', is once carried by judges at the opening of Assizes in the belief that it kept away gaol fever. The plant has a penetrating scent, appreciated by some people, disliked by others. It is a perennial growing about 60 cm (2 ft) high. 'Jackman's Blue' is a specially attractive cultivar with deep steel-blue leaves. The plant is decorative during the cold dark days and only a really severe frost will damage its evergreen foliage. Rue is a great favourite with flower arrangers, and is a useful plant both for the scented and decorative garden.

Above: Leaves and flowers of the common sage.

SAGE *Salvia officinalis*

The common sage, a native of Europe, has been grown in Britain since 1597. The greyish leaves are about 38 mm (1½ ins) long, the purple bell-shaped flowers opening in summer. Sage needs a well-drained soil and grows about 60–75 cm (2–2½ ft) high.

Propagation is by seed or division. It is simple to pull off rooted pieces for growing separately. If the soil is drawn toward the plant, the lower parts of the stems will form roots and they can be severed from the parent plant and grown separately.

While the broad-leaved species is the hardiest and best for drying, there are variegated forms which provide ornamental interest. Non-flowering types are best for drying, flavouring and stuffing.

SAVORY *Satureja* species

Although well-known by name this plant is not widely grown. There are two species, Winter savory, *Satureja montana* and Summer savory, *S. hortensis*. The latter, an annual, is raised from seed in spring. Sow in a sunny position in drills, 30 cm (1 ft) apart. Choose a light, rich soil, and thin the seedlings to 15 cm (6 ins) apart. Winter savory is a perennial. Divide the roots or take cuttings of new shoots in spring. It may

Below: Winter savory

also be raised from seed, the plants flowering in their second year. This is best done on a rather poor soil. Fresh sprays of savory are used for garnishing. When dried, they are used in mixed herbs and for flavouring poultry and veal.

SORREL *Rumex scutatus*

This is a herb for which claims have long been made for its health giving properties. It is said to be of value 'in sharpening the appetite, cooling the liver and strengthening the heart'. Believed to be a source of iron, it used to be thought that cuckoos ate it freely to improve their voice. The leaves are eaten in salads and soups or cooked like spinach.

A hardy perennial growing up to 60 cm (2 ft) it has leaves not unlike those of the

To obtain an adequate crop give plenty of space to sorrel plants

dock. The light green foliage is usually veined red. The reddish-brown flowers are produced in clusters and should be pinched out to make leaves more succulent.

Well-drained soil and partial shade suit the plants, although they will also grow in sunny situations as long as the ground does not dry out badly. If the plants are cut to the ground in late autumn they will produce vigorous new leaves.

'Broad-leaved French' is the best-flavoured strain.

SWEET CICELY *Myrrhis odorata*

A decorative plant with large fern-like leaves, this is well worth a place in the garden. It is a long-lived plant with a penetrating tap root that makes it difficult to propagate vegetatively. The leaves are noted for their sweet aromatic perfume, while they have a pleasing aniseed flavour.

The white flowers are freely produced in terminal umbels during April and May. The seed heads are quite large, and the seeds are dark brown with sharp ribs. Gather the leaves when fairly young and pick the flowers just before they open.

It seeds freely and once plants are in the garden there are usually plenty of self-sown seedlings. It is best propagated by seed sown in April, in a well-drained bed of medium loam which stays moist in dry spells.

Sweet cicely is used in mixed herbs, salad dressings and soups. Chopped finely, it imparts a zestful flavour to food. The roots can also be boiled and eaten with oil and lemon, or included in mixed salads. It is used for flavouring various liqueurs, and herbalists used to recommend it for digestive disorders.

TARRAGON *Artemisia dracunculus*

The common name of this perennial comes from the French word meaning 'dragon', possibly from the flower's slight resemblance to the shape of a dragon's head.

Used with other herbs and salad plants such as lettuce, tarragon imparts an acquired rather 'hot' flavour. Leaves are plucked as required. Avoid stripping individual plants. The sharp flavour is then present but once dried, it fades. Tarragon vinegar is often made by steeping the leaves in vinegar while the foliage is used in preparing French Mustard and Sauce Tartare.

French tarragon growing 60–90 cm (2–3 ft) high is the best for flavour but is not so hardy as the sharper flavoured Russian tarragon.

Not particular about soil, it does best in a sunny situation where the ground is well drained and not too rich. Propagate by division or from cuttings taken in Spring or early summer, as French tarragon rarely sets seed. The inferior Russian variety is the usual kind offered from seed.

THYME *Thymus* species

This family of plants varies in size from the creeping form, *Thymus serpyllum*, to little bushes 30 cm (1 ft) high. All like sun and to be sheltered from cutting winds, while well-drained, humus rich soil encourages leafy growth. Harvest the leaves for drying before the flowers appear.

The garden thyme, *Thymus vulgaris*, a small bushy plant essential in mixed herbs, has had the reputation of 'promoting courage and vitality'. Excellent as a bee flower, it is occasionally possible to get thyme honey. Used fresh or dry, its flavour improves the taste of many culinary dishes and it is invaluable in stuffings, although it needs to be used judiciously. Oil of thyme has a medicinal value.

Lemon thyme, *Thymus citriodorus* has a refreshing, less pungent flavour, and is used in stuffings and with fish. Caraway

Thyme needs a choice position

thyme, *T. herba-barona*, has, as its name suggests, a scent reminiscent of caraway. Apart from its culinary uses, it is an excellent rock garden plant.

Left: Sweet Cicely grows wild in grassy places

Below: French Tarragon

A-Z Guide to Fruit Growing

The majority of gardens are not big enough to have a very large plot set aside for fruit growing, so it is essential to use the space to the best advantage. Fortunately, there are a number of dwarfing stocks on to which apples and pears can be grafted so that they will not grow too large and compete with other features in the garden for light, moisture and nutrients.

Another way of making full use of all the space available is to grow single cordons planted at an angle of 45° against walls or fences or as divisions throughout the garden. Espalier trained trees can also be used, while plums and cherries can be trained as fans against walls and fences. Cultivated blackberries and loganberries are also useful for clothing walls and arches.

The so called Family Trees help to solve the problem of limited space. These are trees on which up to five different varieties are grafted on to one stock. Obviously, not a lot of fruit is produced from any one variety but a single stock can have grafted on to it say, dessert apples or pears that cross-pollinate well to yield a succession of fruits over several months.

As far as possible, it is advisable to group together the same kinds of fruit trees, for this makes spraying and pruning easier. Also, plant close to each other varieties which cross-pollinate well, to ensure a good crop of fruit. It is advisable to discover the size to which particular trees are likely to grow for some are unsuitable for small gardens.

One of the secrets of success is to buy good healthy stock – particularly certified virus-free black currants, raspberries and strawberries. The ground should be dug well and manured, since the trees and bushes will be in position for many years.

APPLE *Malus sylvestris*

The apple is probably the most popular fruit. It was Edward Bunyard, a pomologist of a past age who wrote, 'no fruit is more to the English taste than the apple. Let the Frenchman have his pear, and the Italian his fig. The Jamaican may retain his farinaceous banana, and the Malay his durian, but for us, the Apple.' This assertion seems to limit the enjoyment of apples to the English but this fruit is valued in many parts of the world.

It is thought by some that not only does the eating of apples help to keep the doctor from our doors but helps to keep ourselves from the dentists. No other fruit compares with the apple for the length of its fruiting season, from August to June. By careful selection and storage, it is possible to have *home*-grown sun ripened fruit for ten months of the year.

Climatic conditions affect both flavour and colour, and different varieties reach their climacteric, or peak of flavour, at different times. We cannot pretend that all good-flavoured apples have the same taste. This is evident by comparing 'Cox's Orange Pippin' and 'Blenheim Orange', both long

Fruit tree blossom is of decorative value in any garden

keeping dessert varieties and both of excellent though quite different, flavour. To quote Bunyard again 'there is in Blenheim a mellow constancy, a reminder of those placid Oxford meadows, which gave it its birth in the shadow of Blenheim Palace. Although I like to wear the light blue favour, what can Cambridge put beside the Blenheim? — only a "Histon Favourite" of poor quality, indiscriminate and undistinguished.' There is still room for old favourites but how often do we today come across 'American Mother', 'Gravenstein' and 'Wagener'? All have a superb flavour.

As a result of generous feeding with nitrogenous fertilizers each year the crop weight is usually very heavy, but flavour is almost non-existent. It is not suggested that the manurial system is the only factor involved in the production of flavourless fruit. Rootstocks are to blame in some degree. Soil too, affects the problem. Unfortunately, 'Cox's Orange Pippin' are often planted on soil that is quite unsuitable.

The good grower does not feed his trees, he feeds the *soil* and gives supplementary dressings or foliage sprays only when the trees indicate their need for them. The aim should be to keep the roots really active. If you want good flavoured 'Cox' from store you must go to the man who keeps them for a few weeks only in a barn that probably cost him nothing to erect.

Colour is always a feature of apples, and we have only to think of 'Charles Ross', 'Rival', 'Lord Lambourne' and 'Scarlet Pimpernel' to know how attractive some apples can be. 'James Grieve' and 'Miller's Seedling' are showy, too. While many realize that good flavour is often found in less brightly hued fruits, good colour will remain a lure to us.

Other showy varieties of apples of fairly recent introduction include 'Red Ellison's Orange' a highly coloured bud sport from 'Ellison's Orange'. It was discovered in a tree near Wisbech, showing crimson coloured fruit. The remaining trees yielded fruit typical of the variety. Sufficient wood was available to 'work' a few scions on to a young Bramley's seedling tree. It was possible to increase stock and the fruit produced has the same distinctive crimson colouring while the trees have inherited the valuable characteristics of 'Ellison's Orange'.

Cooking apple 'Bramley's Seedling'

'Scarlet Pimpernel' is another striking new variety which came to Britain from Holland although it originated in America. 'Scarlet Pimpernel' keeps in excellent condition for a month or so after picking. Growth is vigorous and the branches are upright and spreading. It is highly resistant to scab and is not susceptible to canker. It is self fertile and flowers at the same time as 'Egremont Russet'. If fruit spurs are thinned during winter, instead of the end of May which is normal with other varieties, the apples grow to a good size.

RECOMMENDED VARIETIES:

The following is an alphabetical list of the best dessert and culinary apples and those which do well in gardens. The months mentioned are those when the fruit is at its best although often it is eaten beforehand. When buying apple trees check the pollination requirements with the nursery.

'Allington Pippin', dessert, October–December, medium sized, conical yellow flushed red, regular cropper, partially self fertile.

'Beauty of Bath', dessert, early August, medium, flattish pale yellow with a red flush, sweet and brisk flavour, a free bearing early variety, party self-fertile.

'Blenheim Orange', culinary and dessert, November–February, fairly large, handsome, flattish, round fruit, yellow striped and flushed, red and russet, of vigorous growth and a heavy bearer when established; does well on heavy soils, partly self-fertile.

'Brownlee's Russet', dessert, January–March, splendid variety of medium size, brownish-green, tender flesh of good flavour, self-fertile. A good choice for the small garden.

'Court Pendu Plat', dessert, December–May, bright green changing to yellow marked with russet, and rich red on the side exposed to sun, crisp, juicy, rich flavoured; of moderate growth. This variety is hardy and an abundant bearer, flowers late and usually escapes frost damage.

'Cox's Orange Pippin', the best known dessert apple, October–February, raised at Slough in 1830 from a pip of 'Ribston Pippin'. The greenish skin is streaked and flushed with red, especially where exposed to the sun, flesh yellowish, crisp, juicy and sweet. It is not self-fertile so should be planted with other apples such as 'James Grieve', 'Worcester Pearmain' and 'Sunset' to ensure pollination.

'Cox Pomona', culinary, October–

November, yellow streaked bright crimson, flesh white, tender and good flavoured.

'D'Arcy Spice', dessert, March–May, of roundish flattened appearance; yellow covered with brownish-russet, sweet, juicy and aromatic; found at Tolleshunt D'Arcy in Essex many years ago.

'Edward VII', culinary, December–April, large, pale yellow, flesh firm and juicy, vigorous habit, suitable for gardens and orchards; late flowering.

'Egremont Russet', dessert, October–December, golden-yellow with broken russet, flesh greenish-yellow, firm and of excellent flavour; heavy cropping, hardy, ornamental when in flower, a good pollinator for 'Cox's Orange Pippin'.

'Ellison's Orange', dessert, September–October, dull green streaked red. The flavour is reminiscent of aniseed. It grows and crops well, the flowers rarely being touched by frost.

'George Cave', dessert, July–August; showy red skin on the sunny side, overlying greenish-yellow; flesh firm, juicy and sweet.

'Golden Delicious', dessert, December–February, a good variety provided virus free stocks are grown; splendid flavour.

'Gravenstein', dessert or culinary, October–December, yellow, streaked crimson and orange, flesh crisp and juicy with rich aromatic flavour. The tree is hardy, vigorous and a good bearer; a grand old apple of German origin, now coming into favour again.

'Grenadier', culinary, August–September, large handsome fruit, greenish-yellow skin; very fertile variety most valuable for garden and orchard, cooks to a froth.

'Howgate Wonder', culinary, December–February; fruit large, flattish with yellowish-

Dessert apple 'Egremont Russet'

green skin, flushed and streaked red, firm flesh, good cooker, a dependable cropper.

'James Grieve', dessert, September–October, good shaped fruit, with pale yellow skin, flushed and striped with red, juicy and of good flavour; vigorous, compact cropper.

'Kerry Pippin', dessert, September–October, yellow tinged and streaked red, sometimes with russet markings, crisp and juicy, with an aromatic flavour; a good apple but little grown at present.

'Keswick Codlin', culinary, July–September, angular fruit with yellow flushed orange skin, flesh juicy, with a brisk, pleasant flavour; use soon after picking, otherwise it becomes mealy.

'King of the Pippins', dessert, August–September, greenish-yellow with red blush; flesh firm, crisp and of excellent flavour.

'Lane's Prince Albert', culinary, November–April, large, handsome shiny flushed red green fruit; flesh tender, slightly acid; a dwarf grower of spreading habit, very free bearing.

'Laxton's Advance', dessert, August, well flushed skin, with crisp, 'Cox' like-flesh and flavour; a valuable early apple.

'Laxton's Epicure', dessert, September. This variety is the result of a cross between 'Cox's Orange Pippin' and 'Wealthy' and has the 'Cox' flavour. The skin is pale yellow streaked red, flesh tender, sweet and juicy, it will not keep.

'Laxton's Fortune', dessert, September–November, yellow, flushed and streaked red, flesh yellow, 'Cox' flavour; strong growing.

'Laxton's Superb', dessert, December–March, a cross between 'Cox's Orange Pippin' and 'Wyken Pippin', of similar appearance to 'Cox' but rather larger, flesh white, sweet and crisp; a strong grower and good cropper.

'Lord Derby', culinary, November–December, large, yellow-fleshed; cooks to a lovely deep golden colour, sturdy, upright growth, does best on well drained soils; susceptible to scab.

'Lord Lambourne', dessert, October–December, yellow, flushed red firm and juicy, an upright, strong grower and a good cropper.

'Monarch', culinary, December–April, pale green with red flush, heavy cropper.

'Mother'; also known as 'American Mother', dessert, October, medium size, good flavour.

'Peasgood Nonsuch', culinary and dessert, October–November, large and handsome, greenish-yellow flushed and streaked

'James Grieve' is a popular and fine-flavoured variety

red, yellow-fleshed, juicy and well-flavoured, one of the most showy apples in cultivation.

'Rev W. Wilks', culinary, October–November, large, pale yellow, excellent apple for dumplings, hardy, vigorous grower, good bearer, liable to canker on heavy soil.

'Ribston Pippin', dessert, November–January, dull yellow shaded red, with russet markings, flesh yellow, firm, crisp and juicy; an old favourite of superb and distinct flavour; subject to canker on heavy soils; needs regular pruning; grow with other varieties.

'Scarlet Pimpernel', dessert. August, well-coloured fruits of good shape; crisp, juicy and sweet with an acid tang.

'St Edmund's Pippin', September–October, smallish round golden-russety fruit, tender and aromatic; a tip bearer and sometimes liable to scab.

'Stirling Castle', culinary, August–October, pale green, flesh white, and well flavoured, one of the heaviest cropping, early cooking apples.

'Sturmer Pippin', dessert, January–June, the green skin is almost covered with dark brown russetings; excellent flavour; raised at Sturmer in Suffolk nearly 100 years ago from a pip of 'Ribston Pippin'; prolific; leave fruit to mellow as long as possible. Best grown in warm districts.

'Sunset', dessert, October–February, golden-yellow with red and russety markings, delicious 'Cox'-like flavour, and succeeds where 'Cox' often fails; strong growing and a good fertile variety; blooms late and almost always escapes frost damage.

'Tydeman's Late Orange', dessert, April–May, yellow, richly flavoured flesh, deep green brightening to golden yellow.

'Wagener', culinary and dessert, December–July, first class for eating from March onwards; yellowish green with red cheek, fresh, firm, crisp and juicy, easy to grow, rarely affected by pests, mildew or scab.

'Winston', sometimes wrongly known as 'Winter King'; dessert, January–April, skin crimson, flesh firm, crisp and sweet, compact grower and resistant to mildew and disease, keeps well.

'Worcester Pearmain', dessert, September–October, one of the best known apples, skin red, with minute fawn coloured dots, flesh tender, juicy and sweet, free fruiting, hardy and much used as a pollinator for 'Cox's Orange Pippin'.

6 Dessert apples for October–November use
Allington Pippin	Gravenstein
American Mother	Ellison's Orange
Egremont Russet	St Edmund's Pippin

6 Dessert apples for December–January use
Blenheim Orange	Golden Delicious
Court Pendu Plat	Ribston Pippin
Cox's Orange Pippin	Wagener

6 Dessert Apples for January–March use
Brownlee's Russet	Sturmer Pippin
D'Arcy Spice	Sunset
Laxton's Superb	Tydeman's Late Orange

APRICOT *Prunus armeniaca*

Generally speaking, it is more difficult to bring apricots into a fruitful condition than peaches or nectarines. They are cultivated successfully and on a large scale, in France, Italy, parts of the United States and Australia and other countries. Apricots will grow on greatly differing soils but they appear to prefer a medium loam over lying limestone.

The rootstocks on which the trees are grafted have a tremendous influence on their vigour. The most popular commercial rootstocks are the vigorous Brompton and the more dwarfing Common Mussel. St Julien A, a plum stock of East Malling origin, is also first class for producing smallish trees.

Apricots can be raised from stones and it is sometimes possible to get good fruiting trees by sowing in May. Bury the stones at least 5 cm (2 ins) deep, and move the resultant seedlings the following autumn to a sheltered position against a warm, sunny wall or fence. To be sure of fruiting it is best to rely on grafted stock. Trees raised from stones sometimes fail to fruit or if they do the fruit is of poor quality.

Apricots flower early in the year, so the blooms are liable to frost damage. Low lying sites should be avoided, or exposed windy situations which may deter bees and other pollinating insects from visiting the flowers.

A warm sheltered garden is best for growing apricots

Bush trees usually do well in sheltered places and wall trained specimens have the advantage of extra shelter and warmth. Avoid north facing walls.

Since apricots start into growth early, the autumn is the best time for transplanting. Heavy soils are unsuitable although the trees will not flourish where the roots dry out in summer. If a deficiency of lime is suspected, dig in lime rubble or hydrated lime when the site is being prepared. As a guide, wall trees should not be planted closer than about 3 m (10 ft) and the stem should be about 15 cm (6 ins) from the wall.

Prevent frost damage to the flowers of bushes or wall trained trees by covering them with old curtains or fish-netting. If the weather is unfavourable for pollinating insects, hand pollinate the flowers. Most varieties are self-fertile.

Apricots require nitrogen and potash for good results and established trees will benefit from top dressings of a fertilizer, preferably of an organic nature, which is rich in these properties. A mulching of good compost or old manure and peat in the spring helps much to curb fruit drop.

Take care not to knock or bruise the trunk or branches or gum may spill from the wounds. If there are signs of a very heavy crop, some thinning out should be done when the fruit is the size of a hazel nut.

The fruit should be picked when it has coloured well, but before it becomes soft, for then wasps fancy it! Keeping apricots in the warm and light for a day or two after harvesting brings out the full flavour.

Prune with care. The plan for bushes should be to produce open-centred specimens, while for wall trees a good fan-shape is ideal. Because of the tree's susceptibility to die back disease and silver leaf, keep pruning cuts as small as possible, and apart from shortening the leaders, all other cutting should be done in spring or summer. If it becomes necessary at any time to make big cuts, cover the wounds with Arbrex or Stockholm Tar. A simple guide to pruning: cut back one-year shoots to half their length, to just above an upward pointing bud. Nip out with the thumb nail any unnecessary or badly placed shoots.

Die back disease can be destructive; blossoms wilt and later the affected spurs die back.

Brown rot fungus affects both wood and fruit. Its incidence is less likely if no jagged wounds are ever left. Bordeaux mixture sprayed on at the bud swelling stage is a good control. Silver leaf should be dealt with as recommended for plums.

RECOMMENDED VARIETIES: 'Breda', one of the hardiest, producing a heavy crop of orange-flushed, good flavoured red fruit in August; 'Hemskerke', orange-yellow blotched red, good flavour, end of July; 'Moorpark', probably the best known variety, large deep orange with red spots, August–September; 'Royal' or 'Royal Orange', oval shape, good

'Parsley-leaved' blackberries have an excellent flavour

flavour; yellow skin with purple spots, early August; 'Shipley's Blenheim', a strong grower, hardy and prolific; the oval-shaped fruit has an orange skin dotted crimson. It seems to do best as a bush and the fruit is excellent for bottling and jam — mid-August.

BLACKBERRY *Rubus fruticosus*

Apart from their heavy cropping value these most useful plants can be used for covering unsightly fences or for screening an untidy corner of the garden, or for dividing one part of the plot from another.

They need some kind of support on which their long growths can be trained. While they can be planted in a shady position, they prefer an open, sheltered, sunny spot, then crops will be heavy and well flavoured.

Although not particular about soil, drainage should be good and, in preparing the site, it is wise to dig the ground deeply. If humus is lacking, work in plenty of decayed manure. Failing this, any other bulky matter such as peat, leaf mould or spent hops can be used. To this, add sea-weed fertilizer, fish meal or bone meal, to provide nourishment over a long period. Unless the ground is naturally limy, complete preparations by dressing the surface soil with hydrated lime, at the rate of 136 g per m² (4 oz per sq yd).

Where more than one blackberry is grown, it is advisable to space them at least

2.70 m (9 ft) apart, and a post and wire structure is necessary if plants are grown in the open garden. The posts should stand up to 1.80 m (6 ft) above ground level. Three strands of taut wire 60 cm (2 ft) apart are run between the posts. Such a support is suitable for the strongest varieties.

Nurserymen usually supply blackberries as sturdy one-year-old plants and send them out from November to early April. They should be planted immediately on arrival although if the soil is sticky, or frost bound, they can be 'heeled in' until conditions improve. When planting, spread the roots out and retread the soil around the stems after frosts have loosened it.

Once they are planted the canes should be shortened to about 90 cm (3 ft) and tied loosely to their supports. When it is obvious the plants are beginning to grow in spring, it is best to shorten the canes to about 23–25 cm (9–10 ins) from ground level, cutting immediately above a stout bud. This will encourage the production of strong young fruiting canes for the following season. If fruit is required the first year the second shortening of the growths should not be carried out and initially the canes need not be cut back so severely. This will mean less shapely plants and the probability that the following season's growth, or some of it, will develop from the older canes instead of from the base. When stems come from ground level they are easier to train, the fruit is better and annual pruning is easier

as the stems are less tangled.

To prune established blackberries, cut out the old canes and tie in the new ones to bear fruit the following season. Any surplus canes, that is, those which cannot be conveniently tied in or would lead to over-crowding, should be cut out completely. See p. 230 for training systems.

RECOMMENDED VARIETIES: The following varieties return a heavy yield:

'Bedford Giant', ripen in July and August with shiny berries of fine flavour; 'Merton Early', a fine mid-season sort; 'Parsley-leaved', a fairly old variety, vigorous on heavy soil; matures in August and September; 'Himalaya Giant', very robust, producing its excellently flavoured berries from early to mid-season; it should be pruned very severely annually, not only to keep it under control but because most of the fruit is carried on young canes; but beware, for it is extremely thorny.

Thornless varieties include 'Merton Thornless', which requires a really rich soil, and produces sweet fruit in August, and 'Oregon Thornless' which has cut, paeony-shaped leaves and fruits in August and September.

Other berries which may conveniently be included here are some of the more unusual edible fruited *Rubus* species and hybrids derived from blackberries and raspberries.

Fruits of the boysenberry

Boysenberry The Boysenberry is a hybrid which produces large dark wine coloured fruit of good flavour with few pips. A strong grower, the plant bears fruit on long spurs which stand out from the prickly canes making it easier to pick them. A hardy variety, it will succeed on drier soils than other berries. Allow 1.8–2.1 m (6–7 ft) between the canes which, when newly planted, should be cut down to about 30 cm (1 ft) from the ground to induce new growth from the base.

A thornless variety of loganberry is easier to prune, train, and pick from

Loganberry *Rubus loganbaccus* It is nearly one hundred years since Judge Logan of California found this plant in his garden. It was named the loganberry and was introduced to Great Britain well over 75 years ago. It has been grown under varying conditions and has proved to be an abundant bearer and absolutely hardy. The large dark red berries ripen over a period of many weeks in summer. The juicy good flavoured fruit is specially valuable for stewing and jam making.

It is essential to grow a good stock. Perhaps the reason that the loganberry is not appreciated as much as it ought to be, is that poor fruiting stocks are grown – cropping indifferently with poor disease resistance.

When well grown, the true loganberry yields heavily. Although some people like the fruit when it is ripe for dessert, it lacks the sweetness of both the blackberry and raspberry. It is, however, suitable for cooking, jam making and bottling, as well as for the manufacture of fruit juice. Loganberries ripen from July onwards.

Planting can be carried out from November until March, the normal spacing being 1.80–2.40 m (6–8 ft) apart. The canes should be cut back after planting, to encourage strong basal growths to develop. These should be tied into place and not left to flop about for it is on these new canes that fruit is borne the following year.

Where a good vigorous stock is available, it can be propagated by tip layers. Bend the young canes over during July and August and bury their tips in the soil. Leave them in position until the following spring, when they should be moved to nursery beds. After a year they will be good strong specimens, suitable for planting out. Encourage heavier crops by mulching with strawy manure or compost each spring. Once the tips have rooted well and have been severed from the parent plant a new set of canes will develop to furnish further material for propagation.

Obviously only really healthy plants should be propagated. Virus infected stock is usually seen as weak, spindly growth and small anaemic foliage.

Cane spot disease is often spread by the spores falling from the old canes on to the new. This is why some specialists keep the new growths trained more or less upright in the centre of the plants until the old canes have been cut out. Should the disease be suspected at any time, spray the plants with colloidal copper fungicide.

The thornless loganberry was introduced to Britain well over 30 years ago. The fruit is large and good flavoured, excellent for stewing and jam making. Growth is strong and attractive and plants are as easy to grow as the ordinary loganberry. This is the best variety to grow alongside a path.

The attractive wineberry will happily grow against a trellis or fence

The youngberry is a cross between the blackberry and the raspberry

Youngberry This is a vigorous hybrid with large well-flavoured fruit containing few seeds and little core. As the berries ripen they change from deep red to a pleasing black. As the fruit is produced on short stems from the main canes it is easy to gather, and there are few thorns to contend with.

Since the plants are semi-trailing, plant them at least 1.80 m (6 ft) apart, in soil which does not dry out badly in summer. Well-drained, moisture retentive soil encourages heavy cropping.

Propagation is simple: layer the tips of the long stems as previously described.

Wineberry *Rubus phoenicolasius* Wineberry, also known as the Japanese wineberry, is an attractive fruiting plant with bright orange berries that turn a rich crimson when ripe and have a slightly acid flavour. The softly hairy canes assume an attractive reddish hue in winter. Allow at least 1.80 m (6 ft) between the plants.

BLUEBERRY *Vaccinium corymbosum*

The Blueberry is one of several species of *Vaccinium* bearing edible fruit, others being the cranberry and whortleberry.

The finest are the Highbush varieties. Blueberries thrive in acid, peaty soil where little else will flourish; but they cannot stand drought conditions.

The soil should have plenty of humus with moisture always available but it should never be waterlogged. Treated well and pruned regularly, the bushes are kept to a height of about 1.8 m (6 ft). In good conditions, they will fruit well for fifteen years or more. Apart from their fruiting value, blueberries are most ornamental in the autumn when their leaves assume yellow and crimson tints.

Choose an open, sunny situation and prepare the soil thoroughly for the plants are long-lived. Do this well in advance of planting. Small plants move best and those supplied by the growers are usually no more than 15–30 cm (6–12 ins) high.

To allow for future development, they should be spaced up to 2 m (6 ft 6 ins) apart each way. Newly planted bushes should be mulched with compost or decayed manure and peat. In subsequent years a top dressing in early spring is beneficial, but avoid lime in any form.

Little pruning is necessary for the first two years after planting. Subsequently, the older, thicker stems are cut out to encourage basal growths. The white bell-shaped flowers are borne on the previous season's growth. They appear from March onwards and are resistant to frost damage. The fruit ripens from July to September. Established bushes will bear about 2 kg (4½ lb) each year.

Let the fruit mature on the bushes where it will remain in good condition for some days. Ripe berries are a dark bluish colour at the stem end but a reddish tinge indicates immaturity.

General cultivation is simple; keep the ground clean of weeds and net the ripening fruits against birds.

RECOMMENDED VARIETIES: In Holland and Germany research workers have long been engaged in breeding improved varieties to give really worthwhile crops. Apart from wild plants, from which fruits are often gathered, there are a number of named hybrids available in Britain. You can prolong the picking period by planting a selection of these. Some are of American origin, and many have been tested at Long Ashton Research Station. Among the best are: 'Earliblue', strong upright growth and large berries ripening from mid-July; 'Blueray', spreading habit with large pale-blue berries in branched clusters; 'Jersey', an older variety, long sprays of large fruit. Plant with another variety for pollination.

Blueberry 'Blueray' can be eaten raw but is best stewed

BULLACE *Prunus domestica* var *insititia*

These old fashioned fruits are closely related to and grown in the same way as damsons, but sadly are little cultivated today. They were once plentiful in hedgerows but are now rare as land continues to be used for building. In the small garden one bullace tree or bush should be adequate, since all varieties are self-fertile. If more than one is grown, the distance between them should be 4.5–6 m (15–20 ft). They are useful plants, for they prolong the fruit season, and as large bushes form attractive hedges. Bullace are best for stewing or jam-making.

RECOMMENDED VARIETIES: The following can still be obtained from fruit specialists:

'Black Bullace', October, almost black fruit with a purplish 'bloom', juicy but sour.

'Langley Bullace', November, a prolific cropper of good flavour, the large black oval fruit keeping well; introduced by Messrs Veitch in 1902 it is said to be a cross between 'Farleigh Damson' and an early 'Orleans' plum. It makes an upright tree.

'Shepherd's Bullace', October, large round-oval, greenish fruit; growth upright; delicious for fruit pies.

'White Bullace', October, fairly small, attractive fruit with a creamy bloom.

CHERRY *Prunus* species

Although flowering cherries are widely grown in all parts of the country the fruiting varieties are very much less common. There are several reasons. They grow best as standards or half-standards and take nine or ten years to come into full bearing. They are unable to set fruit with their own pollen and only certain varieties will cross-pollinate. Bushes can be obtained but they are of a rather spreading habit. Standard trees too, take up a lot of room and it is not always easy to gather fruit from the higher branches, and birds often take their toll of the crop.

For the smaller garden, the solution to the problem of large trees is to grow cherries as fans, planting them against a wall or fence. Then it is easier to gather the fruit and protect the crop from birds.

Cherries grow best on light loam over chalk, and where potash is not lacking. Over-rich soil can cause the trees to 'gum'.

Established trees and bushes can be encouraged to bear good crops by scattering bone meal over the root area at 56 g per m² (2 oz per sq yd) in February. Dried blood at 28 g per m² (1 oz per sq yd) is also beneficial.

It is best to plant three- to four-year old trees, although two-year old specimens are satisfactory if one is prepared to wait longer for the fruit. November is the ideal planting

The 'Morello' or sour cherry is best for small gardens

month but trees can be moved up until the end of March. Do not attempt to push the roots into a very small hole but spread them out fully and plant firmly. Make sure too, that the standards are supported with stout stakes. These should be in position before the trees are planted to avoid damaging the roots.

If you are planting in established grassland or are going to sow grass seed after the trees are in, leave a circle about 1 m (3 ft) in diameter around the trunks to prevent the grass taking all the moisture and nourishment while the trees are becoming established. Do not over-manure trained trees. They should be kept growing slowly. A spring mulch of ordinary compost or sedge peat will ensure that the roots do not dry out in summer. Manure or very rich compost should not be used since it encourages exuberant stem and leaf growth and over-fed trees are more susceptible to disease.

Little pruning is needed the first year for, at transplanting time, the shape of the head will have already been formed. Whenever pruning is necessary, always cut immediately above an outward pointing bud. Crowded, crossing and rubbing branches should be well cut back.

The only sure way of protecting the fruit from birds is to net the trees. Other methods include automatic bird scarers and scarecrows in the trees, although birds often get used to the latter after a few days. Not all the fruit ripens at the same time, so pick carefully so as not to spoil the unripe fruit.

There are many varieties, several having Bigarreau as part of their name. This name was originally applied to varieties which were two coloured but now it applies to any cherry with firm flesh whether it is white or black. Cherries with soft flesh are often known as Geans.

RECOMMENDED VARIETIES: *Sweet Cherries* 'Bigarreau de Schrecken', late June, shiny black, good flavour. 'Bigarreau Napoleon', mid-July, yellow and red, good cropper. 'Early Rivers', June, crimson-black, juicy, delicious flavour. 'Frogmore Early', late June, yellow marked red. 'Governor Wood', early July, yellow and pink, juicy flesh. 'Merton Bigarreau', mid-July, black, rich flavour. 'Merton Heart', late June, dark red, juicy, good flavour.
Acid Cherries The most commonly grown acid or sour cherry is the 'Morello', which unlike sweet cherries is very well suited to garden cultivation. It matures from August onwards, is blackish-crimson, hardy and excellent for north walls. A reliable heavy cropper, fruit rarely splits.

Sour cherries should always be given a winter tar oil spray, since they seem more liable to aphid attacks than sweet cherries.

CRANBERRY *Vaccinium oxycoccus*

This is another undeservedly little grown fruit in Britain though it is grown in quantity in Holland and North America. However, investigations are being made into the possibilities of growing cranberries on a larger scale in this country, and there is no reason why they should not be grown in gardens. The cranberry is a spreading plant with upright branches of 15–20 cm (6–8 ins) high. It flowers in June and July and the fruit is ready for harvesting from September onwards.

Cranberries have a shallow rooting system, so the soil need not be very deep. They thrive in a layer of shallow peat over sand or clay. While peat may not be absolutely essential, the soil should stay fairly moist throughout the year, but never waterlogged.

The cranberry is readily increased from cuttings. Use shoots 7–10 cm (3–4 ins) long and root them in sandy, peaty soil in late April. For striking a small number, boxes may be used, but for larger quantities insert them directly in rows in frames or in the open ground. Some gardeners leave the cuttings untrimmed since they appear able to root quite well if they are simply scattered on the surface and lightly covered with soil, but undoubtedly it is best to plant them in the ground in the usual way.

Sweet cherry 'Bigarreau Napoleon'

CURRENTS

All currants are species of the genus *Ribes*. The black currant grows wild across the whole of Europe and Northern Asia.

BLACK CURRANT *Ribes nigrum*

One of the most important soft fruits, the black currant is rich in vitamin C and its juice is used in health drinks. The name currant is derived from the ancient Greek city of Corinth. Heavy yields can be expected from healthy established bushes which normally bear well for at least twelve years.

In the garden, there is rarely much choice of site but avoid a low lying shady position. Ideally, provide a deep loamy soil with a high organic content. This will ensure moisture is retained during long spells of dry weather. Black currants like moisture during the growing and fruiting season, but stodgy cold, clay soil will not produce the heaviest crops. Such ground can be made more suitable by working in compost and well rotted manure.

If the bushes are exposed to cold north and east winds insects are discouraged from visiting the flowers and distributing pollen from bloom to bloom, necessary to ensure a good set of fruit. Also the bushes should not be planted where they are in a frost pocket, otherwise the open flowers will be damaged. Prepare the soil well before planting.

At one time black currants suffered

'Hatton's Black' black currant is a heavy-cropping variety

badly from big bud mite and the related reversion disease, but now, because of a scheme worked out by the Ministry of Agriculture, leading fruit specialists supply only certified virus-free bushes. Only grow best quality named varieties.

It is most satisfactory to buy two-year old specimens. These normally have three or four shoots and will establish more quickly than older bushes. One year bushes are sometimes offered. They take longer to come into bearing and it is not so easy to detect any virus infection then. Against this of course, if the cuttings were taken from certified stock, there would be little fear of big bud mite. By the time a bush is two years old the presence of any reversion will have shown.

Although black currants can be planted from late October until the end of March, early planting is preferable, ideally in November. It is advisable to cut down newly planted bushes to within 5 cm (2 ins) of their base in the February after planting. Plant firmly and space the bushes 1.5 m (5 ft) apart to allow room for proper development and free air circulation. Many growers find that a thick annual mulch of farmyard manure gives the heaviest crops.

Black currants are pruned annually, the object being to encourage the production of new wood, preferably from the base. There should be no forming of a 'leg' or central

stem; all shoots should arise from the soil. By cutting down bushes to ground level the first year after planting, a good supply of new shoots during the summer is ensured.

Black currants bear fruit on one-year old, light coloured wood. Unpruned bushes produce only a small amount of new wood, usually at the ends of the branches. This leads to unproductive bushes with much unwanted old, basal wood. Older branches should be cut back to strong young shoots. The dark colour of the old wood makes it easy to determine which is the new growth.

Good soil conditions and adequate nourishment is the way to build up plenty of fruiting branches, but regular pruning is required if a weighty crop is to be produced annually. A few varieties have a spreading habit and produce their branches very near the ground. These will have to be cut right out, or where possible, pruned back to an upright growing shoot.

Some gardeners prune their black currants in winter when, of course, one can see all the growths clearly but the best time is September, after picking the fruit. This early pruning stops the bushes wasting their energy on shoots that will be cut out later and, more important, next season's fruiting wood is able to ripen better.

By growing several varieties, it is possible to extend the picking season and thus avoid a glut. The fruits of some varieties hang longer in good condition than those of other varieties and also keep better in wet weather. The best among them are 'Seabrook's Black', 'Baldwin' and 'Westwick Choice'.

Pick the berries on the 'strig', not separately, then 'strig' them indoors, with a table fork. Time of picking is important, for sometimes the berries look ripe before they are. Harvesting should begin when the top berries on the strig have softened. If gathered too early a lot of weight may be lost, for in the last few days of maturing the berries rapidly increase in size.

Not all the berries on individual bushes are ready at the same time and it is usually necessary to 'pick them over' more than once.

Black currants are usually propagated from cuttings in the autumn. You can also increase them from soft wood cuttings in summer, and by layering the lower branches.

Autumn hardwood cuttings should be made from healthy one-year-old shoots. Do not propagate from old bushes — it is asking for trouble. The cuttings should be 20—23 cm (8—9 ins) long and trimmed neatly, top and bottom, to just above a bud.

Select a well-drained patch of sandy soil and take out a straight backed trench 40—50 cm (15—20 ins) deep. Insert the cuttings so that only a couple of buds are showing. When returning the soil to the trench, make sure that the cuttings are really firm. This deep planting encourages the growth of basal shoots and lessens the possibility of a 'leg' forming. If more than one trench is necessary they should be 60 cm (2 ft) apart. Different varieties should be clearly marked. It has been found that freshly taken cuttings root much better than those taken some time before being planted.

RECOMMENDED VARIETIES:

'Baldwin', one of the best maincrops. It forms a compact upright bush, responds well to good feeding but does not like really heavy soils.

'Boskoop Giant', an established early variety which colours evenly and is not prone to splitting; rather tall growing, becoming leggy if not pruned regularly.

'Mendip Cross', an early variety of great vigour. The large fruits appear on long strigs, making picking easy.

'Seabrook's Black' ('French Black'), an old sort which crops well although it is sometimes shy in producing basal growths.

'Wellington XXX', a heavy cropping, mid-season variety. Growth is vigorous but occasionally sprawling, so prune carefully to counteract this tendency.

'Amos Black' is an erratic cropper but it has the virtue of ripening very late, so extending the season.

RED CURRANT *Ribes sativum*

Although the origin of the red currant is somewhat uncertain it is generally reckoned that three species have contributed to the constitution of present day varieties. These are, *Ribes vulgare*, *R. rubrum* and *R. petraeum*. Less popular than black currants, red currants are used for jams, jelly and pies.

'Laxton's No 1' is a good early variety for the garden

The bushes grow well on ordinary soils but dislike heavy, poorly drained land. Light ground can be improved by adding strawy manure, compost or anything that will increase the humus content. A good supply of potash is needed to colour the berries, produce a good firm wood and to maintain healthy foliage. Leaf scorch — a condition in which the edges of the leaves turn brown — is usually caused by a shortage of potash. Every four years an application of fish manure at 56 g per m² (2 oz per sq yd) in February or early March will keep the bushes vigorous. Wood ash or sulphate of potash at 56 g per m² (2 oz per sq yd) is an excellent alternative.

November or February and early March are ideal months for planting, provided the soil is workable. Bushes are usually available as two or three year olds. A sunny situation suits the bushes but avoid frost pockets and windy positions.

If you intend to train red currants as single, double or triple cordons to clothe a wall or fence, the younger specimens are the easiest to manage.

When several red currant bushes are planted, space them about 1.80 m (6 ft) apart. This will give them plenty of room to develop and allow for the eight or nine strong branches each should have. Single stemmed cordons should be spaced 45 cm (18 ins) apart at an angle of 45°. Apart from growing them against fences or walls they can be trained on light trellis work and used for dividing the fruit from the vegetable garden without taking up much room.

It is best to keep red currant bushes to one leg (clean stem) of about 15 cm (6 ins) before allowing branches to form. Remove all suckers and buds below this point. This also applies to double and triple cordons and espaliers. Red currants trained as espaliers will grow well on north walls where the fruit will ripen later.

With pruning, the bushes should have four main stems coming from the 'leg'. In the first year, cut these back to within 8–10 cm (3–4 ins) of their base to produce a sturdy, bowl-shaped, framework of branches.

RECOMMENDED VARIETIES: There are fewer varieties of red currants than black currants but among the very best are 'Laxtons No 1', a heavy and reliable cropper of medium sized berries; and 'Red Lake', producing long trusses of good quality, bright-red juicy berries. Two really good varieties of Dutch origin that have recently been introduced are 'Jonkheer van Tets', a very early heavy cropper and 'Random' a late season kind reckoned by some to be the best for yield and quality.

WHITE CURRANT *Ribes sativum*

These are grown just like red currants and repay feeding and watering in a dry season. They do well as cordons or fans when grown against a north wall, but net fruits against the birds. There are several varieties, all rather similar.

Handle white currants with care at picking time and afterwards, for the berries are easily bruised. Propagation is from hardwood cuttings taken in early autumn when rooting is usually quick. Select one year old shoots from strong healthy bushes.

Both red and white currants should be grown on a 'leg', and all buds, excepting 4–5 at the top, are removed from the cuttings. Make the cuttings 23–25 cm (9–10 ins) long and insert them 15–18 cm (6–7 ins) deep. If a quantity of cuttings are rooted, space them 8–10 cm (3–4 ins) apart with 60 cm (2 ft) between the rows. Subsequently, the young specimens must be pruned to shape. To do this always cut to an outward pointing bud to ensure an open, bowl-shaped centre.

RECOMMENDED VARIETIES: 'White Dutch' forms a spreading bush bearing medium sized bunches of berries.

'White Versailles' is an early variety, producing long bunches of large, good flavoured fruit.

DAMSONS *Prunus domestica* var *insititia*

The damson is a native of the country around Damascus, hence its name. At one time damsons were grown on a fairly large scale, but present-day growers do not seem to pay much attention to them. While it is true that some varieties have small fruit which seems chiefly composed of stone and skin, there are several sorts which have really good fleshy fruit. Apart from the fact that damsons make excellent jams and are delicious in tarts and pies they are valuable for bottling and canning, especially since they retain their rich, distinctive flavour for a very long time.

The trees make good shelter belts thriving in exposed places and able to withstand the bitterest of winds. As damsons which are

Currant 'White Versailles'

late-flowering, hold their foliage well into autumn, they provide excellent protection for other late maturing fruits.

This tree also succeeds in soils quite unsuitable for apples and pears, which is one reason why it is seen growing in certain exposed and northern districts where the cultivation of other more tender types of fruit might be less successful.

With very few exceptions, damsons are self-fertile but there is no doubt that heavier crops are carried where two or more varieties cross-pollinate. Damsons crop most freely when there are regular and plentiful supplies of moisture available.

RECOMMENDED VARIETIES: 'Bradley's King', a dessert or culinary variety with medium, oval black fruit having a thick bloom. The firm, acid flesh becomes sweet when fully ripe; of moderate growth, it forms dense twiggy heads and is remarkably fertile; raised by Mr Bradley of Halam, Notts; mid-September.

'Cheshire Damson' ('Shropshire Prune' or 'Prune Damson'), a small tree which is sometimes a shy bearer. The oval fruits which taper to the stem are a deep purple, with a dense bloom; first class for canning and bottling. They are often found in hedgerows in the Midlands; September.

'Farleigh', sometimes known as 'Cluster' or 'Crittendens'; has small oval black fruit with greenish-yellow flesh which are excel-

'Prune Damson' makes a compact tree

lent for cooking; growth is compact and very fertile. It was found wild by Mr Crittenden of Farleigh, Kent; mid-September.

'Merryweather', one of the best cooking damsons, the quite large fruit is round and black, the flesh being firm and of the true damson flavour, a good cropper. This variety was introduced by Messrs Merryweather in 1907; September–October.

FIG *Ficus carica*

Most of us are familiar with those tightly packed boxes or blocks of dried fruit so much in demand at Christmas time. They come from the East, the fig being a native of Syria and surrounding countries.

Figs are not suitable for growing in the open ground in all parts of this country. Certainly, a few may be found growing fairly happily against sheltered south facing walls in the south or west, but they thrive best under glass.

Young plants in small pots are offered by nurserymen and although there is usually a choice of varieties 'Brown Turkey' is perhaps the most reliable, followed by 'Brunswick'. The former has brownish-red fruits with red flesh, and is very fertile, while 'Brunswick' ripens rather later, is larger, green in colour with white flesh. Both are vigorous and usually crop well. 'White Marseille' is an early large pear-shaped variety with pale green skin and sweet red fruit.

The end of March or during April are good times to move figs from their pots to the greenhouse border, or into bigger containers.

The greenhouse border should be well prepared and dug to a depth of 60 cm (2 ft) or so, working in plenty of drainage material such as brickbats, stones, mortar rubble, etc. A good loamy soil is suitable while the addition of really old decayed

Figs need care if they are to ripen

horse or stable manure is beneficial. Bone meal at the rate of 85–113 g per m² (3–4 oz per sq yd) well-worked into the compost will provide additional feeding material over a long period.

Fruit is produced on the new season's growth and if the plants are trained into a more-or-less fan shape they will yield well. The greatest amount of the best fruit is usually carried on the lower branches so that some growers encourage the branches to develop fairly near the ground, or to pull them into that position. With this system some kind of support with stakes or wire is necessary, but even with bush specimens, the branches can be trained to encourage them to grow horizontally.

Once established, the fruit begins to ripen toward the end of May and develops on the new shoots which are produced on the previous season's stems which were pruned back. Further fruit develops intermittently during the summer.

Pruning is important both to keep the trees in shape and to provide new fruit bearing shoots. Often, only very little cutting is necessary, this being done during July and August. Although good drainage is essential figs must have plenty of moisture throughout the growing season.

A moist atmosphere during the summer is advisable and can be ensured by frequent overhead sprayings of clear water, which at the same time, will deter red spider mites — which cause leaf bronzing and spoil the fruit. Occasional applications of liquid manure are helpful. The temperature is best kept at about 15°C (60°F) although naturally it will rise during spells of strong sunshine.

Outdoor figs can be grown against sunny walls. The best method of training is the fan system. This means spreading out the shoots and tying them in position. Never crowd the growths since only with sufficient room, sunlight and warmth, will a crop mature. Avoid rich heavy soils for these lead to rank leafy growth with little fruit. Firm, well-ripened wood is needed for crop bearing.

If the trees are to fruit well it is essential to restrict the root system. The bed should be dug out about 60 cm (2 ft) deep and the bottom of the hole filled with bricks or stone slabs. This will allow for drainage but prevent deep probing tap roots. It is essential to bear in mind that fruitfulness is dependent on a restricted root system.

The fig is unique in the way it fruits. A fruiting branch will usually carry quite large figs on its lower portion, and tiny embryo fruits no larger than peas at its apex. The latter are the crop for the next season.

To develop full flavour, figs must ripen on the trees, although there are several, if old fashioned, ways of inducing earlier ripening. One of these is to dip a needle in olive oil and push it into the eye of the fig.

Propagation is from cuttings in September, by layering low-placed shoots or detaching suckers in autumn.

In prolonged severe weather, protect figs by spreading straw around the base of the tree and over the branches. Branches damaged by frost should be cut out.

GOOSEBERRY *Ribes grossularia*

For centuries this fruit has been popular in British gardens. The bushes will grow in almost every kind of well-drained soil. Where possible, provide fairly deep soils with a good humus content that are unlikely to dry out in summer. Make sure the soil is not short of potash, for a deficiency leads to poor development and small leaves, which are scorched at the edges. The rooting system is widespread and near the surface, so do not cultivate deeply.

Planting can be carried out from the end of October until the end of March, the earlier the better. The site should be prepared in advance by deep digging and working in farmyard or other bulky manure; bonfire ash is a valuable extra. Never use quick acting fertilizers, for they will force growth and the soft lush foliage is liable to mildew.

Two or three-year-old bushes usually establish quickly. Spread the roots out well but do not plant deeply, for the bushes are best grown on a single stem or 'leg'. Deep planting results in unwanted shoots from below soil level. These make it difficult to clean the soil of weeds and pick fruit. Allow 1.50–1.80 m (5–6 ft) between the bushes or, if you are growing single cordons, space them about 45 cm (18 ins) apart. Espalier gooseberries will need to be 1–1.20 m (3–4 ft) apart and all trained specimens should be given a support at planting time.

Pruning should be carried out annually. Well-shaped, open headed bushes allow the sun to penetrate and ripen the wood as well as making it easy to pick the fruit. For the first few years, shorten the new growth by about a half. This will lead to the formation of strong branches which will be able to bear the weight of fruit the laterals produce. If the laterals are kept cut back to 5–8 cm (2–3

The popular gooseberry 'Leveller' has an excellent flavour

growers catalogued over a hundred varieties, many having been raised specially for exhibition for the large gooseberry shows that were then very popular. Today it would be difficult to find a dozen different sorts. While a good gooseberry has a distinct flavour, crops are sometimes gathered too early, before the flavour has fully developed. Unripe fruit is frequently offered in shops and markets.

VARIETIES: Of the yellow fruiting varieties, 'Leveller' is particularly good. Red varieties should be eaten for dessert at the right moment; 'Whinham's Industry' and 'Lancashire Lad' are delicious. Of the so-called white sorts, 'Whitesmith' is excellent. Green varieties include 'Lancer' and 'Careless'.

GRAPE VINE *Vitis vinifera*

There is plenty of evidence to show that grapes have been grown for centuries. They were greatly valued by the Israelites who esteemed them for their health promoting qualities. The Romans brought them to Britain and no doubt to other countries too. Good wine from them was once produced in several English regions including Gloucestershire, Worcestershire and East Anglia, and it is difficult to understand why production ceased. Happily, though, new and productive vineyards are being developed on a small scale in the south and west.

It may have been at least partly due to the dissolution of the monasteries, where the cultivation of vines was regularly practised, that their cultivation died out. Gradually it seems, the idea became widespread that grapes could be grown successfully only in heated greenhouses. Whatever the cause, the British seemed to have accepted the idea that grapes needed warm greenhouse culture. However, during the last thirty years there has been a remarkable revival in grape growing outdoors as well as under glass and many people have learned the skills of producing a good crop and making acceptable wine. It is largely due to the work of the Viticultural Research Station at Oxted, Surrey that so much more is now known about the successful growing of grapes outdoors.

Dealing first with glasshouse cultivation, ideally, the site should drain naturally and there should be a good depth of light chalky loam. Much can be done to provide congenial rooting conditions. Gardeners have

ins) from their base, they will make plenty of fruiting spurs. Cut right out all weak and badly placed shoots. Always prune to an outward pointing bud so that the centre of the bush remains open. Cordon, espalier and standard gooseberries must be pruned carefully to keep them to their particular shape.

Pruning can be done once the leaves have fallen. The exception to this is where birds, particularly bullfinches, are troublesome. Then it is best to wait until just before the buds begin to burst.

Although rarely practised commercially, summer pruning is beneficial. Do it from the end of June onwards, shortening all lateral growths to about five leaves. This leads to the formation of more fruiting spurs. Thin the clusters of fruit to get really large berries.

Propagation of gooseberries from cuttings

is simple, the best time being from October to December. Select strong, well ripened shoots about 30 cm (12 ins) long from the current season's growth. Remove all buds except the top four. This ensures that the developing bushes have a 'leg'. If shoots are pulled from the branches with a 'heel' of old wood, they will root very quickly. Having prepared the cuttings insert them 15 cm (6 ins) deep in a shallow, straight backed trench, lined at the base with sharp sand or clean grit. Firm the soil round them.

Once rooted, the cuttings are planted out and training started to develop good framework. Gooseberries are productive for many years if they are properly treated and mulched with manure or compost each spring.

More than a century ago specialist

'Black Hamburgh' is the best greenhouse grape for the amateur gardener

long planted their vines on an outside border and worked the rods through holes in the greenhouse wall to train them on wires in the usual manner inside the greenhouse.

When this is done drainage must be good for vines will not tolerate stagnant moisture round their roots. The one disadvantage in planting outside is that in very wet weather during the ripening period, the fruit may split.

When planting inside the greenhouse some gardeners make sure they have complete control of moisture by making a brick lined planting hole. This should be about 90 cm (3 ft) deep at the back sloping to 75 cm (2½ ft) at the front, in order to prevent waterlogged roots. Width of the site will depend on the size of the house, but should certainly not be less than 1.35 m (4½ ft). Rubble should be placed at the bottom of the hole before filling in with good rich loam, decayed manure and leaf mould plus a good sprinkling of bone meal.

Vines should be transplanted while dormant and it is advisable to buy pot grown plants. These need to be removed carefully from their pots so as not to damage the rods. Some gardeners believe in thoroughly disentangling the coiled up, often pot-bound, roots before planting. Spread the roots evenly, covering them with about 10 cm (4 ins) of soil and making it firm. Then give a thorough soaking of water which has had the chill taken off it.

If growing more than one vine at least 1.80 m (6 ft) should be allowed between the plants while individual rods should not be spaced closer than 90 cm (3 ft).

Vines are natural climbers having tendrils with which to grasp anything they can find for support. They are normally vigorous growers with many branches and leaves. Various methods of training are adopted when cultivating vines under glass and outdoors. If left untrained a vine will become untidy and unproductive. The training starts the first summer after planting. By then the rod and new growth will be supported by a cane, pushed into the soil about 15 cm (6 ins) deep. The top of the cane should reach just past the first horizontal strand of wire to which it is tied. Next a 2.70–3 m (9–10 ft) bamboo cane must be fixed to the top of the cane and wire supporting the vine, and to a wire along the roof. As growth proceeds the young leading shoot should be tied to this second cane as it grows towards the roof.

Keep rubbing out side shoots that grow from the leaf axils until the last leaf from the wire is reached. From this point allow the growths (laterals) to make two or three leaves before the shoots are pinched out.

Keep removing the tendrils for if left in they will grasp the wires, leaves and laterals and become a nuisance. As a result of stopping the laterals they too will almost certainly produce further shoots. These are known as sub-laterals and they in turn are pinched back to the first leaf. After the rod has been stopped, it is quite a good plan to allow some of the sub-laterals to develop. This not only helps strengthen the rod but keeps the roots active, supplying nourishment to the new growths.

Although pruning sometimes appears to be complicated, it is not at all difficult. The thickish lateral buds that form in the axil of each leaf should be cut off at the end of the first growing season. If growth has not been good and the rod seems unable to make real progress cut it back to within three strong buds from ground level. Such action will stimulate good growth the following year.

In subsequent years when the vine has reached its allotted space, each lateral is cut back to two, sometimes one strong bud from which sub-laterals develop the following season. This means that the fruiting spurs gradually lengthen as a result of cutting the laterals back regularly.

Top dressing the root area can do a lot of good. First very carefully remove the surface soil around the vine, taking care not to damage the shallow fibrous roots. Then, top dress with a mixture of three parts good loam and one part each rotted stable manure and bonfire ash, plus a good dusting of lime and bonemeal.

Where heat is available it is possible to start vines into growth towards the end of November. This is done only where grapes are wanted in April and May. Very often however, the vines are not started until early March. This means that fruit will be ready for gathering from August onwards. Early maturing grapes such as the popular 'Black Hamburgh' and 'Madresfield Court' can usually be cut within five months of being started, but the majority of varieties need six months to ripen their fruits.

Some greenhouse vines will not set heavy crops without being artificially pollinated – 'Muscat of Alexandria' is one of these. If

'Black Hamburgh' or 'Alicante' are grown in the same house as 'Muscat of Alexandria' it will be easy to go from flower to flower with a camel hair brush and distribute pollen to fertilize the flowers.

Once fruit has set the berries develop quickly and some thinning is necessary. No rod should be allowed to carry more than ten to twelve bunches, for overcropping can weaken the tree. Having retained the right number of bunches the next step is to thin out the berries. This is best done with specially pointed vine scissors. The shape of the bunches varies according to the variety being grown, some having much broader shoulders than others. Some varieties have very short fruit stalks which makes it difficult to thin the berries if the operation is delayed. With large bushes particularly, it is helpful to tie out the shoulders, especially if grapes are needed for exhibition. When thinning the bunches, avoid touching the berries with your hands.

As soon as the berries colour, increase ventilation without allowing draughts. One problem in giving more air is that birds may be tempted to attack the fruit. They can be stopped by covering the vents with perforated zinc which, incidentally, will keep out wasps. It is unwise to gather the bunches before the berries are mature for then the sugars have not completely changed and the berries are still acid.

RECOMMENDED VARIETIES:

'Alicante', freely produced, large oval black berries, good flavour.

'Black Hamburgh', probably the best known; large tender berries; sweetly flavoured.

'Madresfield Court', an early muscat, freely producing tender, juicy, rich flavoured berries.

'Mrs Pearson', the round whitish-amber berries turn pink when ripe.

'Muscat of Alexandria', inclined to be a shy setter, large oval berries, pale amber with a sweet, rich muscat flavour.

MEDLAR *Mespilus germanica*

Native to southern Europe, the medlar is widely distributed and can be found both wild and cultivated. At one time this tree was to be found in the gardens and grounds of large estates, the fruit being used in sauces and served with game.

The trees vary in size and appearance, probably influenced by the soil and climate.

Generally, the trunk is rough and on the short side. The spreading branches are irregular in shape, and wild specimens are furnished with thorns. The bark is nearly always an ash-grey colour. In early summer the tree bears large showy white blossoms.

The medlar is usually grafted on to quince stock, very suitable for fairly moist soils. Seed is another means of propagation, but it is about two years before seedlings appear. It is better for the grower to concentrate on grafted or budded trees.

Where large standard medlars with a good straight stem are required, seedling pear stocks are used.

Medlar fruits are more or less round with a slight depression at the top crowned by the sepals of the calyx, giving them a distinctive appearance. They are generally reddish-brown in colour and contain five hard, rather rugged kernels.

When the fruit ripens towards the end of the autumn, it is astringent. It is, therefore, advisable to allow them to remain on the trees, gathering them during November after they have been exposed to light frosts. They are ready for picking when their stalks part readily from the fruits. Gathered then and laid on straw or a rack in a dry frost proof place they become pleasant to eat after a few weeks, and have a somewhat vinous flavour.

The best way to store the fruits is to place them eye-end downwards. After two to four weeks they change from green through yellow to brown; the process is known as 'bletting'. They are then ready for use, and will remain so for several weeks. As well as being eaten raw, medlars may be made into jelly or sauce. To reduce the risk of fruit rotting in store, it is advisable to gather it when the weather is dry and sunny. Some growers have found that dipping the stalks in a solution of ordinary table salt, reduces

'Muscat of Alexandria', fine-flavoured grape, needs careful cultivation

or even prevents rotting.

The fruit borne by really old trees is usually small and flavourless, but the trees compensate for this by the showiness of their white or pink blooms.

Well-shaped specimens with an open, evenly branched head are produced by early training and pruning. Once this has been developed, subsequent treatment consists of removing dead wood and rubbing out badly placed shoots.

Medlars ready for picking

Medlars are not prone to any particular pests or diseases. Occasionally leaf eating weevils are troublesome in the spring, but they can be controlled by dusting or spraying with derris.

RECOMMENDED VARIETIES: 'Nottingham' has an upright habit. The fruit is on the small side, but is freely produced and when ripe has a rich sub-acid flavour.

'Royal' is also an upright grower, producing heavy crops of medium sized, good flavoured fruits.

'The Dutch', which is sometimes known as 'Monster', forms a decorative tree with large leaves. It has a semi-weeping habit and the large brownish fruits remain sound longer than other sorts, often keeping until after December.

MULBERRY *Morus nigra*

The black mulberry is an attractive tree. It is almost always grown as a standard as bushes are seldom satisfactory because of their spreading habit.

Mulberries like a good sandy loam, well-supplied with moisture, but never water-logged. They prefer an open sunny situation and the same conditions as for plums.

Mulberries are very juicy fruits

Although the tree may be small at planting time, and grows slowly at first, it will make a fine large specimen after a few years.

Prepare the soil deeply, working in well-rotted manure and compost, and a 113 g per m² (4 oz per sq yd) dressing of bone meal. Lime is not essential, although mulberries thrive when it is present. Planting time is from the middle of October until the end of March, the earlier the better. Where several trees are planted, allow up to 9 m (30 ft) between them. It is advisable to spread out the roots fully and not to cramp or damage them by putting them in holes which are too small. Cover the roots with about 13 cm (5 ins) of soil and stake the tree before refilling the planting hole with soil.

Initial pruning consists of shortening all leading growths by about a third, and cutting back the laterals to within a couple

of buds from the base. Because mulberries are somewhat slow in coming into bearing it is advisable to start with trees which are about five years old.

Once the main framework is formed, little further pruning is needed. This makes early training important and any later cutting should be done immediately after leaf fall. Mulberries are self-fertile and that is why isolated trees are often seen fruiting heavily. Fully established trees regularly bear heavy crops of sweet, raspberry-looking fruit.

Mulberries are among the latest trees to produce foliage in the spring, but they are certainly most showy in the summer, when most other trees are beginning to lose their attractiveness for the season. The fruit ripens over a period of weeks, and when it turns dark crimson during August and September, it is ready for harvest by laying a cloth beneath the tree and shaking the branches. Surplus berries may be bottled.

Mulberries may be propagated in various ways, the simplest being by layering. In this case, healthy young branches are selected and pegged into the ground in autumn. They should remain there until the following autumn, when they may be severed if they have made a good root system.

Take cuttings of young shoots in October. These should be about 20–45 cm (12–18 ins) long and prepared in the usual way. Insert them firmly 13–15 cm (5–6 ins) deep in sandy soil in a sheltered place. Grafting can be done in March, and consists of selecting suitable shoots from trees of good form, and 'working' them on to strong seedling mulberries.

Seed is another method of propagation, and it should be sown in gritty compost in March. Germination however, is often irregular and it could be some years before saleable trees are available.

The black mulberry *Morus nigra* is distinct from *Morus alba*, the white mulberry, which is grown for its leaves which are used for feeding silkworms.

PEACH *Prunus persica*

Of great antiquity, this fruit is said to have originated from China and to have come to this country by way of Persia, Greece and Italy. In records it is referred to variously as peske, peshe and peche. Its popularity has steadily increased in Britain and other European countries. In 1768 Thomas Hitt described twenty varieties of peaches and nectarines. In 1925 Edward Bunyard mentioned 50 distinct kinds of peach and 23 nectarines commonly grown in England.

Much credit for the development of peaches in England must go to Thomas Rivers of Sawbridgeworth, Herts, which is reputed to be the oldest fruit tree nursery in the country. Thos. Hogg, in his Fruit Manual (1875) mentions about 100 varieties of peach and 35 nectarines. Of these, 24 peaches and 13 nectarines were raised at Sawbridgeworth.

Peaches are sometimes spoiled by careless gathering. Edward Bunyard says, 'They should be neither pinched or pulled off but rather stroked off. A fond and delicate hand is applied and a gentle rotatory movement should suffice if they are ripe. A small basket should be their final mission'.

The culture of peaches and nectarines can be dealt with together as the nectarine is really a sport of the peach with a smooth skin and a rather less robust constitution. At one time it was thought that peaches could only be grown successfully in greenhouses or perhaps, against a sheltered wall in a warm district. Now however, they are cultivated in a similar way to plums and there are established peach orchards, usually of bushes, in various parts of the country.

Many growers depend on peaches grafted on to the Brompton plum stock, on which they make quite large bushes. Fruit is produced on spurs which develop as a result of shortening the stems. The Common Mussel stock is useful because it does not produce such large trees as Brompton although it is sometimes inclined to die back and to produce blind shoots.

Because of the peach's pithy wood, the stocks are usually budded rather than grafted. The experts use triple buds which consist of two fruit buds with a shoot bud between them.

When planting peaches dig holes large enough for the roots to be spread out evenly. The soil mark on the stem indicates the depth at which the tree was planted – do not exceed it. After working in some fine soil among the roots, fill the hole very firmly, finally raking the surface level to a tilth.

The best time to plant is November, although the trees can also be moved in March. Two or three-year old trees transplant best. Fan-shaped specimens are useful for growing against a wall. If several are being planted allow up to 5 m (15 ft) between them, spacing them 15 cm (6 ins) from the wall. Any broken or bruised roots should be pared clean.

When buying a peach bush get a tree with an open centre and well-thinned sides. Fruit is produced on the previous seasons shortish wood growth. If any bush shows signs of producing an extra heavy crop, the fruits should be thinned to 10–15 cm (4–6 ins) apart.

Outdoor peaches A few years ago, it was considered a waste of time to grow peaches

Choose a sunny sheltered spot for growing peaches

outdoors in this country. Since the last War however, it has been proved that this crop can in many districts be brought to maturity without difficulty.

Because peaches are exotic fruits, many amateurs are reluctant to grow them, believing that expert knowledge is vital for success. The excellent results obtained by one or two specialist firms which have cultivated bush peaches on a fairly large scale, have not only created much more interest in this fruit, but many gardeners are actually planting peaches, not only as wall trees, but are growing them in bush form with good success. Peaches will grow successfully in similar positions to 'Victoria' plums, producing first-class crops.

A problem which often presents itself to amateur gardeners is how to prune the bushes or train trees. The framework of a

well-shaped tree will have been developed by the grower, skilled in the knifework necessary, during the first two or three years.

For bushes, a stem of 8–12 cm (20–30 ins) should be left clear of branches, the 'feathers' (side shoots) being cut so as to produce a good open head. If for three years the young branches are cut back annually to half their length, a proper framework will be formed, and from this, branches producing the fruiting shoots will develop.

Peaches are very free croppers, and many gardeners are inclined to let heavy crops mature on very young trees, which are then liable to become stunted and badly shaped. Trees under three years should not be allowed to carry fruit. One is sometimes confronted with trees making extremely strong fruitful growth. This calls for corrective treatment. Pinch out branch tips in June to induce the production of fruiting laterals, and remove new unwanted growth at an early stage.

When bushes of fruiting age bear very heavily, some thinning is necessary. Do this when the fruitlets are quite small, say about the size of marbles; some fruitlets fall naturally, too. Once the stoning process is complete, a good liquid fertilizer is beneficial.

Mulching is invaluable, and a thick layer

119

of peat, leaf mould, or compost, applied after watering and feeding, will check rapid loss of soil moisture, which can be most harmful to the developing fruit. Avoid deep cultivation as suckering will often follow root injury.

Peaches flower early when it is often cold and windy, and pollination can be poor through the absence of bees and other insects. It is, therefore, a good plan to hand pollinate. This can be done about mid-day when the blooms are open, using a camel hair brush to transfer ripe pollen on to the female stigmas.

RECOMMENDED VARIETIES: *Peach*: 'Barrington', mid-September, large, greenish yellow with crimson stripes, pale yellow flesh, rich and good.

'Bellegarde', mid-September, large very dark crimson fruit, flesh pale yellow and a rich flavour.

'Duke of York', mid-July, large brilliant crimson with tender melting flesh; a reliable variety which bears well.

'Hale's Early', end July, medium-sized crimson with pale yellow tender flesh, excellent for outdoor and indoor culture.

'Peregrine', early August, large fruit with brilliant crimson skin and melting juicy flesh.

'Rochester', mid-August, good sized fruit of high quality; hardy and prolific. The best choice for growing outdoors in bush form.

'Royal George', early September, large, pale yellow skin with red cheek, flesh pale yellow, sweet and rich, first class under glass and excellent outdoors.

Nectarine: 'Early Rivers', late July, large crimson on light yellow ground; the greenish white flesh has a rich flavour; a heavy cropper, it is suitable for outdoor or under glass.

'Elruge', late August, of medium size, the greenish white skin is flushed deep red, the flavour good; this very old sort does well under varying conditions.

'Victoria', delicious late variety.

PEARS *Pyrus communis*

Pears are a little more difficult than apples and if neglected, deteriorate more quickly but they repay good cultivation. Many varieties are self-sterile, so it is necessary to grow two or more different varieties for pollinating purposes – not always easy in a small garden.

Pears are not simply sweet. Edward

Bunyard said 'the pear flavour must stand as a basis upon which may be laid the various overtones of flavour and acidity. Acid gives pears a zest and raises them to a higher plane. The next addition is musk . . . it requires great discretion in its disposal. Some pears seem to have an almond flavour, others a vinous quality while in some, it is possible to detect a perfume not unlike that of the rose or of honey.'

'If', says Bunyard, 'the duty of an apple is to be crisp and crunchable, a pear should have such a texture as leads to silent consumption.'

Soil plays a great part in determining whether or not pears are going to be successful. Very light ground is unsuitable, and it is not worthwhile growing pears on thin soil that retains little moisture. Good medium or heavyish soil is best, so long as it has been deeply cultivated and contains plenty of organic matter.

Generally speaking, pears need more nitrogen than apples and perhaps less potash. Top dressings of compost or decayed manure are beneficial, while in the spring, 85–113 g per m² (2½–3 oz per sq yd) of sulphate of ammonia stimulates sturdy growth. Pears usually bloom fairly early so avoid planting in exposed areas and low lying frost pockets.

Select varieties carefully. Comparatively few pears are self-fertile and two or more suitable varieties must be grown to ensure cross pollination and a good fruit set.

Pears can be planted in mild weather throughout the dormant season, although November is the best month. Having made sure that the soil has been well prepared by

Below: A heavy crop of nectarines

deep digging and manuring, dig out a hole about 20 cm (8 ins) deep and wide enough for the roots to be spread out fully. Trim back any damaged roots with a sharp knife or secateurs.

Stake standards or half standards before the planting hole is filled in to avoid damaging the roots. Plant the young tree to the depth marked on the stem by the soil in which it was raised in the nursery. Sprinkle a layer of soil over the roots and tread it down firmly, for good anchorage is important. The soil around the stem must be trodden down fairly frequently during the winter, since frost is liable to loosen the roots.

If you have ordered trees from a distance and they arrive and cannot be planted immediately, they will be alright in their bundle for a few days. If the trees cannot be planted for several weeks, unpack them and heel them in, in a trench in a sheltered part of the garden.

Pruning is as important for pears as for other fruit trees. Excepting for a few tip bearers (those which fruit at the tips of the shoots) such as 'Jargonelle', 'Josephine de Malines' and 'Packham's Triumph', pears on quince root stocks produce plenty of fruit spurs and are pruned normally. The strongest growing sorts such as 'Beurré Hardy', 'Bristol Cross' and 'Doyenné du Comice', are pruned more lightly for very hard pruning usually results in excessively vigorous growth.

Remove dead, crowded or badly placed branches from all trees. If standards produce extra long, upright branches, they should be shortened to a suitable length.

Prune hard the leaders of young trained trees during the winter for the first few years, to build up a sturdy framework. Some summer pruning may also be necessary according to growth made. This usually consists of pruning the side shoots to four leaves and to one leaf in the winter. Generally pruning for pears is the same as that described for apples on page 130.

Although there is usually a natural fall of fruit (the June drop), some thinning is advisable if there are signs of a very heavy crop developing. This will prevent many small second quality fruits.

Having grown and harvested the fruit it is disappointing to discover that the flesh is dry and mealy (sleepy) instead of rich and juicy. Externally, the pears look perfectly sound, but it is a different matter when you cut them open.

The trouble in many cases is related to the

Above: 'Doyenné du Comice' is the finest flavoured pear
Below: The best-known variety of pear is 'Conference'

time of gathering the fruit. This seems especially so with late keepers such as 'Winter Nelis' and 'Glou Morceau'. If gathered too soon, and especially if stored under very dry conditions, they are liable to become 'sleepy' before they are edible. Similarly, if 'Pitmaston Duchess' and 'William's Bon Chrétien', are harvested a little too early, perhaps to avoid wasp damage, they may quickly become over-ripe and then sleepy, all within a few days. So rapidly can pears ripen that fruits should be examined every few days. It is often difficult to tell when a pear is ripe. Many varieties are more or less covered with russet markings, so appearances do not always help. A good plan is to cut one or two fruits at short intervals when they are beginning to ripen. This will show up any tendency to sleepiness.

RECOMMENDED VARIETIES: Many of the older varieties are no longer grown but the following is a list, given in order of maturing dates, of first class pears which are still available from fruit specialists:

'Clapp's Favourite', early September, medium-sized, thin smooth skin, pale yellow with bright scarlet flush, very fertile.

'William's Bon Chrétien', September, golden-yellow, russet dots, red stripes; fairly large, excellent flavour, juicy and sweet; good for bottling or canning. Known in the USA and Australia as 'Bartlett'.

'Beurré Hardy', October, large, very fertile and good flavour.

'Louise Bonne of Jersey', October, medium, yellowish-green, red flush, red dots, sweet and delicious. Cross-pollinates with 'Conference' and 'Williams' Bon Chrétien'.

'Emile D'Heyst', October–November, medium, pale yellow, marbled russet, sub-acid, pleasantly perfumed.

'Durondeau', October–November, fairly large, long pyramidal, skin rough, golden-yellow, very fertile. Good for small gardens.

'Conference', October–November, large, long, pear-shaped, very juicy, good for bottling, or canning; sweet, regular bearer, the best mid-season to late variety.

'Beurré Superfin', medium-sized fruits, yellow with russet patches, juicy and sweet, deliciously aromatic.

'Pitmaston Duchess', October–November, very large, yellow marbled russet, very juicy and pleasantly flavoured. Plant with 'Conference'.

'Packham's Triumph', November, medium-sized, greenish-yellow, pleasant flavour sweet, very juicy.

121

'Doyenné du Comice', November, large, pale yellow with fine russet, the best flavoured pear, crop is improved with 'Conference', 'Glou Morceau' and 'Williams'' as pollinators.

'Winter Nelis', November–January, small, rich melting flavour, good cropper.

'Glou Morceau', December–January, smooth pea green skin ripening to pale yellow, good flavour, planted as the most reliable pollinator of 'Doyenné du Comice'.

'Catillac', in season until April, the best culinary pear; large, cooks deep red, no other stewing pear is necessary.

PLUM *Prunus domestica*

Properly grown, plums are among the choicest of fruit for dessert and cooking. They like a reasonably heavy soil with good drainage. It is often thought that all stone fruits need lime but while the soil should not be acid, too much lime or chalk can be harmful. This is apparent in some districts when the foliage turns whitish yellow. The vigour and cropping capacity deteriorates because the trees are unable to obtain enough iron from the soil. Highly alkaline conditions make the iron unavailable to the plant roots. If the soil pH is 8, then lime-induced chlorosis is likely to occur and this, unfortunately, may not be evident until the trees have been planted for three or four years.

It is a good plan to mulch the soil around the trees with sedge peat or leaf mould, but whatever is used, it helps to smother annual weeds; and worms pull some of the organic matter into the soil. When it is decided to enrich the soil, decayed farmyard or cow manure can be used as a mulch, or if these are not available, hoof and horn meal at 85 g per m² (2½ oz per sq yd) can be used. If there are signs of leaf scorch indicating potash deficiency, it can usually be cured by top dressing with wood ash at the rate of 113 g per m² (3½ oz per sq yd), or 34 g per m² (1 oz per sq yd) of sulphate of potash. Avoid situations exposed to high winds and severe frost. Gusty wind can easily break fruit-laden branches.

Whether bush, standard or trained specimens are planted, they move most easily when two or three years old, when they do not have a very large root system, and soon become established after planting. Plant as soon as possible after November, while the ground is comparatively warm. Always stake half and full standards at planting time.

Firmly tied to the supports, the trees will not rock in windy weather and soon produce new fibrous roots. The top of the stake should come just below the crotch, where the branches start. So often the lower branches become chafed by rubbing on ill-placed stakes. Sometimes it is necessary to support heavily laden branches otherwise they break off. Plum wood is brittle and when loaded, branches split easily if not supported.

Many plums produce sucker growths from the base. These should be removed as soon as seen, by tracing them back to their source, and pulling them off the roots from which they arise. If cut off, fresh suckers replace them.

'Czar' is a good cooking plum

Although the temptation is to plant closely, one should remember that bushes and trees make considerable growth over a period of years. Bush plums should not be planted closer than 4–4.6 m (13–15 ft), half standards up to 5 m (16 ft) apart, with full standards about 6 m (20 ft) apart. Fan trained specimens used against walls and fences will need a distance of 5–5.5 m (16–18 ft) between them.

Bush plums yield freely if treated properly. For preference, a bush should have an open centre with low spreading branches. This can be obtained by simple light pruning, the idea being to remove all shoots growing towards the centre and any which cross or die out. It is not essential to tip the shoots for even if the upright leaders are not cut, the weight of the fruit usually brings these branches down to maintain the correct, open shape.

Fruit thinning is necessary, not only to

Still the queen of plums – 'Victoria'

reduce heavy, indifferent crops but to check biennial bearing, a tendency to which many varieties are prone. Before doing so, wait until it is certain that all the fruit will develop, for usually quite a lot falls naturally.

Since it ripens at different times all the fruit cannot be picked at one time. If it is gathered too early the full flavour will not have developed. Do not harvest fruit when it is wet or it will soon become mildewed. All decaying and imperfect specimens should be gathered and destroyed.

RECOMMENDED VARIETIES: Of the many plums in cultivation today the following are the most reliable for general garden culture:

'Cambridge Gage', early September, a

sport from the old Greengage, but a better cropper; partially self-fertile.

'Coe's Golden Drop', end September, oval golden-yellow, dotted red, good flavour, excellent on walls.

'Comte d'Althann's Gage', mid-September, roundish, rich purple, with firm, well flavoured flesh; a good cropper.

'Czar', early August, roundish, almost black, a heavy cropper, greatly used for market, an excellent cooking variety, self-fertile.

'Denniston's Superb', mid-August, round greenish yellow fruit, excellent flavour.

'Early Laxton', early August, smallish yellow fruit, with red flush, sweet and juicy, a reliable cropper, useful for cooking.

'Giant Prune', end September, large, long and oval, dark red, of vigorous growth and a

good cropper; a fine culinary variety.

'Green Gage', (also known as 'Reine Claude') early September, of medium size, leaf-green with a white bloom, the flesh is also green and most deliciously flavoured; well-known and much grown; fine as a standard or for growing on walls.

'Jefferson's Gage', early September, large, oval golden-yellow, with reddish spots, a fine reliable variety.

'Kirke's Blue', mid-September, medium-sized round, very dark purple, golden flesh of rich flavour, sometimes a shy bearer.

'Marjorie's Seedling', late September, blue-black fruits with yellow flesh. One of the best late varieties.

'Myrobalan', late July, the 'Cherry Plum',

Delicious fruits of the 'Green Gage'

both the red and yellow varieties are excellent for cooking and bottling; sometimes known as 'Roblets'; a self-fertile variety.

'Old Transparent Gage', early September, yellowish-green, red spots, sweet and juicy; good for pot culture.

'Oullins' Golden Gage', early August, large pale yellow firm sweet flesh, a good grower and useful for dessert and bottling.

'Pershore Yellow', August, medium-sized, oval yellow fruit; good cooker, first class for jam.

'Rivers Early Prolific', end of July, a roundish, deep purple fruit with yellowish brisk flesh; although really a cooking plum it is fit for dessert when ripe; partially self-fertile; plant with a pollinator such as 'Jefferson's' or 'Cambridge Gage'.

'Victoria', late August, the surest cropping and most reliable all-round variety; large oval pinkish-red fruit, the yellow flesh is firm

and of excellent flavour.

Although a number of plums will fruit freely on their own, many crop more heavily if a pollinator is growing nearby. The following are examples of how to ensure heavy crops.

Variety	Pollinators
'Cambridge Gage'	'Pershore Yellow'
	'Victoria'
'Coe's Golden Drop'	'Denniston's Superb'
	'Early Laxton'
'Czar'	'Marjorie's Seedling'
	'Pershore Yellow'
'Marjorie's Seedling'	'Cambridge Gage'
	'Czar'
'Oullin's Golden Gage'	'Czar'
	'Marjorie's Seedling'
'Pershore Yellow'	'Czar'
	'Kirke's'
'Rivers Early Prolific'	'Denniston's Superb'
	'Early Laxton'
'Victoria'	'Marjorie's Seedling'
	'Rivers Early Prolific'

'Coe's Golden Drop', 'Jefferson's Gage', 'Kirke's Blue' and 'Victoria' often fruit quite well on their own.

QUINCE *Cydonia oblonga*

This old fashioned fruit is seldom grown as much as it used to be. It delights in damp soil but also does quite well in dryish positions. Quince is often grown as a root-stock for pears.

Apart from its fruit it is beautiful when in flower and enhances the shrubbery. It is also handsome as a specimen tree on the lawn, growing to about 4·5–6·5 m (15–20 ft). When it is grown principally for its fruit, it is advisable to thin the branches. Quinces make extremely good jelly, and when cooked with apples the highly scented fruit imparts a pleasing flavour. One quince to twelve apples is about the right quantity.

RECOMMENDED VARIETIES:

'Bereczeki', a remarkable Serbian quince of great size; once established, it fruits heavily and even two- or three-year-old trees carry reasonable crops; vigorous; the fruit is pear-shaped and particularly tender when cooked.

'Champion' is a splendid greenish-yellow, pear-shaped variety.

'Portugal' produces large yellow downy pear-shaped fruits which turn red when

Devote some garden space to the rewarding quince

cooked; not as prolific as other varieties, it is a strong grower and is said to have been introduced to Britain as long ago as 1611.

'Vranja' is almost identical with 'Bereczeki'.

RASPBERRY *Rubus idaeus*

Although raspberries are not really fussy about their growing conditions they give best results in a fairly rich medium-heavy soil containing plenty of humus. This encourages the development of many fibrous roots and strong canes which carry heavy crops of fruit.

Newly planted canes should be cut down to a bud 20–25 cm (8–10 ins) above soil level in early April. The remaining buds will produce a few fruiting shoots but the effect of hard pruning is to induce one or two stout canes for cropping the following season.

Newly planted rows should be mulched with compost or well-rotted manure against spring droughts.

Very light ground, unless generously manured before planting and mulched annually, produces only poor crops. On such soils there is often a lack of potash which shows itself in the scorched edges of the leaves. This shortage can be remedied by dressings of a good organic fertilizer while bonfire ash placed along the rows and lightly pricked in is helpful. Sulphate of potash is sometimes sprinkled along the sides of the rows but not on the crowns of the canes.

Sites are important and if possible, the rows should run north to south. An open, sunny but not exposed position is best. Avoid frost pockets and other low lying areas, otherwise some of the flowers may be damaged and crop will be light. Clear the ground of weeds before planting. If not it will be very difficult to get rid of tenacious weeds such as bindweed, couch grass and convolvulus.

Plant from October onwards. Autumn planting is best since by the early spring the basal shoots are developing and are easily broken off. Even so, many gardeners do plant successfully up until April.

Space rows from 1.2–1.50 m (4–5 ft) apart and allow from 38–60 cm (15–24 ins) between the canes. It is immaterial whether one permits the clumps to grow into each other or keeps them separate. Plant firmly, and no deeper than the soil mark on the stems. Fruit should not be picked the first year, but strong suckers from below ground will bear fruit the following season.

Some means of support is necessary to prevent the canes from snapping in the wind and make it easy to gather the fruit.

The simplest method is to erect posts at each end of the rows running two strands of wire between them, the lowest being about 45 cm (18 ins) from the ground, the second strand being 1.50 m (5 ft) from the ground. If the canes are not very strong use more wires and space them about 30 cm (12 ins) apart.

Once picking has finished, cut out all fruited canes, tying in the new canes to replace them. Allow four or five new canes to each stool, removing all others, particularly those that are weak or small. Always keep the crop well picked, for over-ripe fruit left on the canes is liable to attract mildew and other fungus disorders.

RECOMMENDED VARIETIES: Although many varieties have been grown, not all have stayed the course, but the following are available and are reliable in every way:

'Baumforth's Seedling', sweet berries.

'Deutschland', dark red, delicious flavour.

'Lloyd George', heavy cropping, rich red well-flavoured berries.

There are a number of excellent varieties

'Glen Clova' raspberries ripen early

raised at the East Malling Research Station; these include 'Malling Promise', 'Malling Jewel' and 'Malling Exploit'.

Among the autumn fruiting sorts, 'Lloyd George' must be included, for it frequently goes on bearing until October or later; others are 'Hailsham' an excellent variety with large dark red fruit.

'November Abundance', medium sized, dark red sweet and juicy fruits.

'September' is a firm red variety.

'Glen Clova' is a fairly new early ripening variety cropping over a long period; of

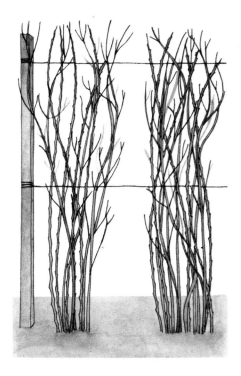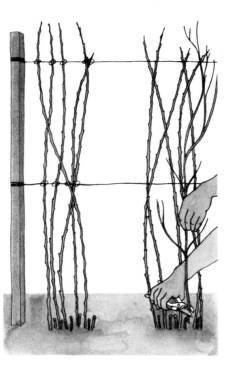

Above: Training and pruning raspberry canes. Below: Ripe fruits.

excellent flavour, it is valued for dessert, jam, bottling and freezing.

Of the yellow raspberries 'Antwerp', although introduced well over a century ago is still very good and in fair demand; it is a firm grower, freely producing large, roundish sweet berries.

There are also a few autumn fruiting yellow sorts:

'Exeter Yellow' produces a good crop of very sweet rich coloured fruit.

'Lord Lambourne' is a splendid sort, rather like 'Lloyd George' excepting colour;

'Fallgold' is a new golden-yellow raspberry bearing a heavy crop of large sweet berries over a long period.

'Zeva' is known as the perpetual fruiting raspberry. Of Swiss origin, it fruits on young canes from July until November; the berries are large and of superb flavour.

STRAWBERRY *Fragaria* x *ananassa*

The delicious strawberry, colourful herald of summer, is probably the most popular of the soft fruits. Whether new plants, or runners taken earlier from one's own healthy plants are used for new plantings, it is never advisable to replant an old strawberry bed. Ideally, change the site every three years, to prevent a build up of pests and diseases. The soil can get 'tired' of strawberries and should be well cultivated before being used for them again.

A fertile, sandy soil is probably most suitable, but success can be obtained in almost any soil, although really heavy land should be drained. It is a good plan, after autumn cultivation, to dig lightly between the rows and place the soil towards the plants, leaving a shallow furrow between the rows, to drain off surplus water.

Select a site which has been recently cultivated and well manured for a previous crop such as early potatoes. Alternatively, deeply dig and manure a patch of ground. If wireworms are present, scatter BHC powder over the soil before planting.

Since deep cultivation will not be possible once the bed is planted, preparation should be thorough and the soil may be further enriched with a 113 g per m^2 ($3\frac{1}{2}$ oz per sq yd) dressing of bone meal. The phosphates this will supply are probably more important than any other ingredient.

Autumn planting should be carried out when the soil is in good condition from September onwards. From an early planting one can allow a fair crop to develop the

125

following summer.

Pot grown runners will be easy to plant with a trowel, but with open ground runners care must be taken to plant firmly. A good method is to plant with a dibber and to press the soil firmly round the roots to remove any harmful air pockets.

The crown of the plant should be kept at soil level; deep planting is as undesirable as shallow planting. Frequently, early frosts lift the plants above soil level and they should be refirmed immediately, or growth may be checked.

Deep cultivation at any time of the year should be avoided for the roots may be damaged. Build up the plant's strength by working a 113 g per m² (3½ oz per sq yd) dressing of bone meal or other phosphatic organic manure into the soil as soon as fruiting is over.

All decayed and drying leaves and runners should be removed, except when the runners are required for propagation. When hoeing, draw the soil lightly towards the plants. This will act as a dust mulch during hot summer days and help to feed the new roots which, each autumn, grow above the previous set.

Many growers propagate their own plants. Where this is done, ensure that runners are taken from strong healthy plants, free from virus diseases, eelworm or aphis. Soon after the stolons (runners) appear, they will produce a cluster of roots at each leaf joint. Peg down the first and strongest plantlet on each runner, cutting back the rest. When well rooted, the plantlets are severed from the parents and moved to their permanent places. If the plantlets are pegged into small pots of rich compost sunk rim-level in the soil, they will crop more readily the first year after planting.

Strawberries can be grown successfully in the greenhouse or the garden frame and will give an earlier crop of really clean fruit than can be obtained from the open ground. Plants for forcing should come from strong runners rooted early directly into pots plunged into the soil. These young plants must be kept well supplied with moisture. They can be severed from the parent plant as soon as it is obvious they are well rooted.

When this has been done move them to a shady spot. Keep them fresh with overhead syringings of water during the evenings in warm weather. After two or three weeks remove them to larger, well drained pots of John Innes No 3 potting mixture. Pot firmly, but avoid burying the crowns. Keep the plants in a shady position for a week or two. Then transfer them to the cold frame, standing them on weathered ashes or similar material exposing them to full sun. Continue watering as necessary and give feeds of liquid manure until the end of September. Do not cover the plants with the frame lights for they must be grown so that they are quite hardy. In late October, lay the pots on their sides with the crowns facing the light. Alternatively, lay the pots on their sides at the base of a north wall, but in either case once severe weather arrives place straw or bracken over the pots to prevent frost damage. And with plants in frames, put the lights on during very wet weather. Frost will not injure the plants. In fact, after frost they will be better for forcing.

Strawberry barrels need little space

About the middle of January the first batch of plants can be taken into the cool greenhouse, warmth being gradually increased as growth develops. Keep the plants on a shelf in full light and take off any early runners so that the plant's strength goes into flower and fruit production. Ventilate freely to avoid mildew and other diseases. Make sure the roots are nicely moist.

Apart from these standard methods of cultivation strawberries may be grown in barrels and by the verti-strawb system.

Strawberries in barrels. Growing strawberries in barrels provides an interesting and often profitable means of obtaining fruit, being particularly valuable where space is restricted or where there is no garden at all. It also gives less active gardeners the pleasure of growing plants with the minimum attention, while weed and pest control is easy. They can easily be covered with netting to prevent birds spoiling the fruit.

First obtain a large barrel. One made of oak, chestnut or similar hard wood will usually last for years. Avoid those which have been creosoted or have contained substances harmful to plant life. Drill the barrel with holes 5–6 cm (2–2½ ins) in diameter, staggering them 22 cm (9 ins) apart.

The barrels can be painted any colour and be used as a feature. To render the barrels weatherproof for a long period, two undercoats of paint are recommended before the final hard gloss colour is applied.

Stand the barrel on bricks, so that water can run away through drainage holes in the bottom. Place a 15 cm (6 in) layer of stones at the base, for drainage. Then fill in with a soil mixture of three parts loam, one part good leaf mould, half part each granulated or similar peat and sharp sand, mixing in about 680 g (1½ lbs) of bone meal, 450 g (1 lb) hoof and horn meal and 450 g (1 lb) of wood ash to each barrel of compost, thoroughly mixing all in a semi-dry state. These organic fertilizers will release their food gradually over a long period.

Ideally, place a column of rubble down the centre of the barrel for extra drainage. A way to do this is to insert a drain pipe, fill it with rubble and pull it out when the barrel is filled with soil.

Planting: Work in the soil firmly and as each hole is reached, insert the plant's roots from the outside, spread them out, and make sure that the growing point is left exposed. Work in fine compost around the roots, taking care not to damage the plants when doing so. Continue to fill the barrel with soil and plants, until each hole is planted. Then the surface of the barrel can be planted.

Little further attention is necessary apart from ensuring that the central drainage duct is kept well supplied with water and occasional doses of liquid manure to help the plants along.

Strawberries particularly suited to growing in barrels include 'Royal Sovereign' and 'Cambridge Favourite', and perpetuals such as 'St Fiacre' and 'Baron Solemacher'. All can be planted from August until November and should yield the following year. Large sized barrels will hold 28 plants and the medium sized, 18, allowing for some on the top of the barrel. White stacking plastic pots are now available which are very useful for this type of growing system.

The Verti-strawb system of culture The Verti-strawb system has been evolved to satisfy the need to obtain maximum crops from limited greenhouse space.

Although the name of the variety used for the first experiments has never been divulged, there seems to be no reason why 'Royal Sovereign', 'Cambridge Favourite' and similar varieties should not be used. Originally strong medium-sized runners, probably from cold storage, were used. In the early part of July, polythene tubing 10 cm (4 ins) in diameter and up to 6.50 m (21 ft) long is filled with suitable compost. This is placed or fixed on raised horizontal supports up to 3.20 m (10½ ft) high.

while for those who have or can make the right conditions.

It has been claimed that the verti-strawb system returns up to 1.4 kg (3 lbs) of fruit per plant, compared with 340 g (¾ lb) from conventionally grown plants. The fruit will be clean, free from weather, bird and slug damage. Verti-strawb plants can also be grown in a sun lounge or on a sheltered patio.

RECOMMENDED VARIETIES:

'Royal Sovereign' has for long been the most popular of garden strawberries, its large scarlet fruit possessing a rich delicious flavour and scent; a medium cropper, some-

'Domanil' also heavy cropping, mid-season.

'Tamella' produces attractive looking berries of good flavour, excellent for dessert, freezing, bottling and jam.

'Grandee' is a vigorous grower with exceptionally large fruit.

Alpine strawberry Although alpine strawberries are much smaller than the standard varieties they are well worth cultivating. They will grow in partially shaded places, specially if the soil contains plenty of compost, peat or other humus-forming matter. They are splendid for edgings and should be spaced 30 cm (12 ins) apart with 45 cm (18

Ripe berries of the variety 'Tamella', protected by straw

Holes are punched in the tubes with a suitable iron 15 cm (6 ins) apart and the rooted strawberry runners planted through them. Feeding and constant but controlled watering is carried out for up to eight weeks, when the autumn crop is ready for picking.

After a rest period, the plants are started into growth again in early January. Warmth, water and feeding will lead to the production of flower trusses in late February. Fruit will be ready for picking in April, the crop continuing for months so that with the July and January plantings, fruit should be available over a very long period. Some of the earliest fruits may not be of perfect shape but quality and flavour is unaffected. This is a novel if rather expensive way of producing strawberries but well worth-

times spoiled by botrytis, susceptible to virus and best grown under really healthy clean conditions.

'Cambridge Favourite' is a widely grown mid-season variety of moderate flavour; a heavy cropper, resistant to disease and suitable for preserving and freezing.

'Cambridge Vigour' is a second early variety bearing medium sized fruit of good flavour.

'Cambridge Premier', an early large fruiting sort is useful for cloche culture.

'Cambridge Rival', good early variety.

'Red Gauntlet' is another vigorous heavy cropping variety.

'Talisman' is quite widely grown.

'Merton Dawn' is a heavy cropping mid-season variety.

ins) between the rows. The fruit is borne on erect stems clear of the ground and is less often attacked by birds.

If the first flush of flowers is picked off, the plants will crop heavily from August to October, a time when the larger strawberries have finished.

Propagation is from seed sown in trays of John Innes seed compost or a similar mixture in spring, or the plants can be divided after flowering, making sure that each offset is healthy with one or two strong buds.

Varieties not producing runners include 'Baron Solemacher', which is the best known variety, and crops heavily over a long period; the smallish dark red fruits have a buttery texture; there is also a white form.

'Red Alpine Improved' is said by some gardeners to be better than 'Baron Solemacher'.

Remontant or perpetual varieties which bear large fruits from September onwards include:

'Hampshire Maid', excellent for dessert and jam.

'Red Rich', strong growing with dark red berries.

'Sans Rivale', vigorous, heavy cropping, often continuing until late November.

'St Claude', sweet, juicy and disease resistant.

Propagating strawberries from runners

Climbing strawberries At one time quite a lot was heard of the so-called climbing strawberries. This is really a misnomer since there are no actual climbing varieties for none have tendrils. One or two of the remontant sorts produce long stolons on which develop a number of little plants. If these stolons are trained upright they can be used to cover low walls, fences, lattice work or similar supports. The top growth will die down in late autumn.

NUTS

As nuts growing wild in the hedgerows become less common, it is a good idea to find some space for a nut tree in the garden.

WALNUT *Juglans regia*

Apart from their elegant appearance and the crops they bear, walnut trees are of value for the timber they produce. It is not essential to grow them as full standards and some nurserymen offer half standards. A large number of walnuts are eaten in this country.

The Romans are said to have known the walnuts as the Nut of Jove or Jupiter from which comes Jooglans, or Juglans, a nut superior to others and fit for the gods. When its cultivation extended to France it became known as the Gaul Nut, corrupted into Walnut by the British.

Once established, walnuts need a good deal of space and are rather erratic croppers. The majority of nuts in England today are grown in woodland conditions, and there is a large nuttery in Gloucestershire, and two or three smaller plantations in Kent.

They will grow in almost any soil provided it is well-drained with a fair lime content. Avoid low-lying ground and frost pockets. November until the end of March are the best months for planting. The ground should be prepared as for other fruit trees. Never allow the roots to dry out, for failure to protect them is a main cause of trees failing to become established. Trim clean any roots damaged at lifting time.

Plant firmly, keeping the graft union just above ground and provide standards with a stout support. Wire netting round the stem will protect the bark from grazing animals or rabbits.

A mulching of compost after planting will prevent the soil from drying out in the spring and summer. Subsequently, it will be helpful if a dressing of bone or meat meal is scattered round the trees at the rate of 56 g per m² (2 oz per sq yd) each spring.

If the trees are grown in grassland, keep the grass well away from the trunks until the trees are really established, when the turf can be allowed to grow right up to the stem.

Walnuts are usually sold as standards or half standards with at least a partially formed head. Trees with laterals (side shoots) on their stems are best, as these encourage the stem to thicken. This avoids the possibility of a large bushy head on a thin trunk. These laterals, or feathered side shoots, should be kept from growing too large or they will compete with the head.

In the second winter's pruning, the shape of the head is determined. This is done by selecting four or five well-placed shoots and cutting them back so that they are 20–23 cm (8–9 ins) long. Cut to an outward or downward bud, so that the resultant growth does not point towards the centre. Remove entirely any vertical shoots to avoid trouble later. Subsequently, until the head is fully developed, cut out badly placed shoots and shorten any that are excessively long.

The feathers on the stem will of course also be removed when the head has formed. Any large scars can be treated with a proprietary protective paint to keep out disease. Never leave snags and keep the trees well supported until they are twelve to fifteen years old and capable of resisting strong winds and storms.

All pruning should be done before the

Walnuts at the immature stage

end of January, otherwise the trees are liable to 'bleed' when cut.

Walnuts bear male and female flowers on one-year shoots on the same tree. The pollen comes from the catkins and the reason why some trees do not fruit well is that the pollen is shed before the sticky stigmas of the female flowers are ready to receive it. There is, therefore, an advantage in having more than one walnut in the vicinity so that the flowers can more easily be wind pollinated.

RECOMMENDED VARIETIES:

'Franquette' starts into growth late, so usually misses May frosts;

'Mayette', a late starter like 'Franquette'. The large roundish nuts have easy-to-crack shells.

FILBERT & COBNUT *Corylus* species

The easiest nuts for the gardener. They are closely related botanically, but are distinguished by the long husk of the filbert, (*C. maxima*) which sometimes almost hides the nut and the short husk of the cobnut (*C. Avellana*), which leaves the nut exposed.

All are easy to grow and do well on most types of soil but crops are smaller where the land is poor. To allow for development the bushes should be spaced at least 3.65 m (12 ft) apart, although if they are being used as hedges or screens space them closer together.

Harvest cob nuts from September onwards

Nut bushes bear male and female flowers so there is no difficulty about pollination. The conspicuous male flowers, generally known as catkins, are easy to see, but the small red female filaments are easily overlooked. It is from these, of course, that the nuts develop. Choose a frost-free site so the female flowers open when the catkins are ripe with golden pollen.

Propagate the bushes from layers pegged down in the autumn and raise plants from seed. The nuts are stratified between layers of sand in a box buried in the soil in autumn. In spring, they are unearthed and sown in drills to germinate within a few weeks. The resultant bushes are likely to vary greatly both in growth and cropping ability.

RECOMMENDED VARIETIES: Cob: 'Cosford', thin-shelled, of excellent flavour, Filbert: 'Kentish Cob', pollinated by 'Cosford'.

WHORTLEBERRY *Vaccinium myrtillus*

This plant is also known variously as the bilberry or blueberry, although the true blueberry is *Vaccinum corymbosum*. It bears racemes of little bell-shaped flowers in early summer. The variety *leucocarpum* has white berries.

Growing about 45 cm (18 ins) high, it is a heath-like shrub with small, ovate foliage

and sprays of pendant pink flowers which are followed by showy bluish-black, round, edible fruit. These are delicious in whortleberry pie topped with cream.

Plants thrive in moisty peaty, lime-free soil and are best transplanted in March or April. Old, badly placed stems should be cut out in late winter or early spring.

Propagation is from half-ripe cuttings 8–10 cm (3–4 ins) long. Insert them under glass where there is bottom heat, in late July or August. Other means of increasing stocks are by offsets, divisions, layering in autumn, or by seed sown in early autumn.

The worcesterberry crops heavily

WORCESTERBERRY *Ribes divaricatum*

Although this American native has long been regarded as a hybrid between a gooseberry and a blackcurrant, it is in fact a small black gooseberry. Certainly the fruit resembles in appearance both these subjects, being smaller than a gooseberry and usually larger than a blackcurrant. The flavour is similar to both. The abundant berries are borne in clusters, and are a deep reddish-purple, often turning purple-black.

The vigorous stems are closely furnished with thorns, undoubtedly one reason why the Worcesterberry has never been popular. If properly trained, however, this is a valuable addition to the fruit garden.

Cultivation and pruning is identical for that recommended for gooseberries. The Worcesterberry is resistant to mildew. Set plants in rich well drained soil containing plenty of humus. For sulphur-shy varieties, like 'Leveller', 'Early Sulphur- and 'Golden Drop', use a colloidal-sulphur spray.

Basic Guide to Pruning and Training

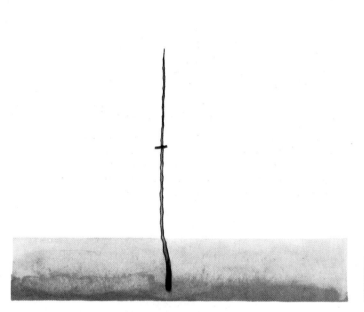

Pruning techniques for apples provide the model for treatment of most fruit trees. The bush is the most easily managed form. The four illustrations show cuts for winter pruning. Above: The maiden tree. Plant to the depth of the soil mark on the stem. After planting, cut back to 60 cm (24 in).

In the next (second) winter, the tree will have put forth several branches. Skilful pruning at this stage will determine the shape of the established tree. Choose up to four branches as leaders, and cut these back by up to two-thirds their length, to an outward pointing bud.

Winter pruning encourages strong growth while directing the tree to a shape which will admit adequate light and air to the developing fruits and facilitate picking the crop. In the third winter, cut back leading shoots again by about two-thirds, laterals (side shoots) to about three buds.

In the fourth and subsequent winters, the extent of pruning depends on the growth made by the tree. Leading shoots of weak trees should be cut back by two-thirds. Vigorous trees (above) should have the leaders shortened by a third their length. Cut laterals back to about three buds.

Red (and white) currants are commonly grown as bushes although, like gooseberries, they can be trained successfully as cordons. In bush form, the aim is to establish about 8 branches radiating evenly from the short central stem or 'leg'. Fruit is borne on short spurs made on the previous year's growth of these main branches.

After planting (above left), cut the branches back to about half. New plants can be grown from these cuttings. Winter pruning of an established bush (above): first cut back side shoots to two buds, then cut back the leaders to about half, more if growth has been weak. Summer-prune sub-laterals only back to five leaves.

Blackcurrants should be encouraged to produce maximum new growth from the base as they produce fruit on one-year-old wood. Buy certified two-year-old bushes and plant slightly deeper than in the nursery. After planting, cut back all the shoots to 2.5 cm (1 in) to direct the plant's energy into producing new shoots.

Established bushes should be pruned annually by removing entirely about $\frac{1}{4}$ to $\frac{1}{3}$ of the old wood to allow the new wood to ripen. At the same time cut down weak shoots. Improve neglected bushes by removing all the old wood and cutting right down to soil level. The best time to prune is after all the fruit has been picked.

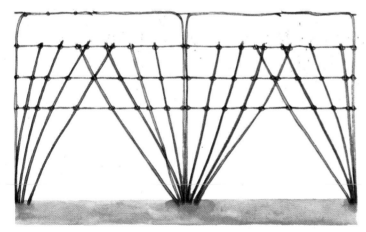

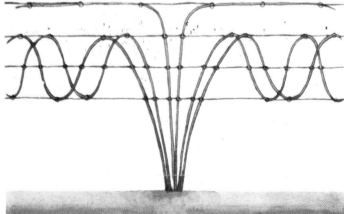

The two training systems shown above are suitable for blackberries, loganberries and hybrids of the two. The aim is to keep old and new wood separate and to train fruiting branches in such a way that the maximum amount of fruit can develop and be picked easily. Wear strong gloves when working with thorny bushes.

Above left: fan training. Current year's growth is tied in along the top wire while the fruiting branches are trained evenly across the wires. Above: weaving. Fruiting branches are woven around the lower wires. After fruiting, cut out the old wood and tie in the new branches in its place. Plant bushes about 3.5 m (12 ft) apart.

Harvesting & Storing Fruit & Vegetables

However successfully crops are grown, care is needed in harvesting at the right time to preserve full flavour and texture. Gathering crops too early or after they have passed their prime will affect their quality.

The following gives some guidance as to when crops are at their best for harvesting.

Broad beans and peas should be tested, opening a pod here or there. The pods should be well filled, but the 'seeds' should be soft. Never let broad beans hang until the seeds go 'black-eyed'; the skins are then tough and the contents mealy.

Round or **stump-rooted carrots** should be pulled as required when the root has developed an orange-pink colour. Main-crop carrots are ready to harvest when the outer leaves are shabby and fall about.

Cauliflowers should be cut before the curds open and discolour. If several cauliflowers are ready at once, pull them up by the roots and hang them upside down in a cool, dark, airy place.

Cucumbers are at their best when the sides are approximately parallel. Immature fruits have a drawn out cone-shape.

Dwarf French and runner beans are gathered when they snap cleanly in half and before the swelling seeds bulge in the pods.

Globe beets are pulled when they are young and tender, before the top of the root goes hard, crinkled and leathery. Harvest main-crop beet in mid-October.

Jerusalem artichokes should also be left in the soil until required, for they become soft unless they are used immediately after lifting.

Lettuce, both cos and cabbage, are ready when the heart feels firm to the touch. When the heart pushes up from the centre, the plant is going to flower and quality deteriorates rapidly.

Marrows are best cut small (as courgettes) when the skin is easily broken with your thumbnail.

Perpetual spinach is gathered when the leaves are fully formed but succulent. Leave the stems to continue growing and yielding leaves until autumn. Never strip all the leaves from one plant and avoid tearing them or soft rot may develop.

Radishes should not be left in the ground for long beyond a usable size, especially in dry soil, or they become hot, woody and hollow.

Summer cabbages develop too strong a flavour if not cut when the hearts are firm and at their peak. The variety 'Winter White' produces solid hearts for October–November cutting. If stored in a cool, airy shed, they will keep in perfect condition for weeks.

Brussels sprouts should be gathered before they become loose and blown.

Parsnips can be left in the ground until required. A touch of frost improves the flavour.

Turnips are best used when the size of a tennis ball, otherwise they become stringy.

Kohl Rabi will not keep in store and should be pulled as required.

Salsify will not keep out of the ground and should be used immediately it is harvested. If some roots are left throughout the winter and pots are placed over their tops, they will produce leaves which can be blanched and eaten in a similar way to asparagus.

Storing Vegetables

Beet (main crop). Lift when the leaves start falling away from the upright position and lose their freshness, which indicates that growth is complete. April and May-sown beet usually matures about the end of September, August-sown beet by November. Having lifted the crop, remove the leaves by twisting, not cutting them off. Store in small dome-shaped heaps in a shed, or in heaps outdoors, covering them immediately with 10 cm (4 ins) of straw, and a week later, with a 5 cm (2 ins) layer of moist sifted soil.

Cross section of a potato clamp. Leave straw vent at top

Carrots (main crop). Lift the crop when you see a natural curling of the foliage and when the dull, listless green outer leaves fall away from the crowns. Cut off the leaves as near the crown as possible without actually damaging it. Crown-paring is disastrous, because the roots shrivel seriously. If not cut closely, the results are equally unfortunate: the carrots start sprouting new leaves and the roots deteriorate.

Store small quantities in boxes on the floor of a cellar or shed. Put down a circular 5 cm (2 ins) layer of sand or leaf mould, following with alternate layers of carrots and storage material. Lay the tops of the roots outwards and cover them well. Larger quantities can be stored in clamps as advised for potatoes.

Celeriac. After lifting in October, cut off the roots. Remove the outer leaves but do not touch the little tufty growing point. To store, spread a 10 cm (4 ins) layer of sand on the floor of a shed or garage. Place a tight ring of celeriac on this and cover them with more sand.

Haricot beans. These should be harvested as they ripen, commencing in August. Pick the pods when they are ripe and swollen. Spread them out in a sunny window or on the greenhouse shelf. Turn them over every three or four days until, without the least forcing, they begin to split. Then the perfectly ripe beans are removed from the pods and stored in air-tight jars or bottles.

Onions (main crop). The usual time for harvesting is early September. Never store bulbs which show an embryo flower stem, which are soft in the neck and those whose outer skin is dotted with small black spots which cannot be rubbed off.

Lift the bulbs on a dry day following a dry spell of at least a few days. After lifting, allow them a fortnight's sunning – laid out in a single layer on a shed roof or other convenient place, covering them against showers. In persistently showery weather, the drying period can be spent in a greenhouse or frame. For a simpler method of storing, clean off roots and tops but do not remove loose skins. Store in single layers on shelves in a dry, airy, frost-proof shed or hang them in a net.

One of the best ways to keep onions is to make them into ropes. Select sound ripened bulbs and remove withered tops and roots. Grade them into sizes so that the larger specimens are at the bottom. Make a rope of three pieces of cord, knotted together at one end. Then braid them together, catching the necks of the onions between the cords as braiding proceeds. It's easy once you get the hang of it. Once completed, hang the rope of onions in a dry, airy, frost-proof place.

Potatoes. First earlies are ready for lifting in June and July, and are dug as required. Lift second earlies about mid-August or when the haulm has yellowed and the skin on the tubers has set nicely. Store second earlies in a dry, dark, frost-proof outhouse, dusting them with fresh slaked lime or flowers of sulphur. Lift main crop potatoes about the end of September or when the haulm has passed from yellow to whitish-brown. Lifting becomes simpler if the haulm is first pulled or cut off with a sickle.

After lifting, leave the crop on the ground for 24 hours. Examine all tubers for signs of disease or pest damage. Set aside all unsound tubers for immediate use, for these will not keep. Store small crops in boxes or sacks or on the floor of a frost-proof shed covered with 10 cm (4 ins) of straw.

Store large quantities in a clamp. Make the clamp in a warm, sheltered, slightly raised position, say on the south side of a hedge. Cover the site with a 25 mm (1 in) layer of small cinders before

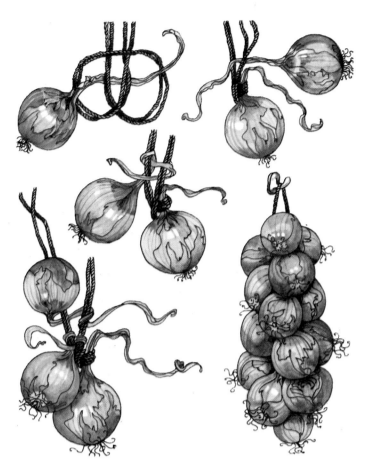

Stages in stringing onions by the knot method

tough and tasteless. Many crops cannot be stored in the usual way but can be deep frozen for use when fresh vegetables are limited.

The shorter the time between picking and freezing the better, so gather only as many as you can deal with at one time. If by chance all cannot be prepared for the freezer as soon as gathered, keep them in a cool, dark place, otherwise they will become limp.

Success in freezing, retaining the flavour and good keeping qualities of vegetables, is determined by variety, the way crops are prepared, correct blanching and speed of freezing.

After cleaning and preparing vegetables for the freezer, blanching is necessary to stop enzyme activity which would eventually cause loss of flavour, colour and nutritional value. This is vital and the length of time required and technique varies according to the crop.

The following are reliable crops for freezing:

Jerusalem Artichokes. Best frozen as a purée for using as soup.

Asparagus. Grade by thickness of stems. Scrape off small scales.

Aubergines. Wash, cut in slices, open freeze, then pack in sealed polythene bags.

Broad beans. Pod and grade, using only small young beans.

Dwarf Beans. Top and tail.

Runner Beans. Slice, cut into 24 mm (1 in) lengths.

Beetroot. Use small roots, wash, remove leaves, skin, pack dry.

Brussels sprouts. Choose tight, small sprouts. Trim off coarse outer leaves.

All kinds of cabbage can be kept in the freezer

building the clamp. Useful measurements for a clamp are: base 1.20 m (4 ft) wide; height 1.20 m (4 ft); width at apex 45 cm (18 ins). The length may be anything that suits the gardener's convenience.

Immediately on getting the tubers in position, cover them with a 15 cm (6 ins) layer of clean straw or bracken, and leave it in this condition until severe frost threatens. Then cover the straw with a 5 cm (2 ins) layer of soil dug in the form of a grip from around the sides of the clamp. When doing this, place a drain-pipe, or a wisp of straw, at 90 cm (3 ft) intervals along the ridge to allow air to circulate round the tubers.

Shallots. These are usually harvested in early July. Give the bulbs a fortnight's sunning to finish ripening and dry thoroughly. Clean off roots and tops before storing. Shallots will keep well for months in bags, preferably of hessian, in open-topped boxes, or wicker baskets, provided these are stored in a cool, dry, airy, frost-proof place.

All stored crops should be examined occasionally and any which are unsound or diseased should be discarded to prevent infections spreading to healthy specimens.

Vegetables for Freezing

However well planned a cropping programme is there will always be more vegetables than can be eaten when the crop is at its peak — tender and full of flavour. Leave them longer and they will become

Cabbage. Discard coarse outer leaves and thick stems. Wash and shred before blanching.

Carrots. Use only small whole roots. Wash and cut off tops before freezing.

Cauliflower. Break into separate florets of even size. Wash in salted water.

Sweet corn. Select tender cobs. Remove husk and silks.

Kohl rabi. Choose small roots, clean and freeze whole, unpeeled.

Leeks. Trim off coarse outer leaves and green tops. Wash thoroughly.

Onions. Peel and slice or chop before blanching.

Parsnips. Thoroughly trim and peel. Cut into strips or dice.

Peas. Select young tender peas. Remove ends from mangetout varieties.

Peppers. Wash, cut off stem, remove seed and membrane. Cut into halves or slice.

Salsify. Scrub clean, blanch, drain, peel and cut into small lengths while warm.

Spinach. Pick over leaves, remove midribs and wash well. Blanch, plunge in iced water, and drain completely. Pack in polythene bags and seal tightly.

Preparing and packing leaf spinach for the freezer

Sprouting broccoli. Trim off larger leaves and cut stems into short even lengths.

Swedes. Young roots should be diced and cooked in boiling water until tender. Then pack into containers and freeze.

Tomatoes. Can be frozen but are unsuitable for adding to salads, although excellent in soups and stews.

Turnips. Peel and trim the roots. Really small specimens need not be cut or diced.

Harvesting and Storing Fruit

Considering the care with which the majority of amateur gardeners grow their fruit trees and bushes, it is surprising how indifferent many of them are to the way in which they gather the crop. Careless picking not only impairs the keeping qualities of the fruit but is likely to damage the trees too.

With soft fruit, one can usually tell by the colour and general appearance when it is ready to gather. Where small quantities are involved, it is a good plan to pick early in the day. Commercially, it is economical to clear the bushes at one or two pickings; in the garden fruit should be gathered as it ripens, which means that some bushes may be 'in pick' for a week or two.

One of the reasons for training fruit bushes and trees is to persuade them to grow in forms that make harvesting easier: this is particularly important with thorn-bearing species like gooseberries and blackberries. Dwarf-stocks of tree fruits will not always need a ladder to gather the harvest.

Blackcurrants are often deceptive when it comes to judging ripeness. They may look ripe before they are, so it is worth testing first.

Red and white currants should be evenly coloured before being picked. Unless the fruit is used immediately, it should not be gathered while wet, otherwise it is likely to rot.

It is usual to 'pick over' gooseberries several times, since all bushes do not ripen their fruits at once. It all depends too, for what purpose they are needed. If required for dessert they must be fairly ripe. If needed for bottling or canning they should be firm, while those for jam, need not be in quite such good condition.

Raspberries are fit to eat when they part easily from the core. The manner and frequency of picking is governed by the use to which the fruit is put. If it is being marketed, only sound, firm fruit should be put in punnets or baskets. This applies whether the fruit is for the open market or for canning or freezing. For jam making, the fruit can be a little riper, but free from moulds and maggots. Since picking raspberries requires a little more care than with most other soft fruit, it is wise to remember that when buying canes, 'Malling Jewel' and 'Malling Enterprise' make fewer canes so that the fruit is easier to see and gather.

With the ever-popular 'Lloyd George', which is a strong grower with many canes, the fruit is liable to be hidden among abundant foliage. 'Norfolk Giant' is, sometimes, a shy fruiter and after the first flush the berries are usually quite small.

For dessert purposes, strawberries must be picked often and thoroughly. This means daily picking when the crop begins to ripen. Net against birds and slugs.

Fruit should be slightly under-ripe when picked unless it is to be eaten immediately. The actual colour will vary a little according to variety but a strawberry is less popular if it is not well coloured.

Supplies of whole soft fruits or purées out of season are among the freezer's most delicious bonuses

Cultivated blackberries and loganberries can be picked and used in the same way as raspberries. Loganberries do not as a rule crop so heavily as blackberries, although the new clonal strains give heavier crops. Most soft fruits can be frozen, either as a purée, or whole by 'open-freezing' first.

Apples and pears are the chief fruits for storing as picked straight from the tree. The problem here is knowing precisely when to pick them. For an apple, the time-honoured test is to lift the fruit gently upwards in the palm of the hand and see if it parts readily from the fruit spur. If it does, it is ripe for eating. Where the fruit has to be stored for long periods there is an advantage in picking it when slightly immature for, the more mature it is, the less likely it is to keep for long periods. Yet if the fruit is considerably immature, it will shrivel and fail to reach perfection in colour and flavour. In many cases the grower has found that the fruit from a certain tree keeps better than that from another. The whole question of timing picking is very difficult; often it is a matter of judgment, rather than science.

The fruit may appear hard to the inexperienced picker, but bruises can be inflicted all too easily, and after a short time in the store the fruit begins to decay. Proper picking containers are essential. The fruit should be picked by grasping it in the palm of the hand rather than with the fingers alone, for it is surprising how much bruising can take place from finger pressure. Long finger nails are an added hazard as these may penetrate the fruit skin.

Fruit for storing must be carefully placed in the containers – never thrown or dropped in.

While commercial fruit growers can provide an ideal store, which may be something quite elaborate such as a cold storage chamber or a gas store, the ordinary gardener will have to make do with something far less grand. This however, does not mean that he cannot store the fruit satisfactorily.

Ideally, the store should be where there is a low, even temperature and where the atmosphere is slightly moist. Old air raid shelters are suitable so long as flooding is not a hazard. Cellars and brick outhouses too, are usually satisfactory. Many amateur growers keep their fruit in attics, sheds or wooden garages. The disadvantage here is that they heat up at times causing the skins to shrivel. Cool fruit that has stood in strong sunshine before it is brought into store.

Wooden trays and boxes are often used and should be kept in the cool and shade and protected from mice and rats.

The advantage of spreading out the fruit on benches or trays is that it is easy to examine and remove any unsound specimens.

Although not essential, some growers wrap apples in special oiled paper although squares of newspaper are just as effective. The advantage of wrapping fruits separately is the reduced likelihood of disease spreading if some fruits decay.

Do not wrap pears and as far as possible never store apples and pears together, for they are incompatible and seem to act against each other, leading to trouble! If they *have* to be stored together, wrap the apples in oiled paper.

Stored fruit can become 'tainted' from the fumes of any strong-smelling substance such as creosote.

The clamping of apples is worthwhile where there is a very heavy crop and where a fruit store or cellar is not available. Late keepers such as 'Laxton's Superb', 'Winston', 'Newton Wonder' and 'Bramley's Seedling' are very suitable for clamps.

Choose a cool, well-drained position and take out a trench about 90 cm (3 ft) wide and anything from 30 cm–1.20 m (1–4 ft) deep, although a clamp can be made without making a trench at all. Line the sides and bottom with plenty of clean straw and then carefully build up a tapering heap of fruits about 90 cm (3 ft) high. Only perfectly sound apples should go into the clamp. Give the heaped fruit about ten days to sweat, first placing a layer of straw over it which can be removed during the day and replaced in the later afternoon. Some growers place newspapers over the fruit before putting on the straw. After the ten days, apply another thick, steep layer of straw, over which should be placed mouse-proof netting, if mice are troublesome. Wait a further week, then apply a casing of soil. This should be 30–38 cm (12–15 ins) thick at the base, and 13–15 cm (5–6 ins) thick over the rest of the heap. In Suffolk and probably elsewhere too, only the bottom of the clamp is soiled, wooden planks or other heavy objects being laid on the straw to keep it in position.

Safely clamped in this way, the fruit should keep in good condition until early in the new year.

137

Garden Friends & Foes

In dealing with garden pests, disorders and diseases the first aim of the gardener is to get rid of them. To do this efficiently it is necessary to identify the culprits.

Very often the severity of attack is due to faulty cultivation or failure to control the pests when they first appeared. Sometimes they gain a hold because of wrong soil care. Also, weak growing plants are more susceptible to troubles than robust ones growing on soil kept well fed with organic manure. The use of quick acting fertilizers induces soft growth which easily becomes the target of many enemies.

It is comforting to realize that there are many friendly creatures about too so do not work on the principle of killing everything.

Among the most useful garden insects are bees whose activities encourage pollination. Wasps eat greenfly, although they can spoil fruits in late summer. Toads, frogs, hedgehogs and the devil's coach horse (a beetle), are our allies, destroying quite a lot of harmful creatures. The earthworm should be encouraged too, although not in the lawn.

Larvae of the ground beetle are beneficial as well. They look like caterpillars, are a dull brown colour and have three pairs of legs. They move very quickly but should not be confused with the harmful wireworm which is lighter in colour and very much less active. The centipede is another friend. It has a rather flat light brown body and moves very quickly. It should not be confused with the harmful millipedes which are either a slate grey or darkish brown colour and

Ladybirds attacking aphids (greenfly)

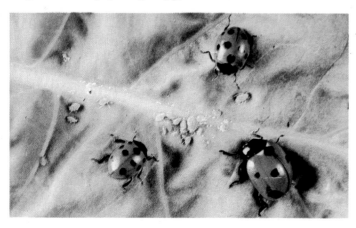

very sluggish. Generally, soil creatures that move quickly are friendly while those that are slow are harmful.

Of the flying insects, the familiar ladybird is one of the gardener's best friends. Both the familiar spotted adult beetles and the tiny rather alligator-like larvae destroy countless numbers of greenfly. Some species of hover fly look rather like elegant wasps, but hang motionless in the air between their quick darting movements when they catch all kinds of pests. Their larvae consume many pests.

Many species of ichneumon fly do a lot of good in the garden. One kind parasites cabbage white caterpillars. The common lacewing has a thin pale green body and is very active destroying all kinds of small insects. It lays its eggs in clusters on leaf stalks and the larvae hatch quickly to mop up aphids.

In a well managed garden there is little to fear from pests and diseases. Good plant hygiene leads to healthy growth and if occasional pest attacks are dealt with early, there will be no repercussions.

Most pests that settle on plants can be killed by stomach poisons, mostly in the form of liquid sprays or dusts. Take special care when using any of these products. Follow closely the manufacturer's instructions for use, and store all poisons under lock and key out of the reach of children and where pets cannot find them. With slugs and snails, poison baits can be placed near the plants to lure the pests to their death. Aphids and other suckers can be destroyed by spraying the plants with derris or pyrethrum. The advantage of liquid derris is that it is easily obtainable and non-poisonous to humans.

Good soil drainage reduces the risk of slugs, snails, millipedes and leatherjackets. There are many predators which do a tremendous amount of good, but unfortunately, they are often unknowingly destroyed.

Some pests favour certain crops, but there are a number which attack all kinds. Similarly some diseases and disorders are common to many edible plants. The following are some of the troubles you are most likely to encounter.

Aphids. There are many species including greenfly and blackfly. They suck the sap, distort foliage, check growth and spoil flowers. Regular spraying with derris is usually sufficient to destroy them. Aphids attack currants and gooseberries (see p. 111) and broad and runner beans, but will infest almost any plant in the vegetable patch as well as the flower garden. Spring and summer are the danger periods out of doors.

Ants. These are attracted to plants infested with greenfly, which they 'milk' for their sweet honeydew. They may carry aphids which spread virus diseases from plant to plant. Various ant killers based on derris and gamma-BHC are effective.

Botrytis. A common fungus, most likely to appear in wet seasons and in cold damp conditions. It may settle on plants which are weak and soft-growing, and it flourishes on dead and dying plants. Burn affected plants and treat healthy specimens nearby with Cheshunt compound.

Caterpillars. Except those that cover themselves with a web, these can be eradicated by the use of derris insecticide. Since caterpillars are so easy to see, the simplest method is to hand-pick them, and also to destroy the eggs which are laid in clusters, usually under the foliage.

Cockchafers. Together with related species such as the rosechafer, cockchafers usually appear in May and June and lay clusters of eggs below the surface of the soil. From these hatch fleshy, dirty-white grubs with brownish-yellow heads. They feed on the roots and lower parts of the stems. Naphthalene forked into the soil at 136 g per m² (4 oz per sq yd) usually clears them. Alternatively, use gamma-BHC dust pricked into the surface.

Symptoms of club root on brassica

Club root. Affects candytuft, stocks and alyssum. Calomel dust controls this soil fungus which spreads easily from these flowering plants to vegetables of the cabbage family, as well as turnips and radishes.

Cuckoo spit. The frothy mass of cuckoo spit seen on stems and leaves of garden plants conceals the pale yellow nymph of the frog hopper, a jumping insect not more than 7 mm (¼ in) long. Both adults and nymphs suck sap and distort leaves and shoots. To get rid of them spray the spittle with soapy water, then dust with derris or pyrethrum.

Cutworms (surface caterpillars). The larvae of several species of moths, they feed at night, attacking the plant stem at or just below ground level, causing it to collapse. Plants with fairly thick stems are usually the victims. Where pests are suspected examine the soil and the plants, for cutworms are easy to see.

Botrytis (grey mould) on strawberries

Damping off. A fungus which attacks crowded seedlings left too long in the seed bed, causing stems to wither at soil level. Avoid over-watering and never grip the tiny stems too firmly. Control by watering the soil with Cheshunt compound.

Earwigs. These sometimes damage foliage and flowers. They are most active at night hiding under rubbish. They can be trapped in inverted pots filled with hay or straw, or eradicated by spraying damaged plants with gamma-BHC.

Eelworms. These damage potatoes, onions, some bulbs and a few annuals. They are microscopic pests which lay their eggs in the tissues of plants. Ultimately the plant dies, first exhibiting twisted stunted growth. Leave affected ground unplanted for three seasons.

Flea beetles. These very active creatures damage vegetables such as cabbage, turnips and radish, and some other crops, especially in dry weather. The remedy is to keep the soil surface moving and to give frequent dustings of derris powder. These pests hide in rubbish; eggs are laid on the soil and foliage.

Protect plants from cutworms with bromophos

139

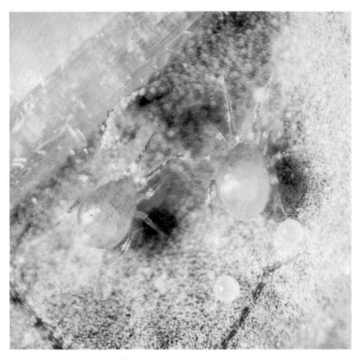

Above: Millipedes. Below: Red spider mites can be controlled by introducing the predator Phytoseiulus persimilis

Leaf hoppers. Minute insects which bite and disfigure foliage: spray with derris.

Leatherjackets. These are the larvae of the well-known crane fly or daddy longlegs. They attack and kill the roots of plants, especially on newly broken ground that was previously grassland. They occur on damp, badly-drained soil. Birds will often clear the larvae. Naphthalene at 85 g per m² (3 oz per sq yd), or Chlordane worked into the ground will usually get rid of this pest.

Mildew. Slight attacks seem to do little harm, but sometimes the white powder-like growth is very bad, causing a whole batch of plants to become disfigured and useless. As soon as the disease is seen, dust the plants with yellow sulphur powder or spray with one of the proprietary mildew specifics such as karathane.

Millipedes. These are common both in the garden and under glass. They usually feed at night, attacking seed-leaves and early growth. They are easily distinguished from beneficial centipedes by their slower movement and greater number of legs. One species, slate-grey in colour, curls up like a watch spring when disturbed. The simplest method of destroying millipedes is to trap them with scooped-out pieces of vegetables, which should be examined daily and the pests destroyed.

Red Spider Mites. These tiny reddish pests attach themselves to the undersides of the leaves producing whitish specklings on the upper surface. Left unchecked, the pests settle on the growing points and may make a fine weblike growth over them. Although excellent sprays are available, killing both the insects and their eggs, the liquid works only by contact. Malathion is also effective and is partially systemic. This is why some growers of greenhouse plants prefer to use an aerosol or smoke bomb based on malathion as it reaches all parts of the plants as well as the crevices of the greenhouse.

Scab. A disorder sometimes affecting apples and pears. A spraying of Orthocide normally controls the disease.

Springtails. These are wingless active jumping insects in various colours. They feed on decaying plant tissues, as well as attacking living plants, especially delicate seedlings. If they are suspected, dust around the plants with pyrethrum powder.

Stem rot. This works through the roots and affected plants must be burned. Cheshunt compound checks the disease.

Symphalids. These small white pests attack the roots. Soil sterilization has little effect. Plants should be drenched with gamma BHC two or three days after planting out.

Thrips. These tiny insects attack few vegetables. Silvery markings on the foliage indicates their presence. They are virus carriers, spreading infection by piercing the foliage. Under glass they can be controlled by fumigation. Outdoors, spraying the plants with a nicotine and soft soap wash is usually effective; derris is also helpful.

Virus diseases. The usual symptoms are stunted, distorted growth and mottled foliage. All plants suspected of virus should be removed and burned immediately, and if greenfly or other aphis are seen on nearby plants, spray them with a derris wash, for aphis often spread diseases as they feed on neighbouring plants.

Whitefly. These are small aphid-like creatures which may rapidly build up into swarms under glass. Biological control by introducing suitable predators such as *Encarsia formosa*, a type of wasp, is the best control. Alternatively, spray every three days for a fortnight with malathion.

Wireworms. These larvae of the click beetle are most destructive. They attack and spoil a wide range of plants, usually eating the roots, but sometimes they damage the stems too. They are prevalent in grassland and uncultivated ground, which is why they seem so plentiful on freshly broken-up soil. Regular cultivation is the best means of controlling wireworms. They can be trapped by pieces of root vegetable placed in the ground, which can be examined frequently so the pests can be destroyed. There are a number of proprietary preparations, most of which contain gamma-BHC which can be dusted into the ground when it is being turned.

Woodlice. These are often present in rubbish. They flourish in damp, dull conditions and are frequently found on decaying wood. The remedy is to concentrate on cleanliness. Woodlice can be trapped by placing pieces of root vegetables in the surface soil and examining them frequently so the pests can be destroyed. Alternatively, dust infested areas with derris.

Whatever the pest, disorder or disease that attacks a plant counter measures must be taken early, before the plants are spoiled. The gardener must also be ruthless. It is no use pulling up infested plants and simply leaving them on the surface. Burn them.

Disorders and Diseases of Vegetables

However well crops are grown, there is always the possibility that diseases may attack. Plants grown under really good conditions and in soil rich in humus are not so liable to be attacked as those which are in poor condition and which are fed only with artificial or inorganic fertilizers. By practising a system of crop rotation it will be easier to prevent diseases gaining a hold. (This also applies to strawberries, which should not be grown on the same site year after year.)

It is always advisable to remove poor looking seedy plants, for not only are they unprofitable but they could be the means by which disease spreads. Old yellowed leaves, too, may provide resting places for fungus diseases.

The following are diseases which can cripple vegetables.

Asparagus rust is to be seen from mid-June onwards and appears as patches of rust-coloured blisters which cause the leaves to discolour and die prematurely.

Broad beans are sometimes attacked by what is known as 'chocolate spot disease'. The leaves, stems and often the pods become heavily marked with brown streaks or spots. Attacks are usually worse during wet seasons and are more likely on heavy, badly drained ground.

As soon as the disease is seen or suspected, the plants should be sprayed with a copper fungicide. As far as possible, broad beans should be grown on a fresh site the following year, preferably one which has been dressed with wood ash or some other form of potash.

Dwarf French and runner beans are sometimes affected by a blight which is technically known as anthracnose. This is seen as dark coloured spots and reddish streaks which appear on the foliage, stems and pods. Often the spots increase in size and eventually merge into brownish patches. This trouble, too, is more likely to be serious in damp seasons and where the soil is wet and cold. Spraying with Bordeaux mixture or one of the proprietary copper fungicides usually controls an attack.

Halo blight causes bean plants to become sickly and wilt. If affected plants are examined, small spots surrounded by a light coloured halo will be seen on leaves and stems. Destroy plants affected.

Botrytis (grey mould) may affect the pods in damp seasons. Burn affected plants and treat healthy specimens nearby with Cheshunt compound.

Above: Wireworms. Below: Rust can attack many vegetables, including broad beans

Cabbages and other members of the brassica family may be attacked by various diseases. Among the most troublesome is club root, often known as 'finger and toe'. The roots become swollen and distorted and when they break open, decayed and badly smelling matter will be seen. When buying cabbage and similar plants, make sure they are healthy, as seedlings are often affected by the disease. All infected plants should be burnt. If, when planting brassicas, a teaspoonful of Calomel dust is sprinkled in each hole, it will help to protect the plant from infection. Alternatively, make a slurry with calomel dust and water and dip the plant's roots in it before planting.

Carrots in store are sometimes affected by a rot. It is most likely to appear on roots damaged at lifting time. To lessen its spread, the clamps or boxes used for storing should not be too large and they should be carefully ventilated.

Celery leaf spot can be quite a serious disease in some seasons. It first appears as minute brown spots which gradually increase in size until the foliage is brown and withered. The trouble sometimes originates from the seed and for this reason most seedsmen supply stocks which have been treated against leaf spot. Even so, any plants which become discoloured should be sprayed with Bordeaux mixture as a precaution against the disease.

Celery root rot may appear after the plants have been earthed up. It is encouraged by slug attacks or by soil getting into the heart of the plants. A similar trouble is known as 'heart rot'. This is initiated by pests which make wounds in the stalks, allowing moisture to enter and set up decay. It is essential to make celery trenches in such a way that water drains away easily. A sprinkling of Borax crystals along the ground where the rows are to be made is a great help in reducing the risk of 'heart rot'.

Cucumbers. Under glass, cucumbers are sometimes attacked by rot or canker at soil level. This gradually eats into the stems causing them to collapse and die. The remedy is to keep soil from settling around the stems.

Slight attacks can often be checked by dusting the stems with flowers of sulphur. Sulphur can also be dusted where mildew is suspected. Plenty of ventilation on all suitable occasions will also reduce the risk of mildew.

Leeks may suffer from rust seen as yellowish spots which turn a reddish shade. Where the trouble has occurred previously, do not plant leeks in the same soil for a period of three or four years. Affected leaves should be removed and the entire plants sprayed with a sulphur-copper wash.

Leeks may also be affected by 'white tip' disease. Here the tips of the leaves die back and turn white. This is one reason why it is advisable to cut off the tips of the leaves of young plants when they are put in their final positions, for it is when the leaves droop towards the ground that they become affected. As a control, the plants should be dusted with copper-lime, which can be used from October onwards.

Remove and burn leek leaves affected with spot

Lettuce are sometimes seen with reddish markings on the stem at soil level. Subsequently, botrytis sets in and the plant wilts and dies. It is more likely to appear on frame grown, winter lettuce. If the plants are put in too deeply they are liable to rot at the centre and this gives rise to botrytis. Sulphur powder or calomel dust is an efficient control.

Ring spot also affects lettuces; brown spots appear on the leaves and holes develop. Where this disease has occurred, it is unwise to grow lettuce on the same site again for a few years. If the soil does not lack potash, there is little likelihood of ring spot appearing.

Another trouble is tip burn. There are various forms. All are related to the water balance within the plant or the size of the root system and degree of soil salinity. The most common form occurs from March onwards during periods of high temperatures and low humidity, when transpiration exceeds the uptake of water, and the tissues wilt. The edges of the leaves covering the heart turn brown and look scorched; rotting by botrytis usually follows.

Latex tip burn may occur under glass from the end of March when sap exudes from the edges of the inner leaves, which turn brown and rot. Veinal tip burn may appear in autumn, caused by water uptake exceeding transpiration. Dry tip burn is a winter disorder in which the opposite condition applies, in that transpiration exceeds water uptake. The leaf edge becomes dry and bitter. A good root system, encouraged by deep cultivation and freedom from pests and diseases, should do much to prevent the development of tip burn and similar disorders.

Onions are affected by several diseases. A white or greyish mildew can sometimes be seen on the leaves, which begin to discolour and collapse. This mildew is much more liable to occur on badly drained than well-drained land in good condition.

If only a few plants are affected, it is often possible to stop the infection spreading by applying a colloidal copper wash. If this is done three or four times at ten to fourteen day intervals, the disease should be controlled.

White rot fungus sometimes attacks the base of the bulbs, causing the foliage to wilt and the bulbs to shrivel and die prematurely. Deal with it as early as possible. Some varieties are more resistant than others, including older sorts such as 'White Spanish' and 'Bedfordshire Champion'. If the trouble has occurred previously, dust calomel along the rows before sowing, although it is better not to grow onions on the same site for several years.

Parsnips are liable to canker, which causes the roots to crack at the top and to become affected by a brown rot which sometimes becomes wet and rotten. Canker is less likely on well-drained ground containing a high humus content. The variety 'Avonresister' should be grown where the disorder has previously occurred.

Peas frequently exhibit variegated and otherwise marked foliage. This discoloration is usually due to virus infection, although it is not easy to discover its origin. Undoubtedly aphids are the chief culprits. Inspect the plants periodically and prevent them colonizing the leaves.

In spite of its name, marsh spot usually appears on light soils which dry out easily. Affected seedlings are distorted and never grow well. Here again, it has been proved that where the soil contains plenty of compost, the disease is less likely to occur.

Potatoes. There are numerous disorders which can affect potatoes. Some of these are inherited and others are cultural. The planting of certified seed ensures a good start. Even so, diseases may attack later in the season.

Common scab is more likely on light soil deficient in humus and where there is a high lime content. Powdery scab, on the other hand, is worse in wet ground. Then there is skin spot, which although not serious, can damage the eyes of the tubers, which, if they are to be used for seed purposes, are spoiled.

Wart disease is very serious and an outbreak must be notified to the Ministry of Agriculture, so always plant immune varieties. Potato blight is a very destructive disease and usually occurs in late July. The crop is greatly reduced. This disease is most liable to occur when the temperature is above 10°C (50°F) and when the air is humid. Control by spraying Bordeaux mixture every ten days from late July to September.

Potato 'blackleg' is a rot which can occur on all varieties, and in all soils, being most severe in heavy wet ground. The stems become black and rotten at and below soil level, and can easily be pulled out. First symptoms may be a yellowing, rolling and wilting of the foliage in June and July. Make sure to plant sound tubers and never use cut tubers where the disease has occurred.

Stem canker is seen as dark brown withered stems at ground level, a white 'crust' often developing. Crop rotation and healthy cultivation should prevent this disease.

Bad weather sometimes damages the foliage. Wind or hail can pit the leaves which then become discoloured, often with marginal yellowing. There are several nutrient deficiencies which also spoil the appearance of the foliage. In potash shortage the leaves become brittle and brown, particularly in sandy soils and a dry season. Nitrogen shortage shows by the leaves becoming yellowish, the edge of the leaflets turning brown and curling.

Manganese shortage produces pale foliage with brown spotting along the veins. Magnesium deficiency causes yellowing of the tissues between green veins. The plants remain dwarf.

Spinach may become affected by downy mildew especially in a wet season on heavy soils. The undersides of the leaves become coated with a grey or bluish-grey mould and the whole leaf turns yellow and dies. Attacks are more likely in ground over-rich in nitrogen. Pick off and burn all affected leaves or in bad cases, destroy the entire plant. Dust the remainder with yellow sulphur powder or spray with thiram.

Leaf spot is caused by a fungus. If not dealt with in the early stages the black or brownish-black spots increase over a large area of the leaves. Remove badly affected foliage and spray the plants with Bordeaux mixture or colloidal sulphur.

Spinach Blight is a virus disease, which causes the leaves to become discoloured and malformed. Greenflies are the carriers and if seen or suspected, the plants should be dusted or sprayed with a derris or pyrethrum based insecticide.

Sweet Corn is subject to few disorders. Sometimes cold winds will cause the leaf edges to discolour but this is only a temporary setback. Occasionally the growing points become stunted and some of the leaves look ragged and twisted. This may be due to low temperatures but is more likely to be the effects of the larvae of the fruit fly having previously burrowed into the tissues of the growing points. Such plants can be sprayed with liquid pyrethrum.

Turnips and Swedes will not tolerate an acid soil which is conducive to the spread of club root. Since the organism responsible can remain

Prevent potato blight by earthing up the plants well

in the soil for years turnips should not be grown in ground previously occupied by other members of the cabbage family. Always grow turnips and swedes on land containing plenty of lime. Dusting the seed bed with calomel prior to sowing reduces risk of attacks. Soft rot sometimes occurs in the centre of turnips, caused by a fungus gaining an entry through wounds or pest attacks.

Dry rot, often known as canker, can occur while turnips and swedes are growing, or while they are in store. It starts in late summer as brown patches. These often enlarge, causing the roots to split or become shrunken. Affected roots should be burnt and a long rotation system practised.

Tomatoes being natives of warmer climes, are subject to several complaints, the most common being cladosporium, a fungus causing a light grey mould on the undersides of the leaves. This spreads and eventually the leaves turn brown and fall. In the greenhouse, good ventilation helps to avoid the disease which does not occur in a temperature over 18°C (64°F). Spraying the plants with colloidal copper is effective. Damping off of tomato seedlings is usually due to sowing too thickly and careless watering.

Tomato canker, caused by *Botrytis cinerea*, occurs where there is a cool moist, stagnant atmosphere. It appears on the fruit as brown rotting spots and on the stems, as swellings. The remedy is good ventilation and low atmospheric humidity.

There are several physiological disorders, including blossom end rot, which is the result of insufficient moisture when the young fruits are developing. Dark brown areas appear where the flower was attached at the base of the fruit. Sometimes, diseased roots prevent the plants from obtaining all the moisture needed.

Blotchy ripening is associated with an unbalanced food supply and one or two dressings of sulphate of potash at 56 g per m² (2 oz per sq yd) will correct the trouble. Greenback is a condition when the top portion of the fruit becomes hard and does not colour. Lack of potash and exposure to strong sunlight encourages this disorder. Grow resistant varieties and take care that the soil does not dry out. Tomatoes must develop under even conditions to be at their best.

143

Fruit splitting is due to sudden changes in growing conditions. Very high temperatures will often cause the skin to harden, as will happen if the roots dry out. Then, when moisture is applied, the skin cannot expand quickly enough and this leads to splitting.

Very occasionally virus disorders occur, when the foliage becomes mottled to a definite pattern. Virus diseases cannot be cured and affected plants should be destroyed.

Pests and Diseases of Fruit

As far as possible, prevention is better than cure when it comes to fruit troubles, since too often the remedy will be the ruthless one of grubbing an infected plant altogether. Always buy certified stocks (where applicable) from a reliable supplier, and never propagate from plants which have shown unhealthy symptoms. When pruning, take great care to leave a clean cut so disease cannot enter. If a large branch is removed from a tree, paint the wound immediately with a proprietary seal.

Apples are most likely to suffer the attentions of aphids (q.v.) and codling moths. The caterpillar of the latter bores into the core of the fruit where it feeds, leaving a small hole in the surface. Spray with malathion in mid-June and again three weeks later. Powdery mildew sometimes distorts young stems and leaves, which are covered with a fine white powder. Regular spraying with benomyl or dinocap will hold this at bay. Sawflies are an unpleasant pest. They leave a small brown scar on the skin, and the grubs feed inside on the flesh. Spray with gamma-BHC immediately after petal fall. Fruit tree red spider mites are another problem, but the mid-June spraying of malathion recommended above should be effective.

Swollen buds of black currant infested with big bud mite

Caterpillar of the codling moth inside apple

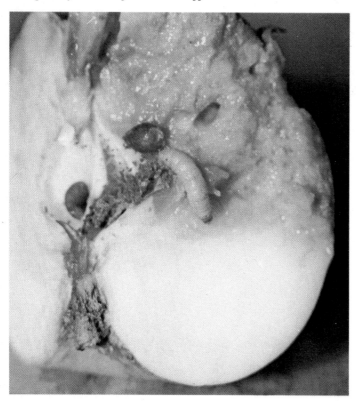

Black currants. Big bud mite causes the buds of young blackcurrant shoots to become abnormally swollen and globular. The mites are microscopic and live within the bud. Infested buds fail to open, so that growth is checked and the bush so weakened and ceases to produce profitable crops. The mites leave the swollen buds at blossom time, spend a short period on the flowers and leaves, and then enter the young buds on the new shoots, in which they quickly multiply. This pest can be controlled, first by removing and burning all infested buds, and then by spraying with lime-sulphur, at the maker's directions. Do this when the blossom is at the 'grape stage', that is, the racemes look like bunches of grapes and the flowers have not opened. Spray annually to protect bushes against this pest. Reversion is a serious virus disease of blackcurrants and is carried by the big bud mite. Infected leaves have fewer sub-veins and serrations than normal leaves. The flowers on 'reverted' branches are often distorted and seldom produce fruit. Bushes showing this trouble should be burned, and of course no cuttings should be taken from them. Various types of aphid attack both red and blackcurrants. One of the commonest is that which, attacking the undersides of the leaves, causes red blisters to appear on the upper surface. Spray the bushes with tar-oil or DNC winter wash while dormant to destroy the eggs. Directly the pest appears spray with derris and, if necessary, repeat at 10-day intervals. The green capsid bug feeds on the foliage of currants and gooseberries as well as on apples and pears. Winter spraying with DNC will kill the eggs.

Cherries. Apart from aphids and, of course, the frequent attacks of hungry birds, the most common problem here is the disease known

The distinctive symptoms of peach leaf curl

graphically as silver leaf. Affected branches should be cut out and burned, and the wound painted with a proprietary seal. If the whole tree is affected, remove and burn it.

Gooseberries. Gooseberry sawfly is a most destructive pest. The adult sawfly lays its eggs on the undersides of the leaves, and the greenish caterpillars, with black heads and spots, quickly defoliate the bush. Two broods of caterpillars are often produced in a season. Spray or dust with derris when the pests are first seen. American gooseberry mildew is a serious disease. The leaves, shoots and fruits are infected and become covered with a whitish, felt-like fungus. Later, it turns a brownish colour and spoils the fruits and causes the shoots to become stunted and distorted. Feeding too generously with nitrogenous manures encourages this disease, as does inadequate pruning to open up the bushes and let in light and air. Infected shoots and fruits should be burned. Spraying with lime-sulphur at 2½ per cent strength before flowering will give protection from early infection. The bushes are sometimes attacked by a disease called gooseberry dieback which causes whole branches to wither suddenly and die, and unless they are quickly removed the whole bush may soon become infested. Dig up and burn badly diseased plants. Magpie moth caterpillars, which are white and black, with a yellow stripe down each side, eat the leaves of currants and gooseberries. If the pests are numerous they can cause considerable damage. Fortunately, they are easily destroyed by spraying or dusting with derris.

Pears suffer from aphids and scab. If fire blight occurs, with cankers at the base of dead shoots, the Ministry of Agriculture must be notified, and will advise on treatment. Brown rot may attack fruits if careless pruning has left snagged wounds.

Plums. Aphids, again, are the main problem, causing distortion of the leaves and shoots. Branches affected with silver leaf must be removed and burned and the wound sealed with a good protective paint. False silver leaf is common, and is caused by poor growing conditions.

Peaches. Aphids and red spider mites may cause trouble and the trees should be sprayed before blossom time with malathion. Peach leaf curl will cause affected leaves to swell up and then fall early in the season. Spray with bordeaux mixture early in the year (February) and again in the autumn before the leaves drop.

Raspberries. The maggots sometimes found in the fruits of raspberries and blackberries are the larvae of the raspberry beetle. A spray of derris when the first flowers open and again 10 days later will be helpful. Cane spot causes purplish spots on the young canes and leaves. Cut out and burn affected canes. Spray with lime-sulphur at 5 per cent when growth starts, with a second 2½ per cent spray just before blossoming. Mosaic is a very serious virus disease; the leaves become mottled with yellow and the plants are stunted and unfruitful. There is no cure. Infected plants should be grubbed out and burned. Replace with certified virus-free canes. Aphids transmit virus diseases and must be kept under control.

Strawberries. Aphids infest strawberries, birds and slugs eat them, and botrytis (grey mould) attacks weak plants in damp weather. Spray with benomyl and malathion in flowering period. Plants affected by virus disease—seen as stunted leaves and distorted stems— should be grubbed.

Gooseberry sawflies are easily recognized

Information Tables

Outdoor Crop Information Chart

Vegetable	Under glass	Time to sow In the open	Time to plant or transplant
Artichokes – Globe	—	—	offsets in March–April
Artichokes – Jerusalem	—	—	tubers in Feb–March
Asparagus	—	April	March–April
Beans – broad	—	November or Spring	—
Beans – climbing French	—	April–June	—
Beans – dwarf French	mid-March under cloches	April–July	—
Beans – runner	April under cloches	May onwards	after frosts
Beetroot	—	April–July	—
Broccoli – green sprouting (Calabrese)	March	April	May–June
Broccoli – purple sprouting; white sprouting	—	April	June–July
Brussels sprouts	February–March	March–April	May–June
Cabbage – spring greens	—	July–August	—
Cabbage – spring	—	July–August	September–October
Cabbage – early summer	February	—	April
Cabbage – summer	—	March	May
Cabbage – autumn (Savoys) and winter	—	April–May	June–July
Carrots	March under cloches	March–August	—
Cauliflower – early summer	September	—	March
Cauliflower – summer	January	March	March–May
Cauliflower – autumn	—	March–May	May–July

Final distance in rows	Distance between rows	Season of use
90 cm (3 ft)	90 cm (3 ft)	June–October
30 cm (12 in)	90 cm (3 ft)	November–March
45 cm (1½ ft)	90 cm (3 ft)	May–June
15–20 cm (6–8 in)	45–60 cm (1½–2 ft)	June–July
20–30 cm (8–12 in)	1.2–1.3 m (4–5 ft)	July onwards
15 cm (6 in)	45 cm (1½ ft)	May–September
20–30 cm (8–12 in)	30 cm (12 in) between each pair of rows; 90–150 cm (3–5 ft) between each double row	July–October
15–30 cm (6–12 in)	30–40 cm (12–16 in)	June–October (fresh); rest of year from store
60 cm (2 ft)	60 cm (2 ft)	August–September
60 cm (2 ft)	60 cm (2 ft)	January–April
60–90 cm (2–3 ft)	60–90 cm (2–3 ft)	September–March
8–12 cm (3–4 in)	30–45 cm (12–18 in)	March–April
30–45 cm (12–18 in)	45 cm (18 in)	April–May
45 cm (18 in)	45 cm (18 in)	May–June
45 cm (18 in)	45 cm (18 in)	June–August
45 cm (18 in) (30 cm for dwarf Savoys)	60 cm (2 ft) (30 cm for dwarf Savoys)	October–February
5–15 cm (2–6 in)	20–30 cm (8–12 in)	end May–October (fresh); October onwards from store
45–60 cm (18–24 in)	45–60 cm (18–24 in)	May–June
45–60 cm (18–24 in)	45–60 cm (18–24 in)	June–July
60–75 cm (2–2½ ft)	60–75 cm (2–2½ ft)	August–December

| Vegetable | Time to sow | | Time to plant or transplant |
	Under glass	In the open	
Cauliflower – winter (heading broccoli)	—	April–May	June–July
Celeriac	March	—	May–June
Celery – self-blanching	March	—	May–June
Celery – trench	March	—	May–June
Chicory	—	May	—
Corn salad (Lamb's lettuce)	—	February–October	—
Cucumbers – ridge	April–May	May	May–June
Endive	—	April–August	—
Kale – curly (Borecole)	—	April–May	July–August
Kape – rape	—	July	—
Kohl rabi	—	March–July	—
Leek	January–February	February–March	June–July
Lettuce	March	March–September	April
Marrows and courgettes	April	May	May–June
Onions – bulb – autumn sown	—	August	
Onions – bulb – spring sown	January	March	April
Onions – sets	—	—	April
Onions – salad	—	August or Spring	—
Parsley	March under cloches	March–July	—
Parsnip	—	February–March	—
Peas – round-seeded	February under cloches	March–June	—
Peas – wrinkle seeded	—	March–June	—
Potatoes – early	—	—	mid-March
Potatoes – second early	—	—	late March
Potatoes – maincrop	—	—	April

Final distance in rows	Distance between rows	Season of use
75 cm (2½ ft)	75 cm (2½ ft)	January–May
30–40 cm (12–16 in)	30–40 cm (12–16 in)	October onwards
30 cm (12 in)	30 cm (12 in)	August–September
25 cm (10 in)	single rows in 40 cm (16 in) wide trenches. 90 cm (3 ft) between trenches	October onwards
25 cm (10 in)	60 cm (2 ft)	Roots lifted from November onwards
15 cm (6 in)	15 cm (6 in)	June onwards
90 cm (3 ft)	90 cm (3 ft)	July–September
30–40 cm (12–16 in)	40 cm (16 in)	August onwards after blanching
60–75 cm (2–2½ ft)	60–75 cm (2–2½ ft)	March–April
45–60 cm (1½–2 ft)	60 cm (2 ft)	May–June
15 cm (6 in)	35 cm (14 in)	mid-June onwards
20–30 cm (8–12 in)	40–45 cm (16–18 in)	November–March
25–30 cm (10–12 in)	30 cm (12 in)	June–October
90–120 cm (3–4 ft)	90–120 cm (3–4 ft)	July–September
15 cm (6 in)	30 cm (12 in)	July onwards
15 cm (6 in)	30 cm (12 in)	September onwards
15 cm (6 in)	30 cm (12 in)	September onwards
0.5–1 cm (¼–½ in)	20–30 cm (8–12 in)	March–April onwards
15–30 cm (6–12 in)	30 cm (12 in)	All year round
15 cm (6 in)	30–45 cm (12–18 in)	November–March
5–7 cm (2–3 in)	60–150 cm (2–5 ft)	May–August
5–7 cm (2–3 in)	60–150 cm (2–5 ft)	July–September
30 cm (12 in)	60 cm (2 ft)	July
30 cm (12 in)	60 cm (2 ft)	August
40 cm (16 in)	75 cm (2½ ft)	October

Vegetable	Time to sow Under glass	In the open	Time to plant or transplant
Radish – salad	—	March–May and September	—
Radish – winter	—	July–August	—
Rhubarb	—	—	Spring or autumn
Salsify	—	April–May	—
Scorzonera	—	April–May	—
Seakale	—	—	root cuttings in March
Seakale beet (Chards)	—	April	—
Shallots	—	—	February
Spinach – New Zealand	March	mid-May	late May
Spinach – summer	—	March–end June	—
Spinach – winter	—	July–September	—
Spinach beet (Perpetual spinach)	—	April and July	—
Swede	—	May–June	—
Sweet corn	April	April–May	May
Tomato	March	—	early June
Turnips – summer	—	March onwards	—
Turnips – winter	—	July–August	—

Quantities of seeds

It is useful to know the number of seeds to 30 g (1 oz), although many seeds are quite small and a full ounce is not always required.

Beet	234
Cabbage	7,000
Carrot	18,700
Cauliflower	7,000
Celery	50,000
Leek	9,370
Lettuce	16,000
Onion	7,300
Parsley	17,500
Parsnip	7,000
Pea	106
Radish	5,000
Swede	8,000
Tomato	7,500
Turnip	9,300

These are only approximate quantities since variations in variety affect weight.

Planting Guide for Soft Fruit

These are minimum spacings between bushes. Allow more room if your soil is very fertile.

	In Rows	Between Rows
Blackberries (Most varieties)	3 m (10 ft)	1.80 m (6 ft)
„ Himalayan Giant	4 m (12 ft)	1.80 m (6 ft)
Black Currant	1.50 m (5 ft)	1.80 m (6 ft)
Blueberry	1.50 m (5 ft)	1.80 m (6 ft)
Gooseberry, bush	1.50 m (5 ft)	1.50 m (5 ft)
Gooseberry, cordon	38 cm (1 ft)	1.80 m (6 ft)
Raspberry	38 cm (1 ft)	1.80 m (6 ft)
Loganberry and other hybrids	3 m (9 ft)	1.80 m (6 ft)
Red Currant bush	1.50 m (5 ft)	1.50 m (5 ft)
Red Currant cordon	38 cm (1 ft)	1.80 m (6 ft)
White Currant bush	1.25 m (4 ft)	1.50 m (5 ft)

Final distance in rows	Distance between rows	Season of use
Broadcast or: 2–3 cm (1 in)	15 cm (6 in)	May onwards
20 cm (8 in)	20 cm (8 in)	Autumn–winter
90–120 cm (3–4 ft)	90–120 cm (3–4 ft)	Spring–Summer
25–30 cm (10–12 in)	40 cm (16 in)	October–March
30 cm (12 in)	40 cm (16 in)	October–March
60 cm (2 ft)	60 cm (2 ft)	Roots lifted from late November onwards
20 cm (8 in)	40 cm (16 in)	July onwards
15 cm (6 in)	30 cm (12 in)	July
60 cm (2 ft)	90 cm (3 ft)	Mid-summer onwards
15 cm (6 in)	30 cm (12 in)	May onwards
15 cm (6 in)	30 cm (12 in)	October onwards (protect from November)
20 cm (8 in)	40 cm (16 in)	Summer and winter/early spring
30 cm (12 in)	45 cm (18 in)	Autumn–Winter
45–60 cm (18–24 in)	45–60 cm (18–24 in)	August–September
45 cm (18 in)	75 cm (2½ ft)	August–September
10–15 cm (4–6 in)	30 cm (12 in)	Mid-June onwards
20–30 cm (8–12 in)	30–40 cm (12–16 in)	Winter

Planting Guide for Fruit Trees

Distances are given in metres and feet. These are minimum spacings. Allow more room if your soil is very fertile.

Subject	Bush	Fan
Apple	4.50 m (15 ft)	3.60 m (12 ft)
Apricot	—	3.60 m (12 ft)
Cherry (Morello)	4.50 m (15 ft)	3 m (10 ft)
Cherry (Sweet)	9 m (30 ft)	6 m (20 ft)
Damson	3.60 m (12 ft)	3.60 m (12 ft)
Gage	3.60 m (12 ft)	3.60 m (12 ft)
Nectarine	—	3.60 m (12 ft)
Nut	3.60 m (12 ft)	3.60 m (12 ft)
Peach	5.40 m (18 ft)	3.60 m (12 ft)
Pear	3.60 m (12 ft)	3.60 m (12 ft)
Plum	3.60 m (12 ft)	3.60 m (12 ft)
Quince	3.60 m (12 ft)	—

Single cordon apples and pears can be planted 75 cm (2 ft) apart at an angle of 45°. Pyramid apples and pears need a spacing of 1.80 m (6 ft), while Espalier apples and pears should have 4.50 m (15 ft) between them to allow for development of the 'arms'.

Chemical terms

Common name

Carbonic acid gas	Carbon dioxide (CO_2)
Gypsum	Calcium sulphate ($CaSO_4 2H_2O$)
Hydrate of lime, slaked lime	Calcium hydroxide ($Ca(OH)_2$)
Nitrate of soda	Sodium nitrate ($NaNO_2$)
Nitrogen	Nitrogen (N)
Salt (common)	Sodium chloride (NaCl)
Sulphate of ammonia	Ammonium sulphate ($(NH_4)_2SO_4$)
Sulphate of iron	Ferrous sulphate ($FeSO_4$)
Sulphate of potash	Potassium sulphate (K_2SO_4)
Superphosphate of lime	Tetrahydric monocalcic diphosphate (H_4Ca2PO_4)
Water	Water (H_2O)

A Glossary of Gardening Terms

Blanching Excluding light from celery, leeks, dandelions and endive to make them more palatable. Also the use of boiling water in preparing produce for freezing.

Bolting Premature running to seed.

Brassicas Members of the cabbage family, e.g., Brussels sprouts, cauliflowers, swedes, kohl rabi.

Broadcast Sowing seed by scattering it over an area as opposed to sowing in straight drills.

Collar Where main stem merges into the root.

Catch crop A quick maturing crop, grown between lifting one main crop and planting another.

Drill A shallow furrow into which seeds are sown.

Chlorophyll The green colouring matter in leaves and stems.

Earthing up Drawing the surface soil towards the stems.

Embryo The rudimentary plant within the seed.

Hybrid Obtained by crossing two selected parent varieties.

Genetics The science of plant breeding.

Haulm Stems of plants such as peas, beans and potatoes.

Habitat A plant's natural environment.

Intercrop A crop grown between other rows of vegetables.

Legume Any member of the pea family.

Mycelium The threads of a fungus.

Mulch A layer of well-rotted organic waste.

Node Joint: that part of the stem from which leaves and shoots develop.

Offset A side bulb or side-shoot formed for reproduction.

Pinching out Removing the growing tip of a stem.

Pricking out Transplanting seedlings from the soil in which they germinated, to another container or part of the garden, to grow on to a larger size.

Radical Proceeding from the roots.

Rhizome A creeping stem, half or entirely buried in the soil.

Seed leaves The first leaf or pair of leaves after germination.

Scion Young shoot used in grafting.

Sport A variation from the variety or species.

Stool Base of plants from which offsets are removed.

Sucker A shoot arising directly from a root.

Sub-soil The stratum immediately beneath the top soil.

Spit A spade's depth of soil – about 25 cm (10 ins).

Soil ball The mass of roots and soil of a pot grown plant.

Tap root The main, usually thick, and proving root.

Tilth Fine crumbly soil prepared for sowing seed.

Top dressing A layer of soil, manure, or fertilizer, applied over the root area.

Variety The popular name for the term 'cultivar' or cultivated variety.

The John Innes Composts

The prime requirement for a good compost is a fibrous textured loam which holds moisture yet drains freely.

To obtain consistently good results the ingredients of loam, peat and sand must be of the right kinds and in the correct proportions, with added fertilizers to boost growth. The loam must be sterilized.

These sterilized composts can be bought ready mixed from garden centres but those who need to use considerable quantities may find it cheaper to make their own. The appropriate formulae are reproduced below:

John Innes Seed Compost

This is needed only for small seeds, e.g. celery, and for sowings of medium-sized seeds, e.g. lettuce, under bad light conditions, roughly between October and January.

Parts by bulk	2 loam, sterilized	+	Superphosphate of lime 42.5 g ($1\frac{1}{2}$ oz)	per 35 litres (8 gal)
	1 peat		Chalk or ground	
	1 coarse sand		limestone 21 g ($\frac{3}{4}$ oz)	

John Innes Potting Composts

No. 1 for plants in 7.5 cm (3 in.) pots, such as tomatoes, lettuce and cauliflower, and for all general sowings.

Parts by bulk	7 loam, sterilized	+	John Innes Base* 113 g ($\frac{1}{4}$ lb)	per 35 litres (8 gal)
	3 peat		Chalk or ground	
	2 coarse sand		limestone 21 g ($\frac{3}{4}$ oz)	

No. 2 for tomatoes in 11 cm ($4\frac{1}{2}$ in.) pots, and dwarf beans in pots for winter cropping, cucumbers, marrows, etc.

Parts by bulk	7 loam, sterilized	+	John Innes Base* 2.27 g ($\frac{1}{2}$ lb)	per 35 litres (8 gal)
	3 peat		Chalk or ground	
	2 coarse sand		limestone 42.5 g ($1\frac{1}{2}$ oz)	

No. 3 for aubergines, capsicums, and tomatoes fruiting in pots.

Parts by bulk	7 loam, sterilized	+	John Innes Base* 240 g ($\frac{3}{4}$ lb)	per 35 litres (8 gal)
	3 peat		Chalk or ground	
	2 coarse sand		limestone 71 g ($2\frac{1}{2}$ oz)	

Notes – Peat means granulated moss or sedge peat, undecomposed and not powdery.

Superphosphate of lime is understood to contain 18 per cent phosphoric acid.

See that the loam is friable and not too wet. Moisten the peat lightly with a fine-rosed can, then sieve both through a 9.5 mm ($\frac{3}{8}$ in.) sieve. Mix the fertilizers with part of the sand before adding them to the rest of the compost.

Do not make up more compost than can be used within a few weeks.

* The John Innes Base is made up as follows:

Parts by weight	2 Hoof and horn, 3 mm ($\frac{1}{8}$ in.) grist (13 per cent nitrogen)
	2 Superphosphate of Lime (18 per cent phosphoric acid)
	1 Sulphate of potash (48 per cent pure potash).

Analysis:
Nitrogen 5.1%, Phosphoric acid 6.4%, Potash 9.7%.

Converting Fahrenheit into Centigrade

With widespread use of the centigrade or celsius scale the following conversions may be useful.

Fahrenheit (degrees)	Centigrade (degrees)
35	2
40	4
45	7
50	10
55	13
60	16
65	18
70	21
75	24

To change Fahrenheit reading into Centigrade readings subtract 32, multiply by 5, and divide by 9.

Greenhouse Spacing for Pots

Size of Pot	1 m (3 ft) length	1.5 m (5 ft) length	3 m (10 ft) length
Staging 60 cm (2 ft) wide			
75 mm (3 ins)	90	150	300
88 mm (3½ ins)	72	120	240
130 mm (5 ins)	36	60	120
156 mm (6¼ ins)	21	35	70
19 cm (7½ ins)	14	27	54
21 cm (8½ ins)	10	16	32
Staging 90 cm (3 ft) wide			
75 mm (3 ins)	140	235	470
88 mm (3½ ins)	108	180	360
130 mm (5 ins)	54	90	180
156 mm (6¼ ins)	32	55	110
19 cm (7½ ins)	18	30	60
21 cm (8½ ins)	15	25	50

These figures are approximate due to differences in the various manufacturers' sizes.

Estimated Yields from a 3 m (10 ft) row

Assuming the soil is in good condition and pests and diseases are under control

Crop	Spacing In Rows	Spacing Between Rows	Yield	Seeds Required for 30 ft
Beans,				
broad	15 cm (6 in)	38 cm (15 in)	11 kg (25 lb)	250 ml (½ pt)
French	22.5 cm (9 in)	1.8 m (6 ft)	4 kg (8 lb)	125 ml (¼ pt)
runner	30 cm (12 in)	75 cm (2½ ft)	16 kg (35 lb)	125 ml (¼ pt)
Beet	15 cm (6 in)	38 cm (15 in)	14 kg (30 lb)	15 g (½ oz)
Broccoli	60 cm (2 ft)	60 cm (2 ft)	5 kg (10 lb)	30 g (1 oz) of seed produces between 1500 and 2000 plants
Brussels sprouts	75 cm (2½ ft)	75 cm (2½ ft)	4 kg (8 lb)	
Cabbage,				
spring	30 cm (1 ft)	45 cm (18 in)	4 kg (8 lb)	,,
summer/winter	60 cm (2 ft)	60 cm (2 ft)	8 kg (16 lb)	,,
savoys	60 cm (2 ft)	60 cm (2 ft)	8 kg (16 lb)	,,
Carrots,				
early	15 cm (6 in)	30 cm (12 in)	1½ kg (3 lb)	10 g (¼ oz)
maincrop	15 cm (6 in)	30 cm (12 in)	4 kg (8 lb)	10 g (¼ oz)
Cauliflower	45 cm (18 in)	60 cm (2 ft)	6 kg (12 lb)	30 g (1 oz) produces 2000 plants
Celery	30 cm (12 in)	120 cm (4 ft)	6 kg (12 lb)	30 g (1 oz) contains 50,000 seeds
Leeks	22.5 cm (9 in)	30 cm (12 in)	5 kg (10 lb)	10 g (¼ oz)
Lettuce	22.5 cm (9 in)	30 cm (12 in)	12 heads	5 g (⅛ oz)
Marrows	120 cm (4 ft)	120 cm (4 ft)	4 marrows per plant	7 plants
Onions	15 cm (6 in)	30 cm (12 in)	4 kg (8 lb)	10 g (¼ oz)
Parsnips	22.5 cm (9 in)	38 cm (15 in)	5 kg (10 lb)	30 g (½ oz)
Potatoes,				
early	35 cm (14 in)	60 cm (2 ft)	5 kg (10 lb)	2 kg (3½ lb)
maincrop	40 cm (16 in)	75 cm (2½ ft)	7½ kg (15 lb)	2 kg (3½ lb)
Rhubarb	120 cm (4 ft)	120 cm (4 ft)	10 kg (25 lb)	7 clumps
Shallots	15 cm (6 in)	30 cm (12 in)	4 kg (8 lb)	1 kg (2 lb)
Swedes	30 cm (12 cm)	45 cm (18 in)	5 kg (10 lb)	10 g (¼ oz)
Tomatoes,				
outside	15 cm (6 in)	30 cm (12 in)	2 kg (4 lb) per plant	20 plants
Turnips	15 cm (6 in)	30 cm (12 in)	3½ kg (7 lb)	10 g (¼ oz)

Index

Page numbers in italic indicate a relevant illustration and caption.

Acknowledgments

The publishers would like to thank the following individuals and organisations for their kind permission to reproduce the photographs in this book.

Bernard Alfieri 14 left, 18, 47 below left, 67 above right, 78 above right, 82 above left, 97 above, 122–123; Bryce Attwell title, 6–7, 10–11, 16–17, 22–23, 30–31, 36–37, 44–45, 90–91, 102–103 below, 132–133, 146–147, 148–149; A-Z Botanical Collection Ltd. back jacket, 13 above right, 35 above and below, 46, 74 below left and above right, 79 below, 96 below left and below right, 98 below right, 101 above and below, 108 below, 129 below; Rex Bamber front jacket; Barnaby's Picture Library 114, 125; Pat Brindley 27 below, 40 above, 45 inset, 63 below, 65 above, 81 right, 93 right, 97 below, 100 above left, 129 above right; R J Corbin 25, 32 left and right, 59, 61, 63 above right, 66 left, 70 below, 72 below right, 80 left, 99 right, 139 left; Eric Crichton 62 below, 66 right; W F Davidson 13 above left; Brian Furner 27 above, 56 above right, 62 above, 63 above left, 67 centre left, 76 above, 78 below left, 82 above right, 87 below right, 92 above right, 94 below centre, 99 below, 124 above, 126, 143; Melvin Grey 135, 136, 137; Iris Hardwick Library 88, 116; G E Hyde 13 below, 21, 60, 83 above, 92 left, 94 below right, 95 centre, 100 above right, 107 above, 118 right, 141 above, 144 above and below, 145 below; Leslie Johns 8, 9, 94 left; Murphy Chemical Ltd. 139 above right; National Vegetable Research Station 138, 139 below right, 142; NHPA (M Savonius) 40 below, 119, (M W F Treadie) 140 above; Ray Procter 43; PWA Services 49; John Rigby 29; Harry Smith Horticultural Photographic Collection endpapers, 14 right, 33, 47 above and below right, 50, 51, 52 left, 52–53, 53 below and right, 54 above, 54–55, 55 above, 56 above left and below, 57 above and below, 58 above and below, 64, 67 below, 68, 69 above and below, 70 above, 71, 72 left, 73, 74 above left and below right, 75 above and below, 76 below, 77, 78 above left, 79 above left and above right, 82 below centre, 83 below left, 84 above left, above right and below, 85, 86, 87 above left, 89, 92 below, 93 above left and below, 94 above right, 95 above, below and left, 96–97, 97 centre, 98 above and below left, 99 above left, 100 below, 101 left, 103 above, 104 left and right, 105, 106, 107 below, 108 above left and above right, 109, 110–111, 111 above, 112, 113 left and right, 115, 117, 118, 120, 121 above and below, 122 left, 123 right, 124 below, 127, 128, 141 below, 145; ZEFA Picture Library (J Pfaff) 65 below.